George Cullum

Elements of military art and history

George Cullum

Elements of military art and history

ISBN/EAN: 9783337280000

Printed in Europe, USA, Canada, Australia, Japan

Cover: Foto ©ninafisch / pixelio.de

More available books at **www.hansebooks.com**

ELEMENTS

OF

MILITARY ART AND HISTORY:

COMPRISING

THE HISTORY AND TACTICS OF THE SEPARATE ARMS;
THE COMBINATION OF THE ARMS; AND THE
MINOR OPERATIONS OF WAR.

BY

ED. DE LA BARRE DUPARCQ,

CAPTAIN OF ENGINEERS IN THE ARMY OF FRANCE,
PROFESSOR OF THE MILITARY ART IN THE IMPERIAL SCHOOL OF SAINT-CYR.

TRANSLATED AND EDITED BY

BRIG.-GEN. GEORGE W. CULLUM,

CHIEF OF STAFF OF THE GENERAL-IN-CHIEF OF THE ARMIES OF THE UNITED STATES;
LATE AIDE-DE-CAMP TO LIEUTENANT-GENERAL SCOTT; AND
CHIEF OF STAFF AND OF ENGINEERS OF MAJOR-GENERAL HALLECK, WHILE COMMANDING
THE DEPARTMENTS OF THE MISSOURI AND MISSISSIPPI.

NEW YORK:
D. VAN NOSTRAND, 192 BROADWAY.
1863.

ENTERED, according to Act of Congress, in the year 1862, by
D. VAN NOSTRAND,
In the Clerk's Office of the District Court of the United States for the Southern District of New York.

JOHN F. TROW,
PRINTER, STEREOTYPER, AND ELECTROTYPER,
50 Greene Street, New York.

PREFACE OF THE TRANSLATOR.

For some years I have been strongly urged by many of my army friends to prepare a work on Military Art and History, suited to our service, for which I had a large amount of material; but not feeling the same confidence in my ability as those who solicited me to undertake the task, I shrank from it, from time to time, till the breaking out of the rebellion of the Southern States, since which my arduous duties have precluded the possibility of preparing such a work, though fully aware of the importance of its being undertaken by some one, especially for the benefit of our volunteer officers, most of whom have not enjoyed the benefits of a military education.

I now submit to our vast army and the public a translation of the best book on Military Art and History I could find among the many excellent productions of the French and Germans, and which will be found far better than any original work I could have produced under existing circumstances.

My time being almost entirely occupied with important professional duties, I sought the aid of a competent translator, and was truly fortunate in securing the assistance of that ripe scholar, Professor W. Chauvenet, formerly of the U. S. Naval Academy at Annapolis, and now of Washington University, at St. Louis, Mo.

GEORGE W. CULLUM, Brig.-Gen.,
Chief of Staff and Engineers of the
Department of the Mississippi.

Headquarters, Department of the Mississippi,
Camp in Corinth, Miss., *July 4th*, 1862.

PREFACE OF THE EDITOR.

IN collecting, under the title of "ELEMENTS," many of the studies of Military Art and History, which my service as Professor at the Imperial Special Military School put it within my power to do, and my particular labors enabled me to improve, I do not pretend to offer a complete treatise, for writing which I do not feel sufficiently prepared. I wish simply to publish essays, carefully elaborated, it is true, though imperfect, and which time alone can improve by successive retouches.

If eight years of a conscientious professorship—if more than ten years devoted to assiduous researches, to grave publications, all relating to the profession of arms, are guarantees—I am authorized to present this work to my chiefs, to my comrades, and to the pupils of the school of Saint-Cyr. May the latter profit by it. May the young officers especially, whose professor I have been, welcome it as an old friend—one of the youthful, smiling friends which they re-find with pleasure at all periods of life. To me, I confess, it recalls happy moments passed with them in the faithful study of an art eleven centuries old, and which even now exercises so much influence over the destinies of our glorious country.

ED. DE LA BARRE DUPARCQ.

1st *October*, 1857.

ELEMENTS

OF

MILITARY ART AND HISTORY.

PRELIMINARY DEFINITIONS.

WAR may be defined, a state of armed struggle between two nations: the nation which attacks makes *offensive* war, and that which defends itself sustains a *defensive* one.

The *art of war* is the art of concentrating and employing, at the opportune moment, a superior force of troops upon the decisive point.

An *army* is a large collected force, raised and paid by a government.

An *arm* is a union of combatants, having the same mode of action. Thus, the union of foot combatants forms the *infantry* arm; the *cavalry* arm comprises all those who fight on horseback; the *artillery* arm those having the management of ordnance; and the *engineer* arm those charged with the construction, attack, and defence of fortifications. A single kind of combatant in each arm is not sufficient for the different circumstances which arise in war; experience demonstrates the necessity of the following subdivisions in the several arms: Light and line infantry; light, line, and reserve cavalry; field, siege, coast, and mountain artillery; and in the engineers, sappers and miners.

In the first three arms, the *unit of force*, or *tactical unit*, is the largest fraction, acting separately, under the command of a single chief: in the infantry it is the battalion; in the cavalry, the squadron; in the artillery, the battery; and in the engineers, the company.

The unit of force, placed on the ground, has a figure called the *formation* or *order*. The part of the troop facing the adversary is the *front*, the opposite side the *rear;* the lateral extremities, the *flanks* of the formation. We call *rank* the line of soldiers parallel to the front; and *file*, the line of men perpendicular to the same front. The number of ranks of a troop determine its *depth*.

Troops are not formed for attack as for defence; there are deep, or *ployed* formations, and thin, or *deployed;* we understand by *manœuvres*, the movements for passing from one to another formation.

The *column* is a disposition of troops whose elements remain placed parallel to each other, and on the same axis. When the axes become different, they are said to be in *echelons*. We ordinarily designate the first and last subdivision of a column as its *head* or *foot*.

The *distance* is the interval between the foot of one corps and the head of that which follows it; or between the toes of one soldier and the heels of the one preceding him. The *interval* is the space between the adjacent flanks of two troops, or of two men in the same line.

Troops placed upon the same front, whether in column or deployed, constitute a line; the line may be either *full* (like *a wall*), or *with intervals*.

The *checker-form*, as its name indicates, is a formation upon many lines, with intervals; the intervals in each line equalling the full spaces; and the lines are arranged so that the void spaces of the one are opposite the full ones of the other.

An *order* is more than a reunion of lines; it is the general and combined disposition of troops of different kinds, grouped together for the same purpose.

Tactics determines the best mode of distributing, arranging, and moving the units of force. The tactics of an arm make known the special properties of this arm, and the most advantageous method of using it. General or grand tactics, show the combinations of the arms, and the *ensemble* of movements, suited to obtain the maximum effect.

Strategy, the science essential to the general-in-chief, is the art of properly directing masses upon the theatre of war, for the defence of our own, or the invasion of the enemy's country.

Logistics is the practical application of the art of moving armies; the science of chiefs of staff.

In a military operation, we ought to attend to three principal things: the line from whence we depart, the point where we wish to arrive, and the line to be followed to reach it.

The line upon which an army is supported, and from which it departs to act offensively, is called the *base of operations*. For example, the French, desiring to attack Germany, would take the Rhine for their base of operations; the Alps, if they wished to enter Italy; and the Pyrénées, if they would invade Spain.

When we are reduced to dispute with the enemy the possession of the base, without going beyond it, this base takes the name of *line of defence*. All the points we desire to reach, and the possession of which would influence the success of the campaign, are called *objective points*, or simply *objectives*.

Since the political concentration of the European states, their capitals form excellent objective points, and, for that reason, many of them have recently been fortified.

The road passed over by the army to reach the objectives, is called the *line of operations;* and takes the name of *line of retreat*, when we are compelled, after a defeat, to follow it in a contrary direction, in order to gain a line of defence, behind which to resist the conqueror.

PART FIRST.

HISTORY AND TACTICS OF THE SEPARATE ARMS.

CHAPTER FIRST.

HISTORY OF INFANTRY.

THE specific history of an *arm* possesses the advantage of exhibiting, one by one, in the order of their discovery or adoption, the several improvements effected in its organization, armament, and mode of combat; and consequently, of indicating successively, in the order of date, each of the properties of this arm. History is thus brought to the aid of theory; and for this reason, the present work contains summaries of the history of each of the arms. The most important, and to us the most interesting of these summaries, is doubtless that which relates to the principal basis of armies—the infantry. It will form the subject of the present chapter.

To unfold it in due order, we shall distribute it

into eighteen sections, each devoted to a single epoch. Thus, Sect. 1 will treat of the infantry of the ancient people of Asia and Africa; 2d, of infantry among the Greeks; 3d, of the Roman infantry; 4th, of the infantry of the barbarous nations who overturned the Roman empire, and especially that of our ancestors, the Franks. From the downfall of Rome, infantry plays a less prominent part than in ancient times: we shall examine it in its decline, under four aspects: 5th, the feudal infantry; 6th, the communal infantry; 7th, the infantry of the soldiers of fortune; and 8th, that of the English archers. In the fourteenth century the Swiss reinstated the infantry, and proved its power by brilliant successes, as we shall show in section 9th; which will be followed, in the 10th, by some particulars respecting the Spanish infantry, the best of the sixteenth century. In the three succeeding sections we shall study the French infantry, under Charles VII., Francis I., Henry II., and Henry IV. In the 14th we shall speak of the diminution of the depth of the infantry by Gustavus Adolphus; the 15th will group together the characteristic features of the infantry in the reigns of Louis XIV. and Louis XV.; the 16th will treat of the improvements made in the Prussian infantry the first half of the eighteenth century; the 17th will indicate the more recent progress; and the 18th and last will contain some remarks on the entire history of this arm.

Our object in selecting, for each epoch, the infantry of some one nation as a type, is to abridge details, and to bring them within the limits of a chapter; citing, nevertheless, in our historic sketch such facts as, for soldiers, are most curious, most characteristic, and most instructive. To have followed the history of each arm, during each period, in all nations, would have involved us too far, and would have produced a narrative which, though perhaps more connected, would most surely have less hold upon the memory.

With this preface, we enter upon our subject.

1. Ancients.—In the oriental countries, where the human race and the art of war had birth, cavalry and war chariots were the most esteemed arms. This was due, 1st, to the level character of the ground, which allowed complete and extended manœuvres of both cavalry and chariots; 2d, to the impression produced by every elevated object, in accordance with which, in those primitive times, the highest combatant appeared to be the strongest.

The character of these countries also modified the formation of the infantry, which was in deep order; that is, more solid than mobile.

The Egyptian infantry was formed in heavy square battalions of 100 men to a side; these battalions were subdivided into fractions of 1,000, 100, 10. The heavy-armed foot soldiers carried each a large shield, a long pike, a hatchet, a helmet; the light-armed foot soldiers were archers or slingers.

The Jews formed their infantry upon a single

line, from 10 to 30 men in depth; the archers and slingers occupied the front ranks, the heavy-armed troops the rear. The troop formations of this people, 1,000 strong, were subdivided into groups of 100 men.

The Persian infantry, originally armed solely with offensive weapons, was composed of heavy battalions, 24 to 30 men deep. Cyrus the elder reduced this depth to 12 ranks, and introduced the use of defensive weapons into his army. The Persian troops were divided into bodies of 10, 100, 1,000, 10,000 men. Thus, among all the early nations we have mentioned, the decimal subdivision appears as the basis of their infantry formations.

Every deep formation upon a single line was, in ancient times, called a *phalanx*. The Jews and the Persians, then, ranged their infantry in phalanx. The Greeks adopted, with some modifications, the Asiatic phalanx, and it is especially among them that we must study this species of formation.

2. Greek Phalanx.—The Greek phalanx was a corps of heavy infantry, formed in a single line 16 men deep, and designed to act *en masse*, and to fall upon the enemy like a solid block. Its organization, instead of being decimal, like that of the Persian, was founded upon the powers of the number *two*. Thus, taking as its primitive element a file of sixteen men,—

HISTORY OF INFANTRY. 15

Two files formed . . . . . . one dilochia;
Two dilochias . . . . one tetrarchia;
Two tetrarchias . . . . . . one taxiarchia;
Two taxiarchias . . . . . . one syntagma;
Two syntagmas. . . . . one pentacosiarchia;
Two pentacosiarchias . . . one chiliarchia;
Two chiliarchias . . . . . . one merarchia;
Two merarchias . . . . . . one phalangarchia;
Two phalangarchias . . . . one diphalangarchia;
Two diphalangarchias . . . one tetraphalangarchia.

TETRARCHIA.

p p p p
p p p p
p p p p
p p p p
p p p p
p p p p
p p p p
p p p p
p p p p
p p p p
p p p p
p p p p
p p p p
p p p p
p p p p
p p p p

The tetrarchia, a body of 64 men, corresponded to our modern company, and was the constituent element of the phalanx. The syntagma comprised 256 men; the chiliarchia, 1,024; the phalangarchia, or small phalanx, 4,096. This last fraction was composed of 16 syntagmas, the syntagma being 16 files of 16 men. The tetraphalangarchia, or complete phalanx, embraced 16,384 men. All these soldiers, when heavy-armed, were called *hoplites*.

It frequently happened that the small Greek states could not set on foot even one phalangarchia, still less a tetraphalangarchia. In such cases the name of *phalanx* was given to any combination of tetrarchias, without fixing any definite number. This facility of organizing any number of men whatever in phalanx, had great advantages.

The hoplite occupied a space, in open rank and file, of four cubits (6 feet) each way; in close rank and file, two cubits (3 feet); in very close rank, one cubit (1½ feet). The phalanx charged in close ranks; it received a charge in very close ranks, a formation called a *synapisma*. The principal arms of the hoplites were the shield and the *sarissa*, a long pike of fourteen cubits (21 feet) in length, which the first five ranks held horizontally, whilst the others held them vertically.

The sarissa being seized at a point four cubits from the but, and each soldier occupying in close rank two cubits, it is apparent that in this close formation the sarissæ of even the fifth rank projected two cubits (3 feet) beyond the front rank of the phalanx. This front, bristling with pikes, presented a formidable aspect.

Besides the soldiers of the rank and file, or hoplites, the Greek phalanx also comprised light-armed troops, designated *psiletes*. In fact, the number of these psiletes was usually half that of the hoplites, or 8,192 for the complete phalanx. They were divided into archers, slingers, and darters or *jaculators*, who threw arrows with the hand. Formed eight men in depth, they skirmished about the phalanx, and were employed in all operations which required lightness and promptitude.

Sometimes the hoplites, imitating the formation of the psiletes, reduced their files to one half, and the phalanx became but 8 men deep; but this mobile order was an exception; moreover, the intervals between the divisions of the phalanx were not strongly marked, and it formed a nearly continuous line.

There was a class of Grecian foot soldiers intermediate between the heavy and the light armed: they were called *peltastes*, from the small round shield (πελτη) with which they were armed; they carried a shorter pike than the hoplites. Alexander the Great made frequent use of them.

The chief end of the Grecian system of education, as well as of the laws and customs, was to make a good soldier of every citizen. Thus, the young were from their infancy familiarized with the idea of war, and their first plays were military exercises; the system of rewards was more honorable than lucrative, and the system of punishments based rather upon sentiment than actual infliction; and hence, the lack of courage, or any censurable act committed in war, even when it was not punished, subjected the soldier to public reprobation, and disgrace with his friends and relatives. In Sparta, mothers rejoiced when they received the announcement of the death of their sons upon the field of battle, and their dead bodies were brought home upon their shields, preferring to see them stretched lifeless upon that defensive arm than alive without it, for its loss was branded with infamy.

The Greek foot soldiers, moreover, excelled in every soldierly quality; robust, skilful, and courageous even to an extreme, he thought nothing more glorious than to die for his country. But it is to be remarked, that the formation in phalanx in a measure counterbalanced these qualities in the hoplite; for this formation upon a single line nearly continuous was not sufficiently pliant to fight advantageously in broken and mountainous countries, where the waverings of the march produced fatal gaps, into which the enemy could penetrate and attack the body in flank and in rear. For this reason, the phalanx was very successful only in level countries. To be just, however, let us add that whenever it was commanded by generals of the highest order (and such always understand how to adapt the arrangement of their troops to local circumstances), the phalanx was equally victorious upon irregular ground; as was exemplified under Alexander the Great, and especially under Xenophon.

3. Roman Legion.—At the first glance we observe a characteristic of the Roman legion which distinguishes it from the phalanx: it is not hampered by close order; its organization breathes mobility.

It forms three lines, each divided into ten *maniples* or companies, ten men deep. The *hastati* are in the front line, the *principes* in the second, the *triarii* in the third. In each line, the maniples are separated by a distance equal to their front, and the maniples of each line behind are placed opposite to the spaces of the preceding line, which produces a checker-board formation. The interval between the lines equals the depth of a maniple; the space between two soldiers, in any direction, is six Roman feet (5 feet 7 inches).

MANIPLE FORMATION OF THE LEGION.

Hastati, 10 ranks and 12 files.	☐ ☐ ☐ ☐ ☐ ☐ ☐ ☐ ☐ ☐
Principes, 10 ranks and 12 files.	☐ ☐ ☐ ☐ ☐ ☐ ☐ ☐ ☐ ☐
Triarii, 10 ranks and 6 files.	☐ ☐ ☐ ☐ ☐ ☐ ☐ ☐ ☐ ☐

In the first two lines, the maniple contains 12 files, which, with a depth of 10 men, gives the maniple a force of 120 men. In the *triarii*, the maniple contains but 6 files, so that it numbers but 60 men.

The light-armed troops attached to the legion were called *velites*, and formed 10 maniples of 120 men each, like those of the *hastati* and *principes*. They constituted the inferior class of the legion, and fought outside and around the lines. It was the reward for brave deeds to be promoted to the regular ranks.

The Roman legion, therefore, embraced 1,200 *hastati*, 1,200 *principes*, 600 *triarii*, and 1,200 *velites*; or, in all, 4,200 foot soldiers. This is the usual number, but there were legions of a smaller as well as those of a larger effective force.

The organization of the legion allowed the ready formation of detachments embracing the same classes of soldiers, and in the same proportions as in the legion itself. Thus, one maniple of *hastati*, one of *principes*, one of *triarii*, and one of *velites*, formed a small legion of 420 men, to which could also be added a *turma* of cavalry, or the tenth part of a cavalry legion. By doubling or tripling the number of maniples, detachments were obtained of 840 or 1,260 foot soldiers, which still retained the likeness of the legion.

A helmet, a shield, a sword, and seven javelins constituted the armament of the *velites*, who fought as skirmishers, either on the front or flanks. They took advantage of the spaces left by the checkerboard formation, to advance and retire.

The defensive arms of the *hastati* and *principes* were a helmet, a brass breastplate, and a convex shield; their offensive arms, two light spears or darts (called *pila*), two javelins, and a sword. This sword was the favorite weapon of the Romans: being broad and strong, it served, in the hands of a vigorous man, the purpose of an axe, and inflicted wide and deep wounds, which terrified the enemy. The *hastati* received or gave the first charge; the *principes* supported them, either by advancing in front of them, by passing through the intervals of the first line, or by simply filling up the spaces, so as to form a full and more solid line; the legion then fought as a veritable phalanx, which not unfrequently happened. This facility of transformation at pleasure, according to circumstances and localities, so as to possess either extreme mobility or great solidity, renders the Roman legion superior to the Greek phalanx.

The *triarii*, who were tried soldiers, were armed with the shield, the pike, and the sword. During the combat of the first two lines, they remained immovable, their pikes resting upon the ground. Their mission was to throw themselves into the weak places, and reclaim a victory about to be lost: they constituted, therefore, a reserve. It was only when the battle was becoming desperate, that they were called into action; and hence the Latin proverb: *Res ad triarios pervenit*, expressive of a final struggle.

The soldier of the Roman legion was a valiant combatant, well skilled in manœuvres and the exercise of arms, and especially inured to fatigue of every kind. The Greek foot soldier, the *hoplite*, ordinarily carried no burden, leaving the transportation of his munitions to servants or slaves; but the soldier of the legion, at least during the better days of the republic, carried not only his arms, but his baggage, a stake, a pioneer tool, and a leather pouch containing his provision of corn for fifteen days. Reckoning the weight, piece by piece, of his arms and all his effects, we find that his load amounted to about 100 pounds, or double that which is usually carried by our foot soldiers.* With these enormous loads the Roman soldiers, nevertheless, travelled some 20 miles or more in a day on ordinary occasions, and in forced marches as much as 33 miles.

The soldier of the legion was, moreover, accustomed to digging the ground; for the Romans were in the constant practice of surrounding their camps with intrenchments, even when they encamped but

---

* In the Russian campaign (1812) the soldiers of Marshal Davoust adjusted upon their knapsacks, already filled, 6½ lbs. of bread, 4½ lbs. of biscuit, and 11 lbs. of flour, thus carrying a total weight of 66 lbs.

for a single night—a prudent habit, to which may be ascribed in a great degree their remarkable exemption from reverses, and which also had the advantage of keeping the soldiers in training, and making them robust and healthy. We may observe, however, that the practice of intrenching camps and positions, though excellent with the projectile arms of the ancients, all of which were destructive only at small distances, presents but unimportant advantages with our modern fire-arms.

The legion, by its formation in small bodies drawn up in several lines, with intervals, always had a reserve, was possessed of great mobility, and could fight upon all kinds of ground. It had, therefore, that character of universality which is indispensable to armies, and especially to infantry: it was a military machine, eminently fitted to serve the Romans in their projects of universal conquest, to which they always aspired, and which constituted their strength,—a machine precisely adapted to their political constitution; for it is worthy of particular remark, that the Romans differed from all other nations, ancient or modern, in this: that whilst other nations made war only to maintain themselves in a position to administer their government, they administered their government solely with a view to making war.

The lines with intervals were objectionable, inasmuch as a quick and resolute enemy might penetrate the open spaces. Convinced of this, Marius, the celebrated conqueror of the Cimbri and Teutoni, substituted for the formation by maniples the formation by cohorts, which assimilated the organization to that of the phalanx. In this new formation there was now but one class of soldiers: the hastati, the principes, and the triarii were mingled, all armed with the *pilum*, and divided into ten cohorts of an equal force. The number of ranks, and the intervals between the ranks and files, remained the same as in the formation by maniples.

Marius formed his legion upon two lines, each consisting of two cohorts, separated by small intervals. Cæsar, as the following diagram shows, disposed the Roman legion in three lines, the first of four cohorts, the second and third each of three cohorts. The third line formed a reserve, and it was for that purpose that Cæsar restored it.

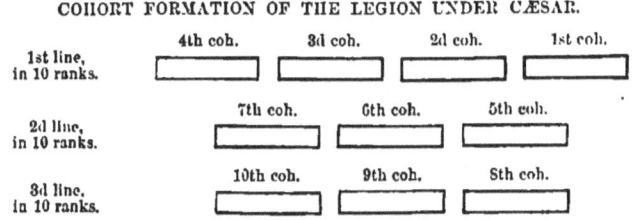

COHORT FORMATION OF THE LEGION UNDER CÆSAR.

In the formation by cohorts, the lines being full, the first could no longer retire between the intervals of the second, as in the formation by maniples. The second line alone could advance and insert itself in the first, the fresh files stepping into the intervals between the fatigued files, so that the front of the legion doubled in number, without increasing its length. The possibility of such a manœuvre depended upon the opening of the ranks and files which characterized the Roman legion, in which each man occupied, as we have said, a space of six Roman feet (5 feet 7 inches); the difficulty was to preserve this space, and hence all their drills were conducted so as to make the soldier preserve his intervals both in rank and file. Under the new form of cohorts, the infantry legion again rendered most excellent service, and gained as much celebrity as under the manipular form. From that time the cohort became so well established as the unit of the Roman infantry, that their historians, and especially Cæsar, frequently say: "We had so many cohorts," without even naming the legion.

During the period of the Roman emperors, the legion deteriorated; and nothing shows this more clearly than the organization of the legion, described by Vegetius.* This legion, of 6,100 foot soldiers, divided into ten cohorts, ranged in the checker form, in two lines, each of five cohorts, embraced all kinds of foot combatants: thus there were in each cohort, in the first rank the heavy-armed troops, in the second the mailed archers, in the third and fourth the velites, in the fifth a projectile machine called *onager*,† flanked by slingers and crossbowmen, and in the sixth the triarii, forming the reserve.

This confused formation could not last. They returned to the isolated cohorts, of an effective force of from 500 to 1,000 men, some composed entirely of infantry, others, of infantry and cavalry. They

---

* In the third century.—*Tr.*

† A machine which threw stones.—*Tr.*

allowed substitutes in the military service, a decided mark of degeneration; they abandoned defensive arms; they exchanged the use of that broad and trenchant sword, which had gained so many battles, for projectile arms, whose light weight agreed better with the effeminacy of the times; they went further, and threw javelins from engines called *carrobalistæ*, the number of which became considerable. Discipline declined; the troops were no longer drilled; they forgot the maxims which had given them victory. The decline was rapid, and the Roman colossus soon succumbed under the repeated blows of enemies, who poured down in such numbers that their native countries were designated in the Latin idiom as the *officina gentium* (the factory of nations).

Let us now pursue the study of infantry among their enemies: those new people to whom custom has given the traditional name of *Barbarians*.

4. Barbarous Nations.—With the exception of the Sarmatians and the Vandals, the barbarians who overwhelmed the Roman empire fought almost exclusively on foot, and we may apply to them the expression of Tacitus, when speaking of the Germans: "*Omne robur in pedite.*"

The German infantry had a decimal organization: it attacked in wedge form, sometimes in phalanx, always with loud cries.

Let us especially consider the infantry of the Franks.

Here is the portrait which historians have left us of the Frank foot soldier: He tied his flaxen hair on the top of his head in a tuft, which fell back and flowed behind like a horse's tail. He shaved his face, leaving only two long and pendent mustaches. His linen clothes fitted closely to his body; a large belt sustained his sword. His favorite weapon was the *francisque*, a battle-axe with one or two edges and a very short handle. His left arm bore a long and narrow shield, the only defensive armor with which he was furnished. He also had a spear, or pike, of moderate length, designated in the Frank tongue by the name *hang*. This pike could be used both at small and at great distances; its shaft was covered with plates of iron, which protected it against the sword cuts of the enemy, and its point was curved in the form of a double claw.

In the fight, the Frank foot soldier threw this

weapon at his adversary: if it caught in the flesh, it was difficult to disengage it, on account of the small iron hooks at its point, and thus it produced serious wounds. When the enemy parried the blow, the hang struck the shield, and fastening in it, drew it down; while, its but end dragging upon the ground, it hung to the shield like a very troublesome weight; which, from its construction, could neither be torn out nor cut by the sword. Then the Frank sprang forward, placed one foot upon the shaft, pressed upon it with his whole weight, and thus forcing his adversary to lower his shield, could easily strike the exposed breast or head. In this advantageous position the arm which held the battle-axe usually aimed at the face or the neck.

The Franks preserved this warlike aspect down to the end of the sixth century.

The Frank infantry, like that of the Germans, fought in phalanx and in wedge form, the latter formation being often little more than a deep and close column; it attacked with terrible shouts, and with a velocity almost equal to that of cavalry. In consequence of its sojourn in Gaul, it adopted by degrees some of the military usages of the Romans.

At the battle of Tours (732), in which Charles Martel conquered the Saracens, the masses of the Frank infantry were drawn up in great depth, whence the celebrated expression: "*God was with his heavy battalions.*" Having to do with mounted enemies, who fought skirmishing, the Frank warrior opposed to them heavy columns drawn up to act with *ensemble*. There is every reason to believe that he was acquainted with and employed the *agmen quadratum* (square formation).

This massing, the source of power in infantry, disappears from the organization of this arm, from the time of Charles Martel.

5. **Feudal Infantry.**—In the wars of invasion of Charlemagne, the grandson and second successor of Charles Martel, cavalry increased, and at the death of that powerful monarch constituted the half of the French armies. The feudal system, which arose soon after, and which was created with the view of maintaining in subjection the recently conquered people, instituted nobles, who desired no other occupation than the honorable profession of arms. They monopolized this vocation to their own profit, and being wealthy, covered themselves with heavy armor and rode upon chargers barbed with iron. All the chiefs adopted this fashion; the taste for mounted combat became general. From that time the infantry was inefficient, for no one attended to giving it a good organization, without which it can never accomplish anything; and it remained especially powerless against the *gensdarmes*, whose armor rendered them invulnerable.

The feudal infantry was composed of the servants of the gensdarmes, and peasants taken from the plough. Their principal and most common office was to pick up their masters when they fell to the ground, and remount them, as also to despatch the disarmed cavaliers of the enemy. Sometimes they skirmished at the beginning of the action. Their offensive arms were the sword, the crossbow, the mace, and the sling; they carried no defensive arms, and nevertheless were often made to face great dangers, as the history of the battles of that period proves. The victors always made horrible carnage of this defenceless infantry.

Two historic facts will show the state of degradation to which the feudal infantry fell:

At the battle of Bouvines (1214), the Count de Boulogne formed his infantry into a hollow square, within which he, with six other cavaliers, after a certain period of combat, retired to recover breath; they came out in due time, refreshed, and ready to renew the strife. This was using their infantry as a kind of rampart.

At the battle of Crécy (1346), the Genoese bowmen, who formed a part of the French army, being thrown into confusion by the well-directed shafts of the English archers, and unable to advance, the king, Philip of Valois, enraged at seeing them retire, called out to the cavaliers: " *Or tôt tuez toute cette ribaudaille qui nous empêche la voie sans raison.*" The French gensdarmes fell upon the unfortunate Genoese infantry; but while they were thus engaged, the enemy gained the upper hand, and they suffered a complete defeat,—a defeat which, together with the sad and fatal names of Poictiers and Agincourt, will ever be for us and our descendants a striking proof of the errors committed by our ancestors, which brought France to the very brink of ruin, and had wellnigh caused us to be to this day a colony of England, instead of boasting the proud title of Frenchmen.

The *condottieri*, those warriors by contract who afflicted the Italian peninsula in the middle ages, also diminished the usefulness of infantry in the interest of their trade; for the petty princes who employed them could afford neither to support a large body of foot, nor to pay their wages; they succeeded, indeed, in reducing the number of effective foot to the tenth part of their mail-clad horse;* a proportion which shows how completely the principles which should govern the mutual relation of these two arms were at that time reversed.

Let us see how the infantry rose from this useless condition.

6. **Communal Infantry.**—In the twelfth century, several European nations, as the English, the Flemish, the Swiss, and the Lombards, still looked upon infantry with favor. In France, they were brought back to similar views by the crusades. In those distant expeditions the foot soldier could not be replaced as upon the soil of the mother country; he became of more value, was armed with more care, and drilled; and henceforth could render services which were appreciated. The introduction of fire-arms soon also favored the regeneration of

---

* *The Prince*, by Machiavelli, chap. xii.

infantry. At the same time the excessive tension of the feudal system brought together the two powers of the political hierarchy before most widely separated, namely, the sovereign and the burghers of the towns. These powers, both incommoded by the system, came to an understanding: the towns were erected into communes enjoying political rights, on condition of paying a tax and raising militia, which should march at the call of the king. Such is the origin of the *communal militia*. The creation of these citizen troops rendered the feudal troops ever after less important, and thus broke down the exclusive use of cavalry.

The communal force, raised by the authority of the commune, sometimes embraced mounted men, but was generally composed of infantry alone; the number of soldiers, or rather, to use the expression of the time, *sergeants* (*servientes*), rarely exceeded 500. Two thirds of the communal infantry carried bows or crossbows; the rest used maces, sticks loaded with lead, and halberds. Moreover, implements of agriculture, or the tools of the improvised soldier, frequently served him as arms, and he even wore in the ranks one of his ordinary garments, the blouse of the field-laborer. The infantry of the communes marched to the army under the parochial banner; an *advowee* of the bishop, or a municipal chief, or a representative of the king, commanded. It was not compelled to go beyond the limits of the commune more than a certain distance, reckoned in days' marches (at most forty days); beyond this distance, its maintenance devolved upon the king or the nobleman who employed it; and in default of the necessary funds for this purpose, the communal troops frequently dispersed. In the order of battle, the communal infantry was placed between the squadrons of horse: this intermixture is all that is known of its tactics.

This infantry proved, in its struggles against the nobles who surrounded a city, that men on foot could contend advantageously with knights completely mailed, whose prestige thus began to disappear. Nevertheless, this infantry was not worth much, although superior to the feudal infantry in organization, armament, discipline, and courage.

Still, the institution of communes did not relieve the dukes and counts from obeying the call of the king and taking part in war. In the rear of their gensdarmes, there always followed a body of infantry, composed of servants and peasants—these continuing to be badly organized, and more ready to pillage than to fight. To put an end to the confusion which reigned among these foot soldiers, Louis IX., in 1226, gave them a commandant under the name of *Grand Master of the Bowmen*, and this office was preserved down to the reign of Francis I., but contributed very little to the improvement of the condition of the infantry: at least, not until Charles VII.

7. Soldiers of Fortune.—Besides the feudal and communal infantry, there arose in France, at the close of the twelfth century, bands of soldiers of fortune, all on foot, known under various names, such as *Cotereaux, Soudoyers, Tard-venus, Malandrins, Routiers, Brabançons, Chaperons, Escorcheurs, Pastoureaux, Ribauds, Tondeurs, Millediables*. These mercenaries, gathered from all nations, formed undisciplined, vagabond troops, who, when not engaged in war, spent their time in pillaging—always taking the part of the sovereign who paid the highest wages. The French king, Louis VII., had as many as twenty thousand in his pay. Their depredations becoming intolerable, Philip Augustus, in 1183, sent an army which overcame them near Bourges. They recruited their force, and continued to fight and steal until the reign of Charles V. This monarch, taking pity on the French provinces which they were laying waste, ordered Du Guesclin to take command of their *grandes compagnies* and to lead them out of the kingdom; which difficult mission the Breton hero successfully accomplished (1366).

At this period, the French infantry, principally composed of crossbowmen, was drawn up in three or four ranks. In the order of battle, it was placed in the first line, in front of, or at the side of the first line of gensdarmes: in attacks it always occupied the front.

8. English Archers.—The English archers who did the French so much harm in the days of Crécy (1346) and Poictiers (1356), constituted one of the best bodies of infantry of the fourteenth century. Their defensive arms were a mailed jacket, a bassinet (or light helmet), and a round shield. Vigorous, and exercised in shooting from their infancy, they carried the long and stout bow, the string of which could be removed when it rained, an advantage not possessed by the crossbow. To arrest the impetuosity of the French gendarmery, they took their positions in front of their cavaliers, in a long line of little depth, each planting before him a stake 11 feet in length, like a cheval-de-frise; thence they discharged as many as ten arrows a minute, aimed at the horses, and dismounted our gensdarmes in a very short time, who, when once on foot, were very much embarrassed by their armor. We thus perceive that the English began to reason upon the art of war.

The Hussite infantry, such as was employed by the famous Bohemian Zisca about 1418, was also one of the first which succeeded in withstanding the gendarmery in open country, fighting behind a barricade of wagons, called a *tabor*.

9. Swiss Infantry.—From the beginning of the fourteenth century, the Swiss were compelled by necessity to resuscitate the ancient infantry, both because they were too poor to maintain cavalry, and because the country was ill adapted to its evolutions. They adopted a compact formation, and made use of a pike 18 feet in length, which they held by the middle with both hands, as our soldiers now hold the musket when crossing bayonets. The Swiss battalion was compared to a *forest of thorns;* it was often called the *hedgehog.* From the year 1386, the Swiss made use of culverins (a kind of long 18-pounder). In 1476, at the battles of Granson and Morat, in which they were victorious, they fought in full squares, having halberdiers, pikemen, and culverin artillerists in various proportions. The halberds were used in the *mêlée;* the pikes rested on the ground to resist the onset of the cavalry; the culverins were employed chiefly on the flanks, occasionally on the front. Their order of battle consisted of three masses arranged in *echelons,* the distance between the echelons being the range of a culverin: thus the cavalry could not break through them. In receiving an artillery attack, they awaited the first discharge,* then, taking advantage of the slow firing of that day, rushed upon the cannon and captured them.

The Swiss always fought with great courage; but this courage, stimulated at that time by the desire of independence, was not all that sustained them against the impetuous horsemen of the Duke of Burgundy. The true secret of the success of their infantry was their discipline, and the ensemble of action which is the result of discipline. This discipline was severe; it prescribed the most absolute silence, and prohibited leaving the ranks under pain of death. Thenceforth, the popular element of *com-*

---

* At Cerisoles (1544) they threw themselves on the ground, so that the balls might pass over them.

bination is found arrayed against the feudal element of *isolation;* but with this exception, the Swiss have not contributed to the improvement of the military art. Nevertheless, we shall find them, subsequently, looked upon as models, and European nations in the following century imitating their formation and taking bodies of Swiss infantry into their pay.

It is therefore to the Swiss that we must ascribe the more extensive introduction of infantry in the composition of armies after the fifteenth century.

10. Spanish Infantry.—The Spanish infantry was the next most celebrated after the Swiss, which it subsequently surpassed. Brave, disciplined, temperate, indefatigable;—such were the foot soldiers of Spain who fought in Italy or in the Netherlands under Charles V. and Philip II. Their contact with the Swiss taught them the art of forming close battalions; their compact order, bristling with pikes, became as difficult to break as the phalanx. Besides the pike, they carried as offensive weapons the sword, the poignard or dagger, and the arquebus: as defensive, a coat of mail. When the Swiss, or the large foot soldiers of Germany broke them, instead of flying they returned individually to the charge, rushing between the ranks of the victors and attacking with the poignard. In these duels and hand-to-hand fights, the Spanish soldier often fell, and always had every chance against him; but his bravery is nowhere more conspicuously proved.

The arquebus, with which the Spaniards were

armed, took the place of the Swiss culverin; it was provided with a forked prop, which relieved its weight while being discharged; whereas, before this time, it was discharged only when resting upon a tripod. This improved arquebus subsequently received in France the name of *mousquet*.

The Spanish infantry, being constantly required to fight, could not be disbanded at the end of each campaign; it therefore became a permanent body, and this circumstance, together with its courage, rendered it so thoroughly disciplined and warlike, that its proud battalions remained for more than a century the terror of the soldiers fighting in Italy and Flanders. The Spaniards often mingled their arquebusiers with the cavalry; a mixture which Gustavus Adolphus imitated, but which is at the present day proscribed.

The Spanish infantry was distinguished for its good discipline and *esprit;* a simple sergeant was obeyed like an officer. When a new recruit arrived, the older ones helped him with their advice and their purse, to put him at once in a condition to do honor to his country. "Their barracks," wrote La Noue, "were like schools, where the ordinary topics were the duties of the soldier and of the officer, honor, and whatever related to arms."

Charles V. had solidly organized the *tercios* (regiments) of his infantry, which out of Spain usually numbered 3,000 men, divided into fifteen companies of 200 men each; the tercio was commanded by a colonel of horse, or the senior captain.

The celebrated emperor had also instituted bounties as rewards for acts of courage, the least of which was two crowns; and the Spanish soldier considered it an honor to obtain them.

Similar organization and usages, it must be confessed, are wanting in the sixteenth century, among the infantry of other nations.

Let us return to the French infantry.

11. Frank Archers.—The Spaniards were not the only people who maintained a standing infantry. In the fifteenth and sixteenth centuries two attempts to establish it in a permanent form were made by the French kings; the first by Charles VII.

This monarch, having recovered his kingdom from the English, desired to consolidate his throne by surrounding it with regular troops. For this purpose he instituted the "free companies" of cavalry, and formed the infantry of the Frank archers. By an edict of 1448, he ordered each parish to raise and maintain one archer, well formed, and skilful in the use of the bow, whose duty it was to practise on Sundays and holidays, and to take the field at the royal command. In consideration of the military service to which he was bound, which was more extensive than that of the communal militia, and attached him exclusively to the king, the Frank archer was exempted from taxes. This exemption was, indeed, an indirect method of paying him; but in active service he received, in addition, the sum of 56 francs per month, which, together with his equipment and armament, was charged to the parish. He wore over his ordinary dress a kind of doublet, which came at least to the knees, formed of thirty thicknesses of linen cloth, enclosed between buckskins. They had great confidence in this defensive article, which, however, was sometimes covered by a steel corselet. On his head he wore a helmet without a crest or a visor. He was armed with the long bow and quiver, and a sword of moderate length.

Louis XI., in 1469, increased the number of Frank archers to 16,000. This force was distributed in four corps of 4,000 men, each commanded by a captain-general, over whom there was a chief of all the archers. France was divided into four military departments; within the limits of each a captain-general had to recruit his soldiers. Each corps of 4,000 was divided into eight bodies of 500. The first of these remained under the immediate order of the captain-general; a captain took command of each of the remaining seven. This reorganization by Louis XI. carried out the views of Charles VII.

This instituting of archers just at the time when portable fire-arms were beginning to spread, is singular enough; but they proved their inefficiency, and finally disappeared, not so much on account of their armament, which reduced them to light troops, as for other reasons. Scattered through the parishes, and drilling separately, the Frank archers could not but remain under the influence of the parish church, losing the habits of the soldier and taking those of the laborer and the artisan. In fact, this came to pass: after having behaved valiantly in some engagements, they could not, when peace came, yield to discipline, and sustain the *esprit du corps:* in short, they could not be soldiers. It became difficult to reassemble them; officers disliked to command them, and, sarcasm lending its aid, the institution was undermined. Toward the end of his reign, Louis XI. substituted for them 6,000 Swiss, 10,000 French soldiers of fortune, and a corps of German foot soldiers known under the name of *lansquenets* (Lands-knecht).

These lansquenets consisted of soldiers of fortune recruited in the German districts, near the Rhine. Being strong and tall, they at first formed bodies of pikemen; but, unlike the Swiss, they held the pike by the end of the shaft, and nevertheless managed it with skill. They were better than the French infantry, and on that account, for want of Swiss troops, they were intrusted with the guard of the cannon.

The infantry having rendered valuable service to Charles VIII., upon his return from the conquest of Naples, the greater part of the crowned heads comprehended the importance of this arm, and formed bodies of pikemen, in imitation of the Swiss. The French kings did not follow this example, but, trusting to the Swiss and the German soldiers of fortune enlisted in their pay, dispensed with the formation of regular national infantry.

Louis XII., however, endeavored to discipline his

infantry, and to give it more importance. He was the first to succeed in dismounting the gentry. At his solicitation, several of the most distinguished cavaliers, among others Bayard, accepted the command of bodies of foot. From that time the prejudices of the nobles against infantry were overcome, and numbers of young gentlemen, of whom Blaise de Montluc was one, exchanged the lance for the pike. This happy reform dates from 1507. By relieving the French infantry from the contempt under which it had suffered, it increased its valor tenfold, and contributed to the success of Louis XII. in Italy.

12. Legions of Francis I.—Francis I. did even more than Louis XII. for the improvement of the French infantry. At the battle of Marignan (1515) he commanded it in person on foot, and, armed with a pike, rushed to the charge, exclaiming, "*Qui m'aime me suive.*" Stimulated by his example, our infantry that day proved their superiority to the Swiss, and conquered them.

It was at this very time that Machiavelli laid it down as a maxim that "well organized infantry could hardly be beaten, except by infantry;" thus proclaiming the superiority of the foot soldiers. The idea was a profound and bold one, especially for one who had never worn a sword.

Francis I., entertaining, doubtless, the same view as the great writer, and unwilling to remain longer at the mercy of the capricious and exacting foreigners, resolved to create a national infantry. For some time he hesitated as to the organization to be adopted; but finally, influenced by the revival of learning, which turned the minds of men back to the ideas of the ancients, he decided to imitate the Roman formation; but he copied it in little else than in name.

In 1534 he formed seven legions, each bearing the name of the province in which it was raised.* Each legion consisted of six *bands*, the band having the following effective force:

OFFICERS.	Captain, ... 1 Lieutenants, ... 2 Ensigns, ... 2		5
NON-COMMISSIONED OFFICERS.	Centurions, ... 10 Corporals, ... 40 Quartermaster sergeants, 4 Sergeants, ... 6		60
4 DRUMMERS AND 2 FIFERS, ...			6
SOLDIERS.	Arquebusiers, . . . 200 Pikemen, ... 600 Crossbowmen, . . . 200		1,000
		Total,	1,071

The entire legion was commanded by one of the six captains of the band. Its force, according to the above schedule, amounted to 6,426 men, and that of the seven legions together to 44,982 men, including officers. The officers and non-commissioned

---

* The legion of Normandy, the legion of Brittany, the legion of Picardy, the legion of Languedoc, the legion of Guyenne, the legion of Champagne (raised also in Burgundy and Nivernais), the legion of the Dauphiné (raised also in Provence, Lyonnais, and Auvergne).

officers were required to be of the province in which the legion was raised.

The arquebusiers formed but the fifth part of the soldiers of a band, but, being frequently detached to fight as *enfants perdus* (forlorn hope), there were assigned to them exclusively one of the lieutenants and his ensign.

Among his privileges, the soldier of the legion enjoyed exemption from taxes to the amount of 20 *sols;* obtained a decoration, consisting of a gold ring, if he distinguished himself by a brilliant action, and attained to nobility by the simple fact of promotion to the grade of lieutenant. Those who were invalided by wounds served in the garrisons under pay, exempt for life from all tax or subsidy.

This project was never fully carried into effect, for it was at that time impossible in France to maintain nearly 45,000 foot soldiers, in addition to the old bands. At the death of Francis I., the legionary formation fell at once into disuse, and was followed by a return to isolated bands.

13. French Bands.—From this period, the band (*bande*) became the only foot corps in France possessing a regular and permanent organization. It was the real unit of formation of the infantry, and as it mostly numbered as many as 500 or 600 men, it corresponded very nearly to our modern battalion.

A captain commanded the band, seconded by a lieutenant, an ensign, quartermaster sergeants, sergeants, and corporals. The band marched to the drum and fife. Among the soldiers there were those distinguished as a first class, called *anspessades*, a name at first written *lanspessades*, derived from the Italian *lance spezzate*, broken lance, and originally applied to dismounted gensdarmes accepting service in the infantry.

The officers and pikemen were armed alike; a long pike, a sword, a helmet covering the ears, corselets or cuirasses, armlets, gauntlets, and cuisses. The arquebusiers had little helmets, mailed frocks and sleeves, and a sword or dirk. The former, therefore, belonged to the heavy-armed troops, or, as we should now say, to the infantry of the line; whilst the latter were of the light-armed kind.

The band was formed in full square, the pikemen in the centre, the arquebusiers outside. The captain took his place in front; the lieutenant stood as file closer; the ensign occupied the centre of the front rank of pikemen. In combat, the pikemen stood fast, while the arquebusiers scattered, under the direction of the lieutenant, and skirmished. If the battle became serious, the arquebusiers took refuge behind the pikemen, who received a charge with crossed pikes, or charged the enemy in close order. In this charge, they went almost shoulder to shoulder, and turned themselves obliquely to break through the enemy—a practice which seems to be a vestige of the ancient influence of the shield, which gave the infantry a tendency to extend itself to the right, because each soldier endeavored to cover himself with the shield of his neighbor.

On the battle field, the imposing masses of infantry were drawn up in large *battailles*,* square or rectangular, varying from 3,000 to 10,000 men. Manuscripts of the time represent these battailles as 42, or even 68 men in depth. The number of men covered with corselets was gradually diminished, and the pikemen were stripped of defensive arms.

It was on account of this formation in full square, that military works of the sixteenth century contained tables of square roots for any given number of soldiers, which tables formed the tactical manual of the epoch.

In these formations, the ranks, as well as the files, were separated by one step. Occasionally, in presence of the enemy, this distance was closed, and they formed in compact order, as in the case of the foot soldiers under Montluc at Cerisoles (1544).

During the religious wars which troubled France under the last Valois, fire-arms were multiplied in the ranks of the French infantry, being better suited to the character of wars consisting of skirmishes, captures and recaptures of posts; but as these arms were then used only for firing, the infantry, deprived of pikes, were incapable of either charging or receiving a charge. Hence this maxim of a contemporary warrior : "The arquebusiers without pikes are arms and legs without bodies." The pikemen were, in fact, retained down to the time when, by the invention of

---

* They already began to use the word *battalions;* subsequently, the name of the whole became the name of a part.

the bayonet, the fire-arm became at once an offensive and a defensive weapon.

The French bands were known under two grand divisions, according to their origin; the bands of Piedmont, which, for more than a century fought for the so much desired conquest of the Milanese and of Italy, and the bands of Picardy, which, on the northern frontier, contended against the Flemish and the English. After Francis I., there were farther distinguished, the bands of Champagne, opposed to the Germans, and the bands of Guyenne and Navarre, charged with the defence of the kingdom, on the side of the Pyrénées, against the Spaniards. Piedmont, Picardy, Champagne, Navarre! glorious names, which the oldest corps of our infantry bore even to the time of the Revolution.

The system of isolated bands was suited to the French character, inasmuch as it allowed the captains to distinguish themselves individually, and did not subject them to any superior authority. It was soon discovered, however, that it was necessary to combine several of these bands under the command of a single chief, in order to give greater impetus to the combatants, as well as to facilitate the direction and administration of the whole. Henry II., convinced of this necessity, tried to renew the legionary organization of Francis I.; but the peace of Cateau-Cambrésis deferred the realization of his projects by rendering them, for the time, useless. It was in the minority of Charles IX., in the early months of 1561, that the first regiments were formed, consisting of several bands—the chief officers receiving the title of colonel. The regimental organization of the old bands was completed in 1569.

The political troubles very much increased the number of regiments from the first, since each influential partisan received a commission to raise one; but these corps usually lasted no longer than the credit of their chiefs, and were disbanded in time of peace. Indeed, until the reign of Louis XIII., there were not many permanent regiments of infantry. The only regiments which, having their origin before this agitated period, survived it unbroken, were those resulting from the fusion of the old bands already known by the distinctive title of the *vieux corps*, which they retained to the end of the eighteenth century—the *moyens vieux* and the *petits vieux* following them in respect of seniority.

The order of battle of a regiment was at first a line of small squares, either full or hollow, each company forming a square. In serious actions the line was made full. For resisting cavalry they had already conceived of the formation in squares arranged in echelons so as to flank each other.

The introduction of the musket was almost simultaneous with the institution of the first regiments of French infantry. The musketeers fought only as skirmishers. Besides the musket, their whole armament and equipment consisted of a morion (small helmet), a buff leather vest without sleeves, a dirk, a knapsack, and a powder flask. To act with greater rapidity, some were mounted upon small horses, thus forming in the infantry regiments an accidental portion of cavalry. The heavy arquebus was gradually superseded by the musket.

The depth of the infantry formation was diminished, as defensive armor and the pike were abandoned. Even with the disposition of the regiment in a line of squares by companies, the depth of the lines could not exceed 10 or 12 men; for this corresponds to an effective force of 100 or 144 men in a company. This depth, habitually preserved, although the intervals were lessened, became the standard depth. Indeed, the depth of ten ranks may be regarded as that of the reign of Henry IV., as the following diagram, extracted from a contemporary author, shows.* It relates to the order of battle of a battalion of 500 men, the *p* standing for pikemen, and the *m* for musketeers.

FRENCH BATTALION ABOUT 1610.

```
mmmmmmmmm   ppppppppppppppppppppppppppp   mmmmmmmmmm
mmmmmmmmmm   ppppppppppppppppppppppppppp   mmmmmmmmmm
mmmmmmmmmm   ppppppppppppppppppppppppppp   mmmmmmmmmm
mmmmmmmmmm   ppppppppppppppppppppppppppp   mmmmmmmmmm
mmmmmmmmmm   ppppppppppppppppppppppppppp   mmmmmmmmmm
mmmmmmmmmm   ppppppppppppppppppppppppppp   mmmmmmmmmm
mmmmmmmmmm   ppppppppppppppppppppppppppp   mmmmmmmmmm
mmmmmmmmmm   ppppppppppppppppppppppppppp   mmmmmmmmmm
mmmmmmmmmm   ppppppppppppppppppppppppppp   mmmmmmmmmm
mmmmmmmmmm   ppppppppppppppppppppppppppp   mmmmmmmmmm
```

In this formation, the musketeers are placed in a position favorable to their action as light troops in skirmishing, and the pikemen still form, as in the old band, a solid centre, capable of sustaining a charge.

* *Principes de l'art militaire*, par J. de Billon, 1622, in 4to., p. 156.

The fire-arms in this battalion constitute two fifths of the whole force. The proportion went on increasing, and became two thirds in the reign of Louis XIII.*

14. Swedish Infantry.—The French infantry, under Henry IV., derived both its formation and tactics, in part, from the Dutch infantry, trained by the celebrated captain, Maurice of Nassau. So, also, the infantry under Louis XIV. borrowed some of its improvements from the Swedish infantry, formed in the school of the great war under Gustavus Adolphus. Let us, therefore, before proceeding to speak of its progress under the greatest of the Bourbons, first consider the improvements made by the conqueror of Leipsic.

Having to deal with the heavy Austrians, who were wedded to the use of large battalions, Gustavus Adolphus turned his attention to *mobility*. He rendered his infantry more manageable by dividing it into small independent corps, under separate commanders, and reducing its depth to six ranks. Sometimes, in battle, he made his files deploy to extend his front, so that the line was reduced to a depth of three ranks. He usually drew up his infantry in two lines, the full spaces of the first corresponding to the vacant ones of the second. This formation is exhibited in the following diagram, in which P denotes the pikemen, and M the musketeers.

* At this epoch the proportion of fire-arms was about the same in the Spanish infantry; for in 1637 the regiment of Jāen numbered 190 men, to wit: 60 pikemen, 90 arquebusiers, and 40 musketeers.

FORMATION OF THE SWEDISH INFANTRY, UNDER GUSTAVUS ADOLPHUS.

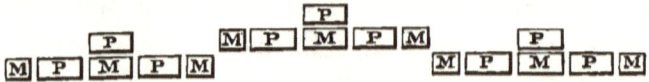

By diminishing the depth of his infantry, the Swedish king extended his front, and thereby increased the effect of the fire-arms; and this effect was the more increased in consequence of the greater number of musketeers in his troops than in preceding formations; for they numbered 72 in a company to 54 pikemen, which gives nearly three fifths as the proportion of portable fire-arms.

With the diminished depth he could also shorten the pike to 12 feet (English). He abolished the cuirasse of the pikemen, leaving as their sole defensive armor the helmet, called a *salade*. He lightened the musket, so that it could be fired without a rest, and carried upon the shoulder without a cushion; he adopted the cartridge carried in a pouch, instead of charges hung upon cords, which frequently became entangled with the soldiers' belts; and introduced firing in three ranks, very much like that of the present day.

All these innovations, increasing the mobility of the infantry, rendered it easy to pass from line into column; and thenceforth, in marches and in battles, the advantage was with Gustavus Adolphus, whose adversaries adhered to the formation 10 ranks deep, and used muskets of such clumsy construction that they could be loaded only by 94 commands.

The king of Sweden also put companies of musketeers between his squadrons of horse, a mixture which at that time, when the cavalry movements were slow, was both feasible and profitable.

15. Infantry of Louis XIV. and Louis XV.—The fire-arms used by the Swedish infantry were muskets with the match or wheel-lock, which had to be borne on the shoulder horizontally: consequently, the ranks could not be closed.

Two inventions appeared which changed this state of things. One was the flint-lock musket, which was introduced into the French army in 1652. The bayonet had already been in existence some years. It was then constructed with a wooden stock, so that, when placed upon the end of the musket, it prevented firing; but it was, nevertheless, an important improvement, inasmuch as it furnished the soldier with a weapon which was at once both offensive and defensive.

These inventions, which date from the time of the *Fronde*, were especially opportune, since Turenne had, in 1640, adopted for the French infantry the Swedish depth of six ranks. Lighter arms and a lighter formation, therefore, in combination, worked rapid progress.

With this depth of six ranks, the French battalion was drawn up as in the times of Henry IV.; pikemen in the centre, musketeers on the flanks. This formation is exhibited in the following diagram, taken from a contemporaneous work.* The battalion here forms a regiment.

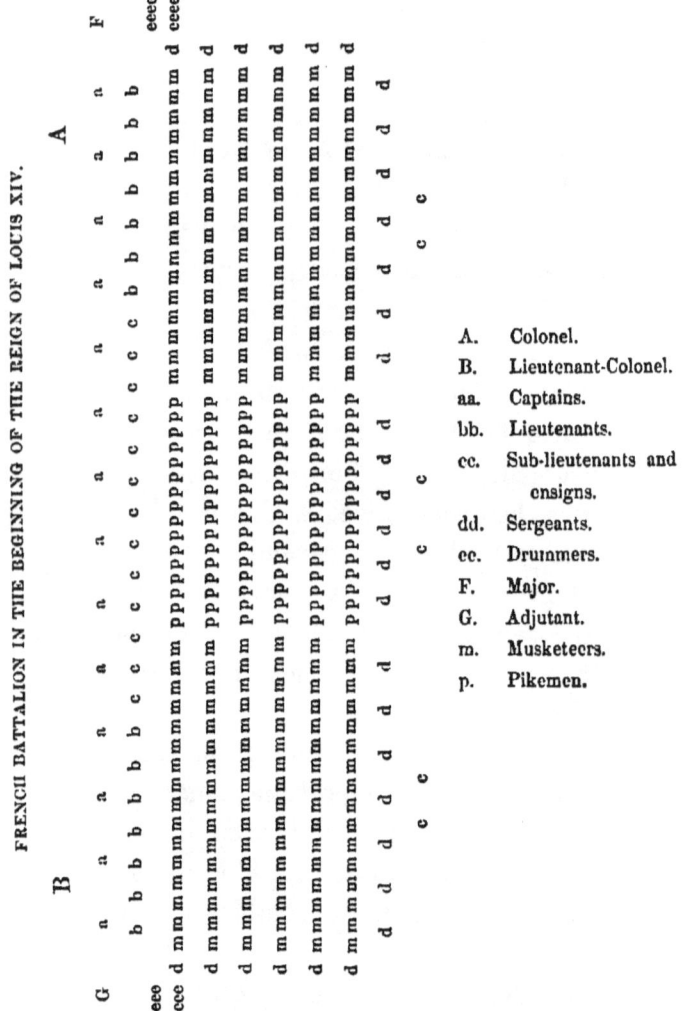

A. Colonel.
B. Lieutenant-Colonel.
aa. Captains.
bb. Lieutenants.
cc. Sub-lieutenants and ensigns.
dd. Sergeants.
ee. Drummers.
F. Major.
G. Adjutant.
m. Musketeers.
p. Pikemen.

In forming a square, the pikemen occupied the centre and the musketeers surrounded them on the

* *L'art de la guerre*, par Gaya, 1689, p. 158.

four sides, as in the following diagram* of a company
of 100 men, 36 pikemen and 64 musketeers.

COMPANY SQUARE (1673).

```
m m m m m m m m m m
m m m m m m m m m m
m m p p p p p p m m
m m p p p p p p m m
m m p p p p p p m m
m m p p p p p p m m
m m p p p p p p m m
m m p p p p p p m m
m m m m m m m m m m
m m m m m m m m m m
```

The new musket (the *fusil*) easily supplanted the old one (the *mousquet*, firelock), which completely disappeared from the French ranks in the last year of the seventeenth century. The bayonet took the place of the pike, but not without a struggle; for it was not until 1703 that Louis XIV., following the advice of Vauban against that of Montesquiou, finally abolished the latter. As the musket was now the only arm of the foot soldier, and its length was much less than that of the pike, it became necessary to reduce the depth of the line, which was now drawn up in four ranks. The diagram on the next page, taken from Puységur,† shows this reduced formation. The commandant of the battalion stands in front of the centre, having behind him the three colors, which are in

---

* From a work entitled *Les Devoirs militaires des officiers d'infanterie et de cavalerie*, par De La Fontaine, 1673, p. 404.

† *Art de la guerre par principes et par règles*, par le maréchal de Puységur, edition in 4to., t. i., p. 120.

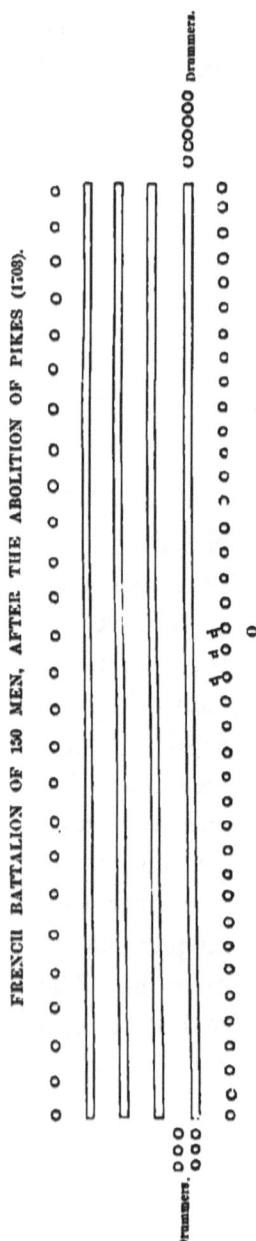

the middle of the line formed by the captains of companies and some other officers; a number of sergeants are placed in a line of file-closers behind the fourth rank. The distance of the ranks is about 12 feet; upon engaging with the enemy the ranks close to about 3 feet, and the officers in front fall back into the front rank of soldiers. The drummers are on the flanks.

Louis XIV. also originated the grenadiers, a wholly French creation, since copied by other nations. The first grenadiers were designed to throw grenades in sieges. In 1670 they became selected soldiers, and each regiment contained one company of them.

At the beginning of the reign of Louis XV.,* therefore,

---

* Light infantry dates from the reign of Louis XV. At the close of 1742, a simple servant, named *Fischer*, collected, near Prague, some of his comrades, and repulsed the attacks of the Austrian pandours. With his handful of men he

the French infantry was drawn up in four ranks, but these were still open ranks. A vast improvement in tactics soon followed, by the introduction of the cadenced and lock step, recommended by Marshal Saxe, which permitted marching and manœuvring in close ranks, each man then occupying the minimum space, both in rank and file. This is, consequently, the period from which we must date the light but compact infantry formation which covers the least possible ground; as may be seen by this figure, extracted from a work of that time.*

COMPANY OF FRENCH GRENADIERS IN ORDER OF BATTLE (1757).

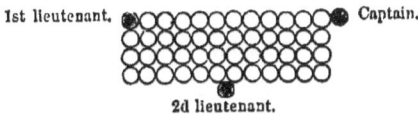

1st lieutenant.   Captain.

2d lieutenant.

16. Prussian Infantry.—At the death of Marshal Saxe, the Prussian infantry was the best in Europe. Trained by the Prince of Anhalt under Frederic-William I., and brought to perfection by Frederic the Great after his conquest of Silesia, it was familiar with marching in order of battle, forming and deploying close columns, and executing rapid firing. The Prussian gun had a cylindrical iron rammer, and a

---

displayed so much bravery and comprehension of military matters, that this small corps obtained, Nov. 1, 1743, through the influence of Count Saxe, rank in the army, under the name of *Chasseurs de Fischer*. At the end of the war, Fischer had under his command 400 foot and 200 mounted chasseurs. He was distinguished in the Seven Years' War. With him originated the foot and horse chasseurs.—*Tr.*

* *Amusements Militaires*, par Dupain, 1757, p. 226.

conical or funnel-shaped vent, which allowed powder to pass from the barrel into the pan, two features which saved two commands in loading, namely priming and reversing the rammer. The soldier being, moreover, trained in the most minute drill, under severe discipline, could fire six times in a minute; a degree of rapidity of execution which gave him the same advantage as if he were nearer, and fired more accurately; and hence firing was the chief mode of action of the Prussian infantry, although, in several battles, it attacked with the bayonet.

Modern infantry tactics came forth completely formed from the Prussian camps of the eighteenth century. The basis and the principles of the manœuvres of this arm, as now practised by the several nations, are the immediate results of the manœuvres either perfected or introduced by Frederic the Great, who was the first to combine precision of movement with celerity.

The Prussian battalion, drawn up in three ranks, was divided into eight equal companies, usually composed only of soldiers from the five companies of fusileers, the grenadiers fighting separately. The consequence was that men of different companies were united into one, and that the soldiers were not always under the same officers in the camp and in the field. To this twofold inconvenience there was added the anomaly of having in each battalion one company of fusileers commanded by a lieutenant, whilst each of the others was under the orders of a first or second captain.

In order of battle the officers in the front rank occupied the interval between the companies; behind them stood a non-commissioned officer. In a single rank, four paces in the rear, stood all the officers and non-commissioned officers who were not between the

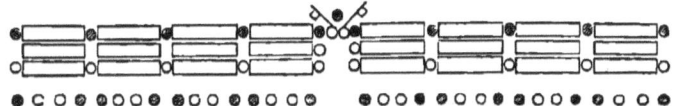

PRUSSIAN BATTALION (1752).

companies. The colors were in the centre, dividing the battalion into two equal parts, called wings, each wing formed of two divisions, and each division of two companies. On each side of the colors, three of the files always reserved their fire. The commandant of the battalion stood in front of the colors. The preceding diagram represents this formation : ● designates an officer; ○ a non-commissioned officer.

The Prussian company, when drawn up separately, was divided into four sections, the supernumeraries forming a separate detachment, in three ranks, in rear of the left flank, as is shown in the following figure.

PRUSSIAN COMPANY.

It was one of the features of the Prussian infantry to execute firing while marching to the charge, a practice since abandoned, as producing more disorder than effect. They were also distinguished for their close-fitting dress and very precise carriage. Under the fire of the enemy, without losing in any degree their quickness of movement, they preserved the most immovable solidity, which, more than once, contributed to save Frederic the Great from impending defeat.

17. Progress to the present time.—From the time of the great Frederic, the history of infantry may be summed up in a few words. The formation in three ranks was definitely adopted in France with the introduction of the Prussian drill among the troops, with a view to giving them uniform instruction.

The principal minister of war of the reign of Louis XVI., Count de Saint-Germain, instituted (1775) in each regiment of infantry, a company of *chasseurs*, a second company of *élite*, to which good soldiers could be promoted, as a reward for distinguished services, without regard to their stature. In 1804 this company, which had disappeared during the Revolution, reappeared, under the name of *voltigeurs;* but there was now one company to each battalion, instead of one to a regiment, as formerly. As each battalion contained also a company of grenadiers, its two flanks, in the order of battle, were each supported by a company of picked men, which rendered unnecessary the select detachment formerly placed in reserve on the left flank, when the depth of the line had been reduced.

In the subsequent campaigns, the French select soldiers, like the grenadiers of Frederic, fought apart from their regiment, no longer forming merely select battalions, but distinct army-corps, used as a reserve.

From this epoch, the infantry organization has remained very nearly the same, with the exception of the number of centre companies of a battalion, and the number of battalions to a regiment, which have varied from time to time.

As to the tactics of the infantry during this period, it may be said to consist no longer in solidity and firing; the Prussian method is disappearing, and the secret of success is possessed by those who best understand marching and attacking. All the wars of the first republic and of the reign of Napoleon I., especially the campaigns of 1796, in Italy, and of 1805, in Germany, clearly set forth this characteristic feature in the progress of modern military art.*

We have yet to point out two essential modifications:

The first is the formation in two ranks, adopted in 1810 by the English; a formation which is particularly suited to their solid and phlegmatic troops. The Swiss infantry has also followed the example of the English, and now forms in only two ranks. The Russian infantry, in great manœuvres, has begun to form in two ranks; but as yet has never appeared upon the battle-field in less than three. In France, we have adhered to the habitual depth of three ranks, as offer-

---

* The secret of Napoleon's success was as much in the *legs* as *arms*—in marching more than fighting. Massing his forces, and profiting by any fault of the enemy, he fell upon his exposed points like a thunderbolt, crushing him at a blow.—*Tr.*

ing better resistance to cavalry; but high military authorities have pronounced in favor of two ranks, which we have, indeed, occasionally employed.*

The second modification relates to the armament. The flint lock becomes sluggish in damp weather, and a continued rain may silence it completely. Frederic the Great, in order to remedy this evil, which was the more fatal because his infantry operated principally by firing, had provided each soldier with a piece of leather as a cover for the lock, to protect it from moisture; but this was but a palliative, for the leather covering, attached to the cartridge-box during a march, soon became unfit for its purpose. The modern invention of percussion arms has more satisfactorily resolved the problem. These arms, adopted in France in 1840, are now in the hands of all European soldiers. In all probability, it will not be long before the fire-arm of the infantry will be constructed throughout the civilized world with the rifled bore, and the foot soldier will thenceforth project the improved elongated ball with such precision of aim, and at such distances, as greatly to increase his importance as a combatant.

18. Remarks.—The rapid history which we have just sketched, shows that the depth of infantry regularly diminished with the progress of the military art. Thus we see that the formation of this arm has passed successively, from the earliest times to the present, from the Egyptian square battalions of 100 men on a

---

* See the following chapter, Sect.

side, to the compact formation of the Greek phalanx, 16 men in depth, and to the subdivided formation of the Roman legion, six men deep; and from the square formation of the French bands, to the thinner ones of six ranks, under Gustavus Adolphus and Turenne; of four ranks under Maurice de Saxe; and of three ranks under Frederic-William I.; while, at the present day, it consists of three ranks among the French, and of but two among the English. There is little probability that this depth will be further diminished until the formation is reduced to a single rank;* nevertheless, the recent improvements in portable fire-arms, and the employment of Congreve rockets against troops, would seem to make such a result not absolutely impossible.

We will remark, in conclusion, that victorious nations, from the beginning of the world, have owed their success to good infantry.

Alexander the Great overturned Darius and his empire with the Macedonian phalanx, thoroughly organized by his father Philip, and the excellent Greek soldiers who accompanied him.

The Romans were correct in their estimate of the Greek phalanx, and conquered almost the whole known world with the legion; for their armies never contained any considerable proportion of cavalry.

Charles V. and Philip II., of Spain, owed their victories to their brave infantry.

Frederic the Great obtained his first successes with the Prussian infantry, formed and disciplined under the reign of his predecessor.

* This would almost amount to converting the whole formation into that of skirmishers.

Napoleon I. conquered at Austerlitz, Jena, Friedland, and Wagram, with the infantry inured by the wars of the Revolution, and trained in the camp of Boulogne.

Finally, without their infantry, the English would not have met with the success that attended their arms in the war in Spain from 1809 to 1814.

CHAPTER SECOND.

INFANTRY FORMATION AND TACTICS.

1. General Principles.—Infantry is capable of fighting upon all kinds of ground, and under all circumstances; it is readily recruited, easily instructed, and maintained at small expense. Whether receiving the enemy's attack, or marching to the charge, it can, *in case of need*, dispense with the other arms. It constitutes, therefore, *par excellence*, the corps which should be the chief basis of an army.

The foot soldier is required to be,—1st, *skilful*, because his arm is effective only when managed with dexterity; 2d, *agile*, that he may be able to overcome all the obstacles of the ground; 3d, *robust*, that he may readily support privation and fatigue; 4th, *intelligent*, that he may not be a mere machine, but a thinking being, whose moral nature may be appealed to. He must be able to fight at all hours, and in all countries, whatever may be the season or climate; in short, he must possess the character of *universality* in the highest possible degree.

His clothing should be simple, convenient, and warm; contrived solely with a view to his health, subject neither to caprice nor to fashion; his shoes should be strong, and well-fitting; his head-gear light, but yet such as to resist the sabre of cavalry.

The percussion gun, with the bayonet, is a portable implement, as perfect (nearly*) as the present state of the mechanic arts permits; the certainty of its fire makes it an excellent arm for the infantry, and the bayonet is the only arm which is suitable for the foot soldier in personal encounters. The sabre worn by the non-commissioned officers and privates of select formations is of very little use except at the bivouac, where it serves, to some extent, as a bill-hook and an axe.

The physical force of the infantry soldier is to be increased by drills, such as those of the manual, marches in line and by flank, various manœuvres, etc.; as also by gymnastics, which impart suppleness to his limbs. His moral force is to be increased by means of discipline, which, properly observed, gives uniform and increased power of action, and also by the inculcation of the most elevated ideas of his strength, his importance, and his superiority over those with whom he has to contend. It is, especially, to be proved to him that with his bayonet he should never fear cavalry, notwithstanding the apparently commanding position of the mounted soldier. He is to be rendered habitually calm in the most critical moments, amid showers of grape-shot, and in despite of

---

* We put in this qualification in view of the rifled gun.

hunger and thirst. His moral education, however, can be properly completed only by war.

An infantry soldier, with a load of 55 pounds,* should be able to march during ten hours of the day: any troop of foot, at this rate, will outdo the best cavalry, and can even overtake it in pursuit in a short time, the horse having more need of repose than man. Thus, in 1805, when the Archduke Ferdinand, upon his leaving Ulm, was pursued by the French, the grenadiers of Oudinot marched as much as fourteen leagues (over 35 miles) a day, never permitting the cavalry of the enemy to rest, and finally causing a part of them to fall into the hands of the French cavalry.

The battalion is the unit of the infantry force, and in the instruction of the soldier, his ultimate destination as a constituent of the battalion must be kept in view. This is to be effected synthetically, by proceeding from the simple to the compound, *from the individual to the mass.* We should begin with a single man, then two men, three men, four men, etc., in a single rank. When they have become sufficiently skilful in one rank, they are to be combined in two and three ranks.

We have observed in the preceding chapter that we owe to Marshal Saxe the introduction of the lock-

* "There are five things from which the soldier must never be separated: his gun, his cartridges, his knapsack, his provisions for at least four days, and his pioneer tool. Let the knapsack be reduced to the smallest size, let him carry in it a shirt, a pair of shoes, a stock, a handkerchief, a tinder-box; but let him have it always with him; for once separated from him, it never returns."—*Mémoires de Napoléon I*, seconde note sur les considérations sur l'art de la guerre.*

step, which enables troops to march and manœuvre in closed ranks; this step is fundamental in all good evolutions. The infantry step is two French feet (28 inches in our service) in length. There are two kinds of step:—the *direct* and *oblique;* the latter is equivalent to a wheel of one fourth and a direct step. With the direct step, the foot soldier goes, in one minute, 50 metres at the ordinary pace, 60 metres at the marching pace, 66 metres at the quick pace, 81 metres at charging pace, and 100 metres (109 yards English) upon a run. He occupies a space, in the rank, of one half a metre (20 inches); and in the file, with his knapsack, the same space; there is an interval of $0^m.32$ (14 inches) between the ranks. But we need not dwell any longer upon these special details.

The formation in three ranks gives more firmness than that in two, chiefly for resisting cavalry, and for attack in line, and on this account it has been preserved in France down to the present time, excepting for the *chasseurs à pied*. The English draw up their infantry in two ranks, and a number of authorities have advocated it;[*] but the French formation com-

---

[*] Napoleon I. in his *Mémoires*, and in a letter to Marmont, Oct. 13, 1813; Marshal Marmont (*de l'Esprit des institutions militaires*, p. 40); Marshal Gouvion Saint-Cyr (*Mémoires*, vol. i., p. 16); Generals Jomini, Chambray, and Decker.

General Dufour, who has been at the head of the federal army of Switzerland, expresses a preference for three ranks, for the infantry of his country, as stronger and more defensive, although the official depth is there but two (see his *Cours de Tactique*, 1851, p. 59). Marshal Bugeaud (*Aperçus sur la guerre*) thinks that infantry should have both formations, so that either may be employed according to circumstances and the views of the general. Marshal Saint-Arnaud, at the commence-

bines the advantages of both, since it is easy to pass from the formation in three ranks to that in two. As for the reason why the three-rank has prevailed over the six-rank formation of Gustavus Adolphus, and over the still deeper ones of antiquity, it may be given in a few words: it is, that our predecessors had but a single mode of formation, whereas we have several, and can pass from one to the other, by means of *manœuvres*.

But although the infantry is, as we have above remarked, that arm which is, *par excellence*, the basis of an army—the only one which, *in case of need*, can rely upon itself alone—it must, nevertheless, not be supposed that it can by itself produce, in all cases, the *maximum of effect;* for, in pursuit, the enemy will often escape from it;* and, when overcome, it will be easily picked up by the cavalry.† Without cavalry, the infantry will be perpetually harassed by the enemy, fatigued by the advance guard-duty which its own safety requires, and very much exposed, in case of defeat, in an entirely open country. It is apparent, therefore, *à priori*, that infantry and cavalry are necessary to each other, and should be considered as indispensable parts of the same whole, whether of an army-corps or an army.

ment of the war in the East, adopted the formation in two ranks for his troops, and proclaimed it in the orders of the day. The Imperial Guard usually manœuvres in two ranks.

* At Bautzen (1813), for want of cavalry, the result of our victory was not as complete as at Austerlitz.

† At Rivoli (1796) we picked up the Austrian battalions which had become separated from their cavalry and artillery.

2. Modes of Action of Infantry.—The infantry has two modes of action, or, if the expression be preferable, two methods of operating. It operates:

1st. By firing, distant or near.*
2d. With sabre or bayonet.

The present sabre of the infantry, however, is a very poor arm, and is, besides, given only to the non-commissioned officers and the soldiers of the select companies. We may, therefore, consider the attack or defence with the bayonet, as the only mode of action of the infantry in close fight.

The bayonet should be sparingly employed; it is, after all, but an extremely inferior weapon; and it can hardly be required of soldiers to expose themselves to a hand-to-hand fight whilst the means of defence are so imperfect.

The French have, indeed, gained a well-deserved reputation abroad by the energy of their charge with the bayonet; for this mode of attack agrees admirably with their character, and is perfectly suited to the *furia Francesa:* thus with some reason the bayonet has been distinguished as the "weapon of the French."

The bayonet attack is only good when it is required to make a sudden demonstration. We may even say that, in general, it is but a demonstration, inasmuch as very few cases are cited in which it was really a charge,—that is to say, in which there really was a *collision*. The only authentic case, indeed, is that in

---

* NEAR, that is, at a very short distance, as for example, in the defence of a military *crest*. See, hereafter, Part III., Chap. viii., sec. 2.

which the grenadiers of Oudinot, at Amstetten, in 1805, met the Russian rear guard of Bagration.

This demonstration generally forces the enemy to fall back, by the moral effect produced by such a charge;* and it is in this sense alone, *compelling the enemy to fall back*, that we use the phrase *bayonet charge*, in cases where this attack occurs between considerable bodies of troops. Nevertheless, there are cases in which the bayonet charge has not only been followed by collision, but has degenerated into a *mêlée;* as, for example, in 1800, during the siege of Genoa, on the part of the troops of Soult, the day of the 10th Floréal (April 30th).†

If, then, the bayonet is only to be used in moderation, the distant mode of action remains the principal mode of action of infantry. Frederic II. placed victory in well executed firing, as Marshal Saxe placed it in the legs (marching and manœuvring); and these two celebrated warriors were both right: for while the legs prepare the victory, firing secures it.

There are two kinds of firing,—simultaneous, by battalions, companies, &c., and firing at will. The former, when executed by the three ranks, produces the *maximum effect*, but on account of the attention it requires on the part of both officers and troops, is with difficulty practised in the field. Firing by command

* General Duhesme, at the battle of Caldiero (1805), finding himself exposed to the fire of an Austrian corps, superior in numbers, made a demonstration with the bayonet; the Austrians fell back, *although an impassable ravine separated the two armies.*

† In this contest "they fought hand-to-hand; they even seized each other by the hair." Thiébault, *Blocus de Gênes*, 3d ed., 1847, vol. i., p. 231.

is divided into firing by battalions, by half battalions, and by companies, succeeding each other in alternation, in such a manner as always to keep a portion of the pieces loaded.

Firing by battalions, or even by half-battalions, is used either in an offensive movement, or in retreat. The force halts, delivers one or more rounds, then renews the march. This kind of firing may also be used with advantage before coming out of an ambuscade. Firing in a charge must be the most destructive possible, and consequently should consist of the simultaneous firing of three ranks.

Firing by divisions, or by companies, is especially suitable for infantry in position, when repelling feeble attacks.

Firing by command by ranks, which was tried in the early part of this century against cavalry, has been abandoned as ineffective.

But all firing by command can continue but a short time in battle, and becomes impracticable in any brisk action; for the orders of the different officers are confounded together, and the noise of the artillery and even of the musketry, the excitement of the combat, increased by the cries of the wounded, make it impossible for the soldiers to give the attention necessary for loading and firing together. Moreover, all firing by command, ends in firing by two ranks; and even the latter cannot be long maintained in the mode prescribed by the French regulations—for the man in the third rank is loth to part with his habitual arm, and, becoming impatient at not taking part in the combat, at last takes to firing on his own account, instead of loading for the man in the second rank. Again, if the man in the third rank remains in his place and fires horizontally, he runs the risk of wounding the men of the first and second ranks; if he remains in his place and fires high, his fire does not reach the enemy, and becomes useless; finally, if he pushes into the second rank, he crowds it, and impedes its action, whence result disorder and accidents. The advocates of the formation in two ranks argue from these facts in favor of their views. It follows that the fire *by file* is the most destructive, gives the soldier the best chance of loading and aiming, and is suited to all cases; being, in fact, that into which any other kind of firing degenerates; in short, it is the veritable *feu de combat.*

Firing, as the reader is aware, may be either *direct* or *oblique;* but one should never fire on the march, which only produces disorder, and but little effect. Besides, when a movement is made on the battle field, it is with a view to reach a certain position, and then it should be reached with the least possible delay.

We will terminate these details respecting firing by two maxims, extracted from the *Aperçus sur quelques détails de la guerre* of Marshal Bugeaud:

1st. Firing at too great a distance is the mark of bad infantry; good soldiers are sparing of their fire.

2d. The waste of ammunition is the greatest fault with which infantry can be reproached.[*]

---

[*] Marshal Bugeaud also recommends loading with two balls, and advises that every infantry officer should, in the field, carry a double-barrelled piece, as practised in the Austrian army.

Marshal Saxe long ago condemned excessive firing (*tirerie*); an opinion the more remarkable, that, in his day, the successes of the Prussians were ascribed to their firing. He says, speaking of the abuse of firing: "*En tirant, on fait plus de bruit que de mal et on est toujours battu.*"*

3. The Battalion.—The battalion is the *tactical unit* of infantry. In France it is composed of 8 platoons,† which, grouped two-and-two, form 4 divisions.

"The battalion is the true military element, the unit in the battle; we move and manœuvre by battalions; we fight by battalions."

"Two conditions are to be observed in the numerical constitution of the battalion: 1st, it must not be unwieldy; and 2d, it should be of such size that, when deployed, the voice of the commander may be heard at both extremities."‡

According to this principle, the front of the battalion should not exceed 170 yards, which embraces a force of about 1,000 men,§ if formed in three ranks; which is the maximum limit calculated with reference to the unavoidable losses which a body of troops suffer in passing from the inactivity of the garrison to the laborious life of the camp.

It is one of the advantages of our modern bat-

---

* *Rêveries*, chap. i., art. 6.

† The French platoon corresponds to our company.—*Tr.*

‡ Marmont, *Esprit des institutions militaires*, pp. 38, 39.

§ A front of 170 yards, or 155 metres, at the rate of two men in the rank for each metre, gives 310 men in a rank, 930 in three ranks, and 1,000 men for the total force, if we count 70 file-closers, that is, about one file-closer for each two metres of front.

talion, that its subdivisions, for administrative discipline and for evolutions, are identical; so that the soldiers are always under the orders of the same officers: thus the *régime* of the camp and the *régime* of the field are in entire accordance. It was not so in France under the reign of Louis XIV., nor in Prussia during the wars of the great Frederic.

Moreover, all the subdivisions of the battalion are symmetrical and equal, which is a great convenience in evolutions.

4. Manœuvres.—By a *manœuvre* we understand any movement, the object of which is to change a body from one condition or position to another. Tactics consist of manœuvres.

In order to secure their successful performance, especially in war, they should combine simplicity, clearness, promptness, and facility of execution. The manœuvres prescribed by the French regulations fulfil these conditions.

The training of troops to manœuvres, and familiarizing them with the most rapid and complicated movements, are among the most important duties of the officers, in which they can succeed only by continual and often wearisome repetitions; but so many unforeseen causes of disorder occur on the field in the presence of the enemy, that we cannot be too careful to provide in advance against their ill effects, by regularity, ensemble, solidity and steadiness in manœuvres—qualities acquired only by numerous drills practised in times of peace.

Every body of troops during a manœuvre is in a condition of danger; for, while manœuvring, they cannot defend themselves. This axiom is especially applicable to infantry. Manœuvring must therefore be effected in the shortest possible time; all manœuvres should, when practicable, be covered, and executed, in preference, in rear of the line of battle.

To prevent innovations and secure uniformity, the instructions to be given to the men are invariably fixed by the regulations for each arm of the service.

5. Order of Battle.—To resist the enemy, a number of battalions of infantry are drawn up in two lines; the first line deployed with but small intervals of about 50 feet between the flanks of the battalions; the second line of battalions is ployed in double column, in order to be the more able to come to the aid of the first, which is its proper duty. When the first line yields, the second advances and takes its place; or else, if the first line breaks, it can disperse through the intervals of the second, and the latter, once unmasked, deploys and receives the charge of the adversary. In order to do this effectively, the second line must have been kept fresh during the engagement of the first, and hence it is posted about 300 yards in its rear,[*] at which distance the enemy's fire will hardly reach it. If the broken character of the ground covers the second line, it can be brought within 100 yards of the first, but seldom nearer. To take it beyond

---

[*] The distance of the two lines is thus about double the front of a battalion.

300 yards would deprive the first of its support; this distance, therefore, should not be exceeded; but if the second line, even 300 yards in rear, suffers too much from the artillery of the enemy, it should be deployed. It is usual to extend the second line beyond the first, in order to protect the flanks of the latter.

ORDER OF BATTLE OF THE INFANTRY.

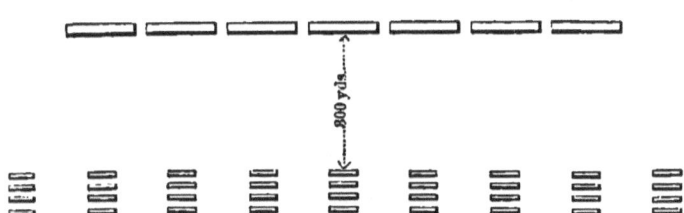

The regulations of 1831 respecting the manœuvring of the infantry, treat first of the evolutions in a single line, and then of those performed in two lines. But the second line is dependent upon the first, inasmuch as it should perform the same movements to keep itself in the same relative position. The two lines, however, execute their movements separately, and in practice it can hardly be otherwise, since the difference of the ground which they severally occupy may occasion modifications in the details of execution.

6. **Marching formations.**—The infantry has four marching formations:
1st. Marching in line;
2d. Marching by flank;
3d. Marching in column;
4th. Marching in square.

A battalion (and *a fortiori* a larger body of troops),

in consequence of its extended front and slight depth, cannot long march in line without suffering injurious breaks, produced either by the march itself, or by encountering various obstacles: besides, there are very few localities sufficiently wide and clear to permit the execution of such a march without inconvenience. A battalion will therefore never march in line except to charge with the bayonet, or when, having engaged the infantry of the enemy, it may be necessary to advance or retire progressively a few hundred paces.

Marching by the flank allows the battalion to pass through the narrowest roads; but in this kind of march, as soon as the step is broken, which quickly happens, the distances are lost and the column is lengthened, so that if it were required suddenly to face to the front, the line which it would form would be irregular. Besides, in the march by flank of a battalion, the front and the rear are too far apart for mutual support in case of attack. Hence, a battalion should never march by the flank in presence of the enemy, unless it be to lean to the right or to the left a few steps only, and not even for that purpose, if it is seriously engaged.

Marching by column is not subject to the same inconveniences as marching in line or by flank; it is consequently the most appropriate for movements or manœuvres. The column by sections or by platoons, at full distance, is the best marching column. The march of a column is quite simple; taking care only to preserve the distances. The men may march at ease and carry their guns at will. Changes of direction are made either by *turning* or *wheeling*, according as the new direction is or is not on the side of the guide.

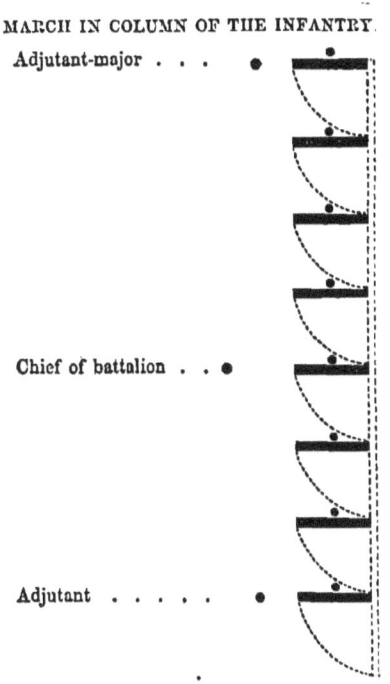

MARCH IN COLUMN OF THE INFANTRY.

Adjutant-major . . . ●

Chief of battalion . . ●

Adjutant . . . . . ●

It is a general principle respecting columns, and an essential one for columns on a march, that they never occupy a greater space from the front to the rear, than they would occupy in line, so that it may always be easy to pass from one order of formation to the other.

Marching in square is employed to reach a shelter not far distant, during a respite from attacking cavalry. It is often more prudent, in open country, to march in square than to re-form the column. To march in square, the two *lateral* lines relatively to the direction of the march, form *by the flank*, and the fourth faces to the front. The march in square is always undulating and uncertain: it should be regarded as purely accidental. In the wars of the Revolution and Empire, squares were marched with success; we need only recall in this connection the battles of Heliopolis (April, 1800), Auerstädt (October 14, 1806),

Lutzen (May 2, 1813). In Egypt they marched in squares, even for days; but this was for the purpose of assuring the soldiers against a new enemy, and to cover the sick and wounded, and the artillery; and with this object the squares were at first formed with six ranks, a superfluous depth, which was afterward reduced to three, and even to two ranks.

7. Formations of Attack.—We shall consider five kinds of formations of attack for the infantry:

1st. Attack in line;
2d. Attack in column;
3d. Attack as skirmishers;
4th. Attack in echelon;
5th. Attack in squares.

Attack in line.—This attack permits the troops to make use of their whole fire, to come upon the enemy upon a greater front, and thus to menace him with danger at all points; to render his defeat more complete and more certain; finally, it offers less exposure to the enemy's artillery.

These are real advantages, and the attack in line, executed by *solid and well trained* troops, ought to be preferred in a variety of circumstances.

To these considerations we may add this formal opinion of Marshal Bugeaud: "The *deployed* order is the veritable order of combat."

The attack in line will generally be employed against infantry: nevertheless, it has occasionally succeeded against cavalry badly managed, but it then requires very solid infantry.

But this order is not suited to all kinds of ground. The greater part of the officers and non-commissioned officers are in the position of file-closers; the others are inserted in the ranks: the soldier is thus deprived of the stimulus of their example. Artillery and musketry may produce voids in the ranks, which can be filled only at the expense of the rapidity of march; it may, perhaps, become necessary to halt, and thenceforth there is no longer any impetus; and, the natural instinct of the soldier prompting him to use his arms at the sight of danger, firing begins in spite of the officers, and the charge fails. In such a case, a battalion may be defeated, and cause a general rout, by uncovering the flanks of the neighboring battalions.

Attack in column.—The inconveniences of the attack in line which we have just stated, frequently lead to a preference for the attack in column.

The best offensive column is the *double-central*, as prescribed by the regulations; which is very quickly formed and deployed, and in which the grenadiers and voltigeurs constitute a reserve in the rear, which can be formed and deployed in face of the enemy, while kept at a distance by the fire of the fourth and fifth

DOUBLE-CENTRAL COLUMN.

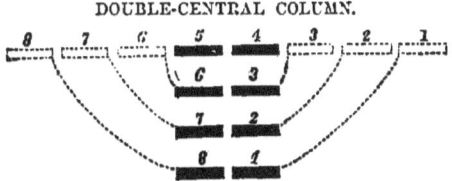

platoons on the line of battle. This last advantage is important, for generally, after the charge, it is necessary to deploy the column of attack, to preserve the point which has been gained.

There are also employed, occasionally, columns by platoons or by sections, at half distance, which can fight with advantage on narrow ground. When several of such columns are made to act upon broken ground, it is prudent to throw one or more companies of skirmishers on the front and flanks of each column, to unite it with the neighboring columns, and protect its march against the skirmishers of the enemy.

According to Guibert, the depth of an offensive column should not exceed eight subdivisions. Since this writer, the experience of the nineteenth century has caused this depth to be reduced to four subdivisions only, as shown by the figure of the double-central column.

In the column, the officers and non-commissioned officers, being all placed between the platoons or divisions, or on their flanks, exercise a very powerful physical and moral influence upon the soldiers.

Once in motion, the column of attack should neither stop to fire nor to deploy; on the contrary, taking advantage of its first ardor and the impetus given by its depth, it should be precipitated in compact form upon the enemy, sweeping away all opposition. To stop within reach of the enemy to deploy would be a dangerous operation, which might lead to defeat in case the enemy knew how to profit by it.

The formation in column offers three principal advantages: 1st, the men being grouped *en masse*, are more easily electrified with enthusiasm than in the thin and extended formation in line; 2d, the leading division of the column has more boldness, because it feels itself followed and supported, and is conscious that it cannot stop without being overthrown; 3d, the other divisions, seeing themselves covered by the first, march resolutely. As to the loss of fire in this formation, it is compensated by throwing out skirmishers on the flanks.

The column acts by a succession of efforts depending upon its depth; nevertheless, the first subdivision has no greater velocity than those which follow it; for if it had, the velocity of a column would increase with its depth, whereas just the contrary takes place.

The order in column allows marching without wavering; is adapted to all kinds of ground, and may take advantage of the irregularities of the surface, to shelter itself from the fire of the enemy. Columns, moreover, can resist cavalry, and the destruction of one column does not, necessarily, involve that of the others. All these are advantages which the order in column offers over the order in line, as an offensive formation.

Troops who are but partially trained may be made to fight in column; for it is not essential in the attack in column that the soldier should know how to march well; it is sufficient that the guides and officers are intelligent, firm, and have sufficient authority to restrain the soldier.

The French have obtained their most notable successes by the attack in columns, which is perfectly congenial to their national character.

Infantry attacks intrenchments in numerous columns, of little depth and narrow front; it exposes thus fewer to the enemy's fire lining the parapets, and reserves to itself the power of reënforcing the attack upon the weakest point.

The great objection to columns of attack is their liability to suffering from the fire of artillery, especially in a flat country; and this often becomes so serious as to compel them to deploy without delay.

We have sometimes employed, in dangerous operations, an order of attack compounded of the attack in line and the attack in column, which we have just analyzed. It consists in marching one battalion in line, while two others, in column, occupy each of the flanks of the deployed battalion; thus, in each group of three battalions, the advantages of the two methods are combined, and their disadvantages lessened. It

MIXED FORMATION.

3d.　　2d bat.　　1st.

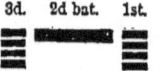

was in this order that the French army, in 1797, forded the broad bed of the Tagliamento in presence of the Austrians; and that a part of the Russians fought at Eylau (1807).

In several modern battles, particularly at Wagram (1809), offensive columns composed of a large number of battalions have been employed; but they should be regarded as exceptionable formations, for under the sweeping fire of the adversary's artillery they are always cruelly decimated, even in case of success.

Attack as skirmishers.—In mountainous and woody countries there are positions which can be attacked neither in line nor in column, the ground being too much covered or cut up by ravines and escarpments to allow any order of march to be observed. They are then attacked by skirmishers; but these must be in large numbers; thus battalions, sometimes even regiments, or a whole brigade, are detached for this purpose, and in this case they are designated as skirmishers *en grande bande.**

Much greater skill and valor are required of the soldier for fighting and advancing in this manner, than in combats in close ranks, where the touch of the elbow and the unity of the command sustains him.

The influence of the officers being purely moral, they can do no more than set the example of bravery. The soldier has here every facility for lagging behind, wandering away, and hiding from the surveillance of his superiors.

The men feel themselves less supported and more exposed to the chances of hand-to-hand combats than when they form parts of a mass, where the danger threatens no individual specially.

In this sort of combat, if the soldiers are not brave and enthusiastic, they will fire a whole day without advancing, and will squat behind trees, hedges, and walls, doing very little mischief, and scarcely receiv-

* We shall again speak of these skirmishers at the end of this chapter, Sect. 10, when treating of the different kinds of skirmishers.

ing any. Such attacks are without vigor, and must often fail.

The bayonet, which is of no advantage to the soldier, in the rank, against cavalry, may become the principal arm in the hands of skirmishers against detached horsemen, for these skirmishers have the greatest freedom of movement.

Attack in echelon.—The order in echelons is favorable for attack, because it readily conforms to the nature of the ground, and does not necessitate engaging more than a part of the forces; it is adopted for the purpose of attacking a particular point of the enemy's line. In this order, the battalions may be either deployed or in column. The echelons should mutually flank each other, even with musketry, and hence their distance should not exceed some 200 yards; it would not do to reduce the distance below 100 yards, for then two echelons would be engaged at the same time.

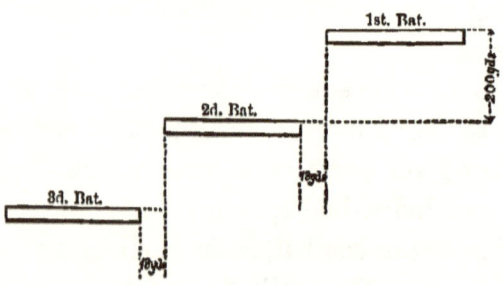

ORDER IN ECHELONS.

The intervals between the echelons should be at least 18 yards.

A line may be broken up into *direct echelons* or *oblique echelons*. In any case, the possibility of an attack by cavalry forbids the formation of echelons of more than six battalions, or a brigade. For, in order to resist the cavalry, they will have to form squares; but, supposing the echelons to consist of a brigade, and each to form *one* square, they will be too far apart to flank each other properly; if formed into *two* squares, of a regiment, they will imperfectly flank each other; and it will be impossible to place *six* squares, each of a battalion, upon 200 yards. Thus, six battalions may be well considered as the maximum of force which should compose each echelon.*

Attack in squares.—Whenever a square can march, it may also act on the offensive. In the campaign in Egypt (1799–1800), the French army not only marched in squares, but also attacked in squares. The attack in squares may,† then, be ranked among the forms of attack for infantry; its special employment is against cavalry.

According to Jomini,‡ the square by battalion is the best for the offensive.

A long square of a front of three companies, closed on one side by the grenadiers, and on the other by the voltigeurs, gives a good formation for a battalion to attack in square.

---

* This is based upon the supposition that the front of the battalion measures a little over 150 yards.

† In this kind of attack the protecting artillery will save its ammunition for the critical moment which may arrive unexpectedly, but during which it will be necessary to act with all the energy possible. The French artillery observed this rule in the battle of Heliopolis (April, 1800), gained by Kleber over the army of the Grand Vizier. (*Tactique des trois armes, par le colonel Favé*, p. 208.)

‡ *Précis de l'art de la guerre*, t. ii., p. 229.

8. Formations of Defence.—We shall consider five kinds of formations of defence, for infantry·

1st. Defence in line;
2d. Defence in column;
3d. Defence in square;
4th. Defence in echelon;
5th. Defence in checker-form.

Defence in line.—The infantry assumes the thin order for combat, whenever its business is to occupy and defend an advantageous position; it then cuts off the approaches by covering them with its fire, which is directed upon the attacking columns.

Infantry adopt the deployed line for defence, especially against troops of the same kind; they then cover the ground which the enemy must traverse to reach them, with skirmishers; and when the adversary has been worried by a stubborn resistance, the infantry move and march to the attack at charging step.

Circumstances may also sometimes require that a body of deployed infantry, though acting upon the defensive, should follow up their fire by a bayonet charge. This case occurs when they are stationed near and behind the crest of a hill, awaiting a column which is ascending the slope. We shall return to this point when speaking of the defence of heights.*

Again, infantry employ the thin order when firing to defend intrenchments, natural or artificial, by lining the parapets with one or two ranks of muskets; but this *passive* means of defence is not sufficient, except when combined with the *active* and judi-

* Part III., Chap. viii.

INFANTRY FORMATION AND TACTICS. 87

cious employment of reserves outside the intrenchment, as was done by Masséna in his energetic defence of Genoa in the year 1800.

Defence in column.—Infantry in column can withstand neither artillery nor deployed infantry, the former raking its great depth with its horizontal fire, and the latter riddling it with its musketry. The column is, therefore, useful in defence only against cavalry.

A defensive column will often change to the square.

*Defence in square.**—The square is the true formation of the infantry against cavalry, because it is closed, and resists on all sides. The double column at half-distance forms, in the presence of cavalry, a *hollow square*. The mode of forming it, according to official regulations, is shown in the annexed figure.

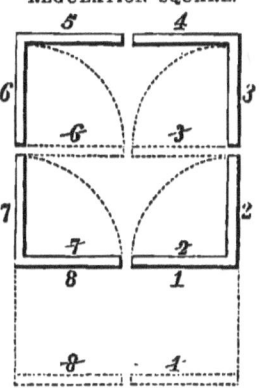

REGULATION SQUARE.

This square may also be obtained directly from the line in *order of battle*, without the intervention of the column, as is shown in the following figure, extracted from General Schramm's *Album de manœuvres d'infanterie*, Paris, 1850, p. 15.

---

* The Russians, and the English in Spain, occasionally substituted the following manœuvre for the square against cavalry. The infantry (even in two ranks) awaited the cavalry in line; the first rank fired upon the charging horsemen; the second rank threw themselves upon the ground until the cavalry, riding at full speed, had passed them, then rising discharged their fire at the backs of the horsemen. This

SCHRAMM'S SQUARE.

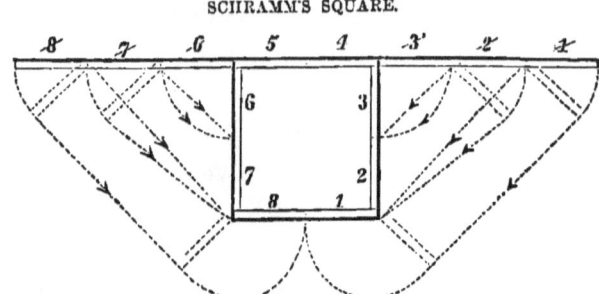

The *square half full* is nothing more than the regulation *column against cavalry*.* This formation is assumed by a column closed *en masse*, so suddenly threatened by cavalry as not to have time to resume the regular distances required in forming a square in the usual manner. It then forms a provisional square, by breaking as many files from the right and left of each company as may be necessary to close the intervals.

General Jomini considers the square by a regiment the best for the defensive, whilst, as we have said, the square by a battalion is the best for the offensive.

"A large square," says Marshal Bugeaud, "has not an increased fire in proportion to its size, and is no stronger than a small one. The only portion of the charging cavalry really to be feared is that which can strike the face of a square; the portions extending beyond are *null*. By extending the face of a square, though we do indeed increase its fire, we increase in the same proportion the number of its ene-

manœuvre may answer, but requires for its execution soldiers of great coolness and experience.

* *Evolutions de la ligne.* No. 925.

mies.· A large square broken, is as much lost as a small one, and everything is thus risked at once. For these reasons, I think, we should form none but deep squares of a single battalion." The annexed figure illustrates the square proposed by the conqueror of Isly.

The weak points of a square are not the angles, which are protected by the oblique fire of two faces,* but rather the middle of the faces, which present but a front fire, and have more void space behind them.†

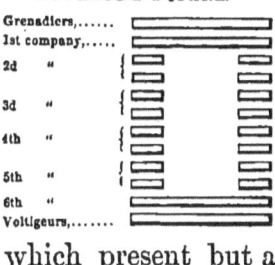

BUGEAUD'S SQUARE.

Grenadiers,......
1st company,......
2d "
3d "
4th "
5th "
6th "
Voltigeurs,........

The infantry of a square should find its defence rather in its fire than in the bayonet. During the war in the East, instead of the regulation fire of two ranks, the preference was given to a fire *d'ensemble*, aimed at the horses' noses at forty paces, after which they were received upon the bayonet.

When several squares are to act together, they should be *echeloned*, so as to flank each other.

Artillery is the most formidable opponent of the square. Nevertheless, in favorable circumstances, brought about by skilful manœuvres, cavalry alone may break a square without the assistance of artillery; as happened, for example, at the battle of Dresden (1813).

---

* In a tactical square, there are no sectors totally deprived of fire, since we can admit oblique firing, which is not done in fortification.

† Upon the heights of Elbodon (Spain, 1811) the cavalry of Montbrun charged an English square upon three of its faces.

The formation in square is often designated by the term *formation of resistance.*

In conclusion, we will remark that a square, notwithstanding its mobility, acts, in fact, as a redoubt, and has the same disadvantages; its faces, for example, stand in need of flanking. In order to flank them, Desaix, when in Egypt, placed on the prolongations of the diagonals of the great square four small squares, each composed of 200 men, to which were added, in case of attack, the companies of skirmishers.

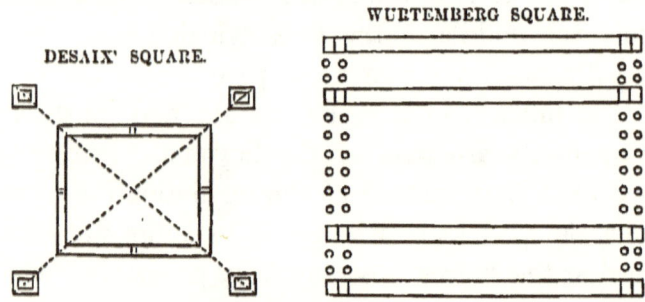

We may also here notice a good formation of the square, adopted by the army of Wurtemberg. The 2d division closes in mass upon the 1st, the 4th upon the 3d, the 3d being at double distance from the 2d. The 3d and 4th front to the rear, the files of the extremities front to the right and left, and the flanks are filled out by the file-closers and picked sharpshooters. This square is strong, and marches with more ease than the ordinary square.

Defence in echelon.—The order in echelons, which we have spoken of in connection with attacks, answers also for defence. It is especially employed in retreating slowly and gradually, after receiving a check.

What we have said above respecting the relative disposition of the echelons and the distances between them, is also applicable here.

Defence in checker-form.—The column, square, and echelons are all suited both to offensive and defensive operations. The order in checker-form, on the contrary, is purely defensive. The regulations with regard to manœuvres prescribe its employment in retreats; but, as it requires level ground, its application is often limited.

CHECKER-FORMATION.

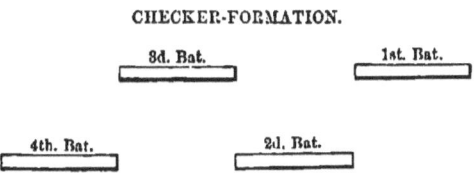

The advantage of this formation consists in allowing the force to retreat in successive portions, obliging the enemy, meanwhile, to remain in a position *parallel* to the line of battle; its disadvantage is, that it offers feeble resistance to cavalry, which can easily enter between its several parts.

In this order the odd battalions (1st, 3d, etc.) occupy the first line, nearest to the enemy, and the even ones (2d, 4th, etc.), the second line.

9. Light Infantry.—All light troops, at the present day, are regularly organized, and have a system of tactics; even Austria has decided to methodize her Croatian and Tyrolean Chasseurs.

In France, the light infantry is composed of the *chasseurs à pied*, who are accustomed to performing their manœuvres at the double-quick pace (*pas gymnastique*), and running; they are drilled in all kinds of leaping; are formed in two ranks, and always fire at will. They are all armed with the rifled carbine,* whose extreme range, upon masses, is as great as 1,300 metres (over 1,400 yards), and they are trained to great accuracy of aim. The battalions of *chasseurs à pied* are created for outpost service, and that of skirmishers. In their evolutions they follow a special system, established by the ordinance of July 22, 1845. Their organization is, in one respect, peculiar: in each company, placed in two ranks, an odd file and its adjacent even file together form a group of four men, who are designated by the name comrades of battle (*camarades de combat*); the company deploys as skirmishers, and rallies *by fours*. Upon encountering foraging cavalry, the rally by fours takes the place of the rally upon the reserve; each group of four men assumes a *radiated* formation, in which, placing their right feet together, the four men mutually support each other; and each, taking the position of charge bayonets, fires from the place he occupies, without moving his foot. We give a view of the rallied group seen in perspective, in order to illustrate more clearly the respective position of the four comrades.

DEPLOYED GROUP.   RALLIED GROUP.

* By a recent decision the Zouaves are also furnished with this arm.

In combats of skirmishers, besides the signals given by the bugle, which may often fail to be heard in consequence of the firing, or a contrary wind, the officers and non-commissioned officers are authorized to use a whistle, to communicate with their men.

RALLIED GROUP, IN PERSPECTIVE.

The selection of suitable men to form the best light infantry, is a matter of some importance. The recruits should be quick of hearing, keen-sighted, light-footed, and clear-headed. In France, we find these several qualities best combined in the inhabitants of the mountainous and forest-covered departments.

The light infantry soldier requires more time for his instruction than the soldier of the line; for both his physical and intellectual faculties must be developed with the greatest care. He must be taught to climb, to run, to leap a barrier, or a brook, and to scale a wall or an escarpment. He will be instructed in the method of reconnoitring a piece of ground, exploring a copse, and examining a house, a farm, or a village. He will learn what kind of obstacles may serve as covers, how they are to be occupied; and, in short, how *to see without being seen*. One of the Russian writers even requires that he should be taught something of topography. Moreover, his quickness of sight is to be cultivated, and accuracy of aim imparted, by frequent target practice. It is only by this detailed instruction of each soldier, that light infantry can be formed fully able to discharge the service required of it in war—a service which embraces watching the movements of the enemy, reconnoitring, beginning and finishing combats, covering retreats, escorting convoys, giving secure repose to the troops by performing patrol duty in advance of and about them, acting as flankers, advance guards, etc.

10. Skirmishers.—Before closing this chapter, we must say a few words more, especially in relation to the branch of infantry designated as skirmishers.

All soldiers fighting dispersed or scattered, are called skirmishers, whatever may be the object they have in view. A body, detached as skirmishers, always leaves a reserve of one third of its force in the rear of the point upon which it spreads, as a centre upon which to rally.

Those soldiers make the best skirmishers who develop the instinct of the *chasseur* and the partisan, in taking advantage of peculiarities of the ground, and employing judicious ruses.

The skirmisher, unless covered by the broken character of the ground, should not stand still while loading his piece; and, when necessary, he should lie flat upon the ground, to avoid the fire of the enemy. The battalions of *chasseurs à pied*, who take the place of our former light infantry, will furnish the best skirmishers; nevertheless, we should add that in France even the soldier of the line may be used for this service, for which he is well fitted by his vivacity of spirit, his activity, and his skill.

There are three classes of skirmishers: skirmishers of march, skirmishers of battle, skirmishers *en grande bande*.

Skirmishers of march.—These skirmishers perform the duty of reconnoitring on the flanks and on the front and rear of columns in march; of giving warning of the approach of the enemy; of masking the movements and formations of the troops; of skirmishing against the enemy, in order to gain time for making defensive dispositions. When the two parties are marching at a short distance from each other, as, for example, in a pursuit, both throw out skirmishers, and the result is a petty warfare. These skirmishers necessarily travel two or three times as far as the columns, and that over the most broken parts of the ground, thus rendering their duty extremely arduous. They must, therefore, be frequently relieved, and, consequently, must not be detached in too great numbers.

Skirmishers of battle.—When two bodies or two armies are drawn up in line face to face, each detaches upon its front a line of skirmishers, designed to drive back the advanced posts of the adversary, and to try the strength of his position. If allowed to approach, these skirmishers should harass the enemy by well arranged attacks, which can be met only by the skirmishers on the other side. However, it is rare that anything decisive results from the action of skirmishers on either side, since they generally neutralize each other; and this is a reason why, in this case alone, they should not be detailed in greater numbers than are actually necessary to repel those of the enemy.

Skirmishers en grande bande.—The chief business of the first class of skirmishers is *to see, and to give warning;* that of the second class, to initiate the combat; that of the third, to carry a position, that is, to perform the real business of war. The distinction between them is thus distinctly marked. The employment of skirmishers *en grande bande* occurs as far back as the sixteenth century; they were used by Coligny, Montluc, and Henry IV. Disused during the seventeenth century, they were again revived by the wars of the Revolution; and this is not surprising, as their action is especially appropriate in the case of intrepid though imperfectly drilled troops.

If a formidable position is to be captured, instead of approaching it by the front, at the risk of great loss, skirmishers will be thrown upon the flanks—either a battalion, a regiment, or even a whole brigade—whilst a body of troops, drawn up in column beyond the reach of the artillery, menaces the front of the position. These skirmishers *en grande bande*, climb the slopes, surmount obstacles, assail the position in flank or rear, and, having arrived within musket range, rush with the bayonet upon the defenders, who, held in check on the front, are obliged to retire.

As examples of the employment of skirmishers *en grande bande*, we may cite the battle of Jemmapes (November 6, 1792), when they were used with success by Dumouriez; and the battle of Hanau (October 30, 1813), in which there were at one time more than 5,000 French skirmishers engaged in the great forest, two leagues from the town.

CHAPTER THIRD.

HISTORY OF CAVALRY.

WE shall here be more brief than in the history of infantry; and shall treat the subject under three heads only: antiquity, middle ages, and modern times.

1. Antiquity.—As the military art had its origin in Asia, a country abounding in arid plains, where manœuvres even of chariots were easy, mounted combatants at first prevailed. War chariots appeared first, because the art of guiding horses in harness presents fewer difficulties than equitation; cavalry proper is of later origin.

Mounted upon the platform of a car, the warrior overlooks the field of battle, has the free use of his arms (the horses being managed by a driver), and can strike his adversary as he comes suddenly upon him. This method of combat was well suited to warriors who were of a select order—warriors d'élite. The Egyptians and Persians made great use of chariots for thus conveying the combatants; but there were also two other kinds of war chariots: those armed with scythes, which mowed their bloody swath through the ranks of the enemy; and those carrying warlike machines, which may be said to have composed the portable artillery of those times. The Greeks and Romans made but little use of war chariots; they opened their lines to let those of the enemy pass. They also employed against these chariots rows of stakes, placed along their front, and caltrops.

Mounted horse existed in China more than twenty centuries before our era. The elder Cyrus was the first who (560 B. C.) introduced a cavalry corps into Persia.

The Greeks began to make use of cavalry in the earliest period of their history; but until the battle of Leuctra (371 B. C.), although they had made great advances in the art of war, this people were yet ignorant of the advantages to be derived from numerous and well instructed cavalry, and their armies were composed almost entirely of foot soldiers.

The Theban general Epaminondas was the first who had a just appreciation of the importance of cavalry in charging and in pursuing. He, with great perseverance, trained a body of 5,000 regular horsemen, and habituated them to fighting *en masse*. His efforts were crowned with success; for, thanks to his cavalry, he was victorious at Leuctra, and Mantinea, and undermined the old reputation of the Spartans.

These two victories opened the eyes of the other Grecian states, and they increased the number of their mounted troops. From that time, improved cavalry sustained a more important part in the wars of Greece.

Two nations of Greece distinguished themselves by the excellence of their cavaliers: the Thessalians, whose numerous cavalry contributed to the success of Philip of Macedon and Alexander the Great; and the

Etolians, whose renowned squadrons rendered so much service to the Romans in their struggle against Macedonia, at the beginning of the second century B. C. The Thessalian horsemen were invincible when they fought in line, massed, but were worthless when once broken; the contrary was the case with the Etolian cavaliers.

According to the Greek theorists, the cavalry should be one sixth of the infantry; and this proportion was adopted by Alexander at the time of his entrance into Asia; for, of the 35,000 men which composed his expedition, 5,000 were horsemen; but, more frequently, the proportion observed in the Greek armies was one eleventh.

The first Roman cavalry was but mediocre, and served either on foot or on horseback, according to circumstances. Subsequently, when they fought altogether on horseback, they were interspersed with foot soldiers. These vicious methods of employing cavalry were not attended by any bad consequences in the wars of Rome against the people of the Italian peninsula, but they well-nigh proved disastrous in their efforts to repel the attacks of the Gauls and of Pyrrhus.

We may well be astonished at this mediocrity of the Roman cavalry; for, in Rome, to be a horseman, or rather *knight*, required the possession of a certain income. In the social hierarchy, the order of knights came next after that of senators, and each knight wore a gold ring, as a distinctive badge.

It was not until the wars with Carthage that the Romans began to understand how much could be done with good and numerous cavalry. They enticed into their service the foreign cavalry, which constituted the force of the Carthaginians; and from that time the face of things was changed. Hannibal had maintained himself in Italy victoriously for thirteen years, by the aid of his excellent Numidian, Spanish, and Gallic cavalry; but when these useful auxiliaries passed over to the Romans, fortune deserted his standard.

From this time Rome maintained two kinds of cavalry: one composed of Roman citizens or knights, the other furnished by their allies. The former, which was attached to the legions, was always mediocre; the latter became skilful, and distinguished itself under the designation of auxiliary cavalry.

The proportion of cavalry which formed a part of the legion varied from a tenth to a twentieth; but at each epoch the number of cavalry attached to each legion was almost always invariable and independent of circumstances and localities: a practice to be condemned, for the cavalry of an army should be more numerous in level than in mountainous countries, and it was not always possible for the Roman consuls to find at hand all the auxiliary cavalry which they needed.

The cavalry of the Greeks and Romans was divided into heavy and light cavalry: both used the shield. The heavy cavalry also wore either a helmet and cuirass, or complete armor; in the latter case, the horse was protected by iron plates. The light cavalry wore the helmet, as well as a small cuirass of metal or leather. As to their offensive weapons, the heavy-armed cavaliers had the sword, the javelin, and the double-lance, with iron on both ends; this lance was held at a point about one third of its length from one end, so that, if the longer part broke, the other part might still be used. The light cavalry used the sword, the javelin, the bow, and even the sling.

The ancients paid little attention to swiftness in the action of cavalry, and this explains why, in the formation of this arm, they multiplied the number of ranks. The Greeks extended their preference for the deep order to their mounted troops, to which, however, it is even less appropriate than to infantry.

The Greek cavalry was drawn up in 4, 5, or 8 ranks; the Thessalians adopted this last depth. As to the formation of this cavalry, it was sometimes a square or a rectangle; sometimes, also, a triangle, which was the favorite form with Philip of Macedon and his son Alexander. The triangle, the point of which was directed toward the enemy, in order to break them with more certainty, is supposed to have originated in the imitation of the figure formed by a flock of birds flying through the air. The habitual form of the Greek squadrons appears to have been the lozenge, which offers the advantage of fronting on all sides. This form is represented in the annexed diagram, in which the chiefs are denoted by the letter *o*.

THESSALIAN LOZENGE.

```
         o
        c c c
       c c c c
      c c c c c c
     c c c c c c c c
    c c c c c c c c c
   c c c c c c c c c c
  o c c c c c c c c c c o
   c c c c c c c c c c
    c c c c c c c c c
     c c c c c c c c
      c c c c c c
       c c c c
        c c c
         o
```

The Romans divided the cavalry of a legion into ten *turmæ*, or squadrons; each *turma* was composed of 30 soldiers and 5 chiefs; the whole drawn up in three ranks, as shown in the annexed figure (the letter *o* denoting a chief).

ROMAN TURMA.

o
o c c c c c c c c c o
c c c c c c c c c c
c c c c c c c c c c
o   o

Sometimes the turma contained 32 men, and was formed in a similar manner, in four ranks. In combat the turmæ were placed on the front or the flanks of the legion. The auxiliary cavalry adopted in its formations either the square, the lozenge, or the triangle; but in every case its depth was less than among the Greeks.

The best among all the cavalry which figures in the Roman armies is unquestionably that of the Numidians and the Gauls. The latter rendered important services to Cæsar, and maintained its preëminence during the period of the Roman emperors, to such an extent that at the commencement of our era all the terms of *manége* most in use were Gallic.

In the latter days of the empire, cavalry increased beyond measure in the Roman armies.

The barbarian nations who overwhelmed the Roman empire had but little cavalry; adhering to their practice of fighting on foot, they displayed great skill in that kind of combat. But the establishment of the feudal system, which happened soon after, produced a marked preponderance among them of cavalry, which is said to have composed one half of the armies in the reign of Charlemagne.

The ancients were not acquainted with the saddle; they used, instead of it, skins or housings, placed so as to afford the rider a firm seat without hurting the horse. The saddle was invented under the reign of Constantine; and this led, naturally, to the use of stirrups, which could be more firmly sustained by the saddle than by housings. The invention of stirrups is attributed to the Franks,* and their use caused the hernias and the numerous diseases of the legs, with which horsemen were afflicted, to disappear. Besides lessening fatigue, the use of stirrups enabled the horseman to remain a longer time in the saddle, and also, by giving him a point of support, permitted him to give more certain blows to the enemy. The absence of stirrups is, indeed, a distinctive feature of the ancient cavalry; without them, the heavy feudal cavaliers had perhaps never existed.

2. Middle Ages.—During the middle ages, the history of cavalry is interwoven with that of the feudal system and chivalry. We are not here required to treat of chivalry under its political aspect; but will merely remark that this institution, during a period of trouble and general anarchy, powerfully contributed to the suppression of violence and the purification of morals; and that the knights-errant themselves, notwithstanding the absurdities of some of their number, so well satirized by Cervantes, were useful to society, for their generous protection of the weak, wherever they went, was really the only police

---

* Before this invention the cavalier mounted his horse by the aid of one of the milestones disposed along the Roman roads, or else by means of a projection, provided for the purpose, near the but of his lance.

which could be exercised in the rural districts and on the high roads.

It was not in the nature of the feudal system to employ methods of warfare based upon observation and reflection: the distribution of power, as then constituted, is alone sufficient to explain this remark. Besides, tactics and chivalry could not exist simultaneously; the fundamental principle of the former being *ensemble*, the employment of masses; that of the latter, individual courage, the isolated feat of arms—prowess.

The nobles who held fiefs owed their military service to the king, for a period of sixty days, at their own expense; beyond that period, it was at the royal charge. At the call of the monarch, they repaired to the army, accompanied by mounted combatants taken from the nobility of their fiefs, and bearing the name of cavaliers, or knights. Each knight had a retinue armed with the long bow or the crossbow, constituting the light cavalry, whilst he himself, wholly cased in iron mail, pursuant to the privilege of his rank, fought in line, face to face with the enemy.

To aspire to the dignity of knighthood, it was necessary to be a gentleman, to have given proofs of courage, and to have reached the age of majority. The induction of a knight into his office was accompanied with pomp and ceremony; but, most singularly, this induction took place on the eve of battle, a practice plainly unjust, and destructive of emulation. This custom was infringed by Francis I. when he caused himself to be knighted by Bayard the evening after the battle of Marignan (1515); Montluc was also knighted by the Duke of Enghien after the battle of Cerisoles (1544). Any knight could confer the order of knighthood upon a compatriot.*

The knights were divided into *bannerets*, those sufficiently powerful to raise a banner, and *bachelors*, or lower knights, gentlemen less powerful than the preceding, who carried only an ensign, called a pennon, attached to their lance. The force of an army was estimated by the number of its banners and its pennons; the infantry not being thought worth counting. To rise to the dignity of a banneret, the knight had to be able to embrace under his command 5 or 6 *lances*, in all 30 or 36 horses.

A *lance* was the term applied to a small band formed by a man-at-arms and his attendants, the latter consisting of a *coutillier* (so named from the long, broad dirk in his belt), one page or varlet, and three archers. The coutillier frequently marched on foot and conducted the baggage horse; the page, or varlet, brought the war-horse to the knight when he was going to battle, carried his lance and shield, and guarded his prisoners; the archers were young gentlemen entering upon the military career, and aspiring to become men-at-arms.

The man-at-arms was covered with iron, when his fortune allowed it, and wore, as much as possible,

---

* A case is cited in which an English chief, the Count of Suffolk, at the combat of Jargeau (1429), knighted the French gentleman, Guillaume Renaud, before surrendering to him. But, in my opinion, we should not draw any general conclusion from this instance.

only armor from Milan. The details of this armor are as follows: Over a vestment of leather, called a *gambeson*, he buckled on a shirt of mail called a *hauberk*, and over this a *cuirass*. In addition to the cui-

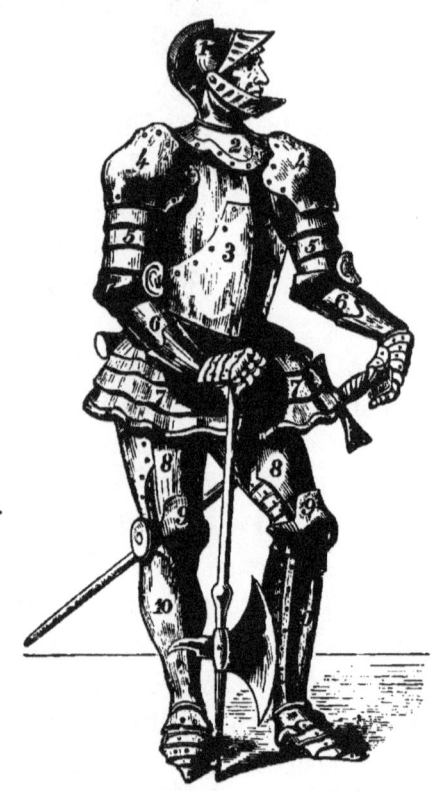

KNIGHT IN ARMOR.

1. Helmet.
2. Gorget.
3. Cuirass.
4. Épaulières.
5. Brassarts.
6. Gauntlet.
7. Tasses.
8. Cuishes.
9. Genouillères.
10. Greaves.

rass, the complete armor embraced the *gorget*, which defended the neck; *brassarts*, which protected the arms; *épaulières*, covering the shoulders; *tasses*, protecting the lower part of the body; *cuishes*, for the thighs; and *greaves*, for the legs. Over the whole was sometimes thrown the *sagum* (*saye*), a kind of embroidered doublet, made of woollen cloth (*serge* or *say*). A *helmet* and a shield, either round, oval, or demi-oval, completed the defensive armor. As offensive arms the knight carried the sword, the mace, the battle axe, and the lance, the latter being about 15 feet in length. The lance with which the gendarme unhorsed his enemy was regarded as a noble arm, and was forbidden to *villains*, or serfs. Upon a march, the knight did not wear his armor, which would unnecessarily fatigue him in advance; but it was carried after him upon a horse or in a wagon. For a like reason, he then rode upon a small horse, called a *courtaud;* but on the day of action he armed himself cap-a-pie and mounted his war-horse, an animal of lofty stature and great strength.

The French cavalry charged in a single line—a formation which resulted in part from the tendency of the feudal lords to consider themselves as equals, possessing equal rights. This claim of equality was satisfied by the formation in a single rank, which gave each knight a free field for attacking the enemy and displaying his own prowess. The pages, or varlets, ready to support their chiefs, formed a second rank behind that of the gensdarmes; but the latter attacked alone, which necessarily occasioned successive charges of a small number of horses.

The cavalry ignored the laws of tactics, and submitted but little to discipline; still, such was the defective organization of the infantry, that the former bore all the burden of war, and not only fought battles, but also laid sieges.

Toward the middle of the fourteenth century, and the beginning of the fifteenth, the expert English archers and the excellent Swiss pikemen, all foot soldiers, frequently forced the chivalry to convert itself into infantry; and this lasted so long as armies did not contain a body of infantry, properly so called, sufficiently compact to sustain a charge. This was illustrated at the battles of Poictiers, Cocherel, Monteil, Agincourt, and Formigny. When the knights dismounted, they often shortened their lances to five feet, to render them easier to manage, and of stouter resistance; they took off their spurs, to use them as caltrops, planting them in the ground, rowels up. Moreover, the men-at-arms, with their heavy mail, made but clumsy foot soldiers; they could march against their adversaries only by resting several times on the way. They were obliged to fix in advance the number of *poses*, or *rests*, of which an attack should consist. It would have been impossible for them to perform a long march; and when dismounted, they were compelled to divest themselves of their armor.

After the crusades, chivalry fell into decline, the principal causes of which were the destruction of the feudal system, the establishment of the communal militia, the invention of fire-arms, and the ignorance and vices of the knights. This decline ended in complete extinction about the middle of the fifteenth century, when the modern epoch begins.

3. **Modern Times.**—Dissatisfied with an intractable nobility frequently absenting itself from the

ranks, the kings soon began to supplant the feudal armies by permanent troops more obedient to their wishes. In the middle of the fifteenth century more correct ideas of organization, and the employment of armies, effected a revolution in war, which again became an art.

In France, Charles VII. was the first to institute permanent troops of infantry and cavalry. He succeeded better with the latter than the former, for the corps of cavaliers which he created lasted as long as the old monarchy.

In 1445 he organized fifteen companies of cavalry, called *compagnies d'ordonnance*, each containing 100 *lances*. Counting six men in a lance, this gives 600 combatants per company, and 9,000 for the whole body estalished, not including the supernumeraries or candidates who followed voluntarily, in the hope of one day becoming full gensdarmes.

Besides the captain, there were in each company a lieutenant, an ensign, and a guidon, all chosen from the gentlemen most reputed for valor. There was also a quartermaster.

Every gendarme had four horses: one for his servant, one for his baggage, a war-horse, and a *courtaud*. Each archer had two horses. The gensdarmes were paid after a review, or muster, held by a special commissioner; and the means for that purpose were raised by a tax called the *gendarme tax*, levied upon the people of the towns and the rural districts.

After the institution of these companies, the feudal lords no longer brought their vassals into service.

Except in the rare cases when the king summoned the *arrière-ban*,* the use of banners and pennons ceased, gentlemen of high rank preferring the position of captain of an independent company (which conferred a real command) to that of cavaliers.

The companies thus created by Charles VII. were imitated by the neighboring nations; but, with the exception of those of the duchy of Burgundy, the foreign companies never reached the excellence of ours.

Upon the accession of Francis I., the French gendarmery still formed in a single rank; a formation too thin, especially for resisting German squadrons, which were sometimes drawn up in squares, but always in deep order. The depth of these squadrons was usually seventeen ranks. Charles V. reduced it to ten, and finally to eight ranks.

This deep formation of the German squadrons resulted from their being composed entirely of the common people, to whom the reasons which led the French gendarmery to form in a single rank, and which we have above explained, were no longer applicable.

. Fire-arms began to be introduced in the cavalry. In Germany, about the middle of the sixteenth century, they reckoned one arquebusier for every four lances. They also began to employ special corps of light cavalry for skirmishing, who, when necessary, dismounted. They were called *chevau-légers* when they carried the lance, and *stradiots* when they

---

* Body of *arrière-*vassals, or inferior feudatories of the sovereign.—*Translator*.

served as scouts. There existed also *cranequiniers*, or mounted crossbowmen, who used a hook called a *cranequin* to draw the cord of their crossbow; *malandrins*, mounted soldiers of fortune, armed with a bow; *argoulets*, horsemen carrying the *escopette* (wall-piece with wheel-lock and rifled barrel); *carabins*, when the escopette was changed to the carbine; and, finally, *reitres*, or *pistoliers*, when armed with the pistol.

The origin of dragoons dates also from this epoch, since history informs us that, in 1543, in the environs of Landrecy, Peter Strozzi placed 500 arquebusiers on horseback, *in order that they might not be fatigued.* This fact explains how dragoons were at first but mounted infantry; and this character they preserved for a long period, sometimes serving as horsemen, and sometimes as foot soldiers.

The deep formation of the German squadrons was attended with little inconvenience in the sixteenth century, on account of the feebleness of artillery; and these masses of cavalry did, in fact, contribute to the success of several battles. Defeated by these squadrons on the days of Pavia (1525) and Saint-Quentin (1577), the French gendarmery were compelled to abandon its single-line formation, although the deep order wounded to the quick the self-love and susceptibility of the cavalier. From that time a remarkable change is observable in the organization of the cavalry. All the European states, France included,*

---

* In France this adoption took place as early as 1556; but this power returned occasionally to the single-line formation, especially at the battle of Saint-Denis, in 1567.

adopted the German formation of eight ranks deep; the cavalry immediately lost a part of the mobility it had possessed in the times of chivalry, when the knights charged at the fastest gait, and now manœuvred at a walk or trot, and made more use of fire-arms than of other weapons.*

The first deep squadrons were very strong in number. They rose to 1,500 and even 2,000 men-at-arms, all equal, all cavaliers without a retinue. Reflection soon showed how little effect was produced by these heavy, almost immovable masses. This, together with the ravages produced in these elevated living rectangles by the projectiles of improved artillery, led to the reduction of the depth to six ranks. Henry IV. further reduced it to five ranks, and formed no squadrons of more than 600 horses.

Louis XIII., in 1635, organized the companies of light cavalry into regiments, each commanded by a colonel. The *compagnies d'ordonnance* continued to form the body of the gendarmery.

Gustavus Adolphus made several improvements in the cavalry, dividing it into small squadrons, forming it in four or three ranks, ordering it to fire only when very near, and to charge with the sabre. This new system of tactics struck the Imperials with astonishment, who with difficulty accustomed themselves to it; and yet the Swedish cavaliers still charged only at a trot. The king of Sweden, to resist the heavy cavalry of the Austrians, placed companies

* Nevertheless, according to La Noue, if the *reitres* charged at a trot, the French cavalry of that period sometimes " galloped."

of musketeers between his squadrons of horse; but this mixture of the two arms has since been abandoned as incompatible with the diversity in the nature and tactics of these two arms.

The cavalry retained for a long time its depth of three ranks, which it still possessed at the close of the reign of Louis XIV., and during a part of the reign of Louis XV. The annexed cut shows the order of battle of a company of French cavalry about 1750.

COMPANY OF FRENCH CAVALRY IN ORDER OF BATTLE, (1750).

In the time of Louis XV., the armament of the cavalry was very different from that of the fourteenth century. Down to Henry IV., the gensdarmes were still armed cap-a-pie, and their horses were barbed; whilst the light-horsemen wore either simple cuirasses or coats of mail. From the reign of this monarch, the armor was gradually simplified, and the defensive pieces with which the cavaliers were covered, one by one, shared the fate of the deep squadrons. Under Louis XIII. the lance was no longer used; under Louis XIV. only the cuirass and the helmet were retained; under Louis XV. the buff-leather vest took the place of the cuirass, and the sabre-proof cap supplanted the helmet; helmet and cuirass reappeared only during the Consulate, and were worn very nearly as at the present day.

Marshal Saxe paid great attention to the improvement of cavalry, insisting especially that they should not charge as foragers, as was in his time the practice of the French cavalry; but he had not sufficient authority to produce any important amelioration, and the reform came finally from Prussia.

Before Frederic II., the Prussian cavalry was neglected, except for parade. They charged only at a trot, firing with the pistol or musketoon. This monarch, himself a good horseman, proscribed this routine method of fighting, and gave orders that, without paying any attention to the firing of the Austrian squadrons, his cavalry should rush forward at a gallop and fearlessly attack them, sword in hand. The superiority which this mode of action gave him on most occasions, confirmed what his genius had foreseen, and which others stubbornly refused to appreciate; namely, that *the real qualities of cavalry lie in the charge, and not in firing.*

Frederic always retained in his army some squadrons formed in three ranks; nevertheless, by the advice of Seydlitz, he adopted the formation in two ranks for the greater part of his regiments. Seydlitz deserves to be considered as the first general of cavalry of modern times; he brought equitation again into repute, and perfected fencing upon horseback; then, starting from this basis, he imparted to evolutions the regularity, ensemble, rapidity, and certainty which permitted them to be executed in the face of the enemy with the same precision as on the drill-ground; moreover, in spite of the opinion of Frederic the Great, he placed the guide upon the flanks instead of the centre, an arrangement ever since preserved.

The adoption of the formation in two ranks goes back to the year 1766, and took place simultaneously, after several attempts, in France, Hanover, and Prussia. It was brought about by the fact that, with the rapid gait recently adopted, the second rank could not keep a sufficient distance, unless the third rank remained in the rear, or even halted; in which case it became useless. The result of trials was that in two ranks the movements of cavalry were both more rapid and more precise.

The formation in two ranks did not become general in Europe until 1790. The Austrians* and the Russians were the last to adopt it. Since that time, cavalry has advanced in the science of manœuvres and the tactics of battle, and its progress has rendered it formidable. The campaigns of the Revolution and of the Empire have definitively established its formation in two ranks.

There is, besides, an essential difference between the cavalry of the nineteenth century and that which existed at the close of the eighteenth century; the uniform of the horsemen at the present day is loose, and the burden carried by the horse is equally distributed before and behind.

Let us now proceed to consider the details of the present formation and tactics of cavalry.

* It even appears that the official adoption in Austria only took place in 1806, upon the recommendation of the Archduke Charles.

CHAPTER FOURTH.

CAVALRY FORMATION AND TACTICS.

1. Use of Cavalry.—In mounting on horseback, the soldier sacrifices several advantages to gain speed: thus he can no longer make an efficacious use of his fire-arms, and all are an obstacle to him. It is in rapidity, then, that his strength chiefly consists: we do not say *wholly* consists, for boldness is a quality equally indispensable to him.

The ordinary use of cavalry is to complete a success prepared or obtained by infantry, assisted by artillery; it is, consequently, an *accessory* arm. To accomplish this end, it must *rout* the already broken masses of the enemy, and then *pursue* them. To produce a rout, cavalry must take the initiative, and attack at the propitious moment.* Indeed, the offensive is its only practicable mode of combat; for, if it awaits the enemy, it will be infallibly overthrown by the velocity of its adversary, if cavalry,† and by

---

* At Marengo, the prodigious effects of the vigorous and timely charge of General Kellermann with his 400 horse would have been lost if he had charged but *three minutes* later.

† At Guada-Hortuna (Spain), July 25, 1823, 1,200 Spanish horse,

the amount of its fire, if infantry. For this reason Frederic* and Napoleon wished their cavalry to attack continually; but in attacking, the great matter is to seize the opportune moment, whence the designation applied to cavalry of *arme du moment*.

From the twofold use of cavalry, routing and pursuing, results the division of this arm into at least two kinds : the one, adapted for the charge, composed of men and horses of great stature, provided with defensive armor—this is the *heavy cavalry;* the other, for the pursuit, composed of smaller men and horses, wearing no armor—this is the *light cavalry*. Between these extremes there is an intermediate species—*mixed cavalry*—employing men and horses of a medium height which takes the place, in case of need, either of the heavy or of the light cavalry; and when it accompanies these in war, serves to save the former from unnecessary fatigue, and supports the latter by giving it greater solidity.

The heavy cavalry embraces the *carabiniers* and the *cuirassiers*. Its business is to *appear upon the day of battle and make decisive charges*, as was done at the battle of Austerlitz by a corps of 4,000 French cuirassiers. It may, in case of need, be employed to sustain light cavalry; but this must be done in moderation. Heavy cavalry should be saved from unne-

having awaited a charge, were overthrown by 450 French horse, commanded by General Bonnemains.

* This monarch said, at the beginning of the Seven Years' War : " C'est le diable que mes officiers n'agissent que défensivement, mais j'y mettrai bon ordre, à quoi il a bien réussi." (Warnery, *Commentaires sur Turpin et Montecuculli*.)

cessary fatigue, even on a march; but on the field of battle, it will be charged with the most perilous duties.

The dragoons, theoretically speaking, now compose all the mixed cavalry; for they only wear a single piece of defensive armor, the helmet. For a long time the dragoons were intended to fight both on foot and on horseback. A consequence of this ambiguity of character was a total loss of confidence in themselves, which made them indifferent troops.* At the present day they are exclusively horsemen. Being better mounted than the light cavalry, they support the chasseurs and hussars against the numerous cavalry of the enemy, fight the dragoons with equal arms, and can even measure themselves, with some chance of success, against cuirassiers, whom they surpass in lightness. Since dragoons have become altogether horsemen, all the cavalry seems to have abandoned forever the idea of dismounting and fighting on foot. This rule should not, however, be exclusively followed; for there are circumstances in which a real advantage may be gained by some platoons of cavalry temporarily dismounting; as, for example, in the attack or defence of a bridge, a wood, or a defile. "I have seen one occasion," says Warnery, "where a regiment of hussars were surprised and beaten in their camp, because they had been refused 30 foot

---

* When engaged as foot soldiers, it was difficult for them to regain their horses in case of defeat; as is illustrated in the case of the 14 squadrons of French dragoons sent to retake the village of Franquenies at the commencement of the battle of Ramillies (May 23, 1706).

soldiers to defend a defile." In a reconnoissance among the mountains around Hostalrich, in 1808, Gouvion Saint-Cyr, having fallen into an ambuscade of guerillas, would have been destroyed, had not his dragoons dismounted, and rapidly scaling the heights, in spite of their heavy boots, put the Spaniards to flight.

The light cavalry embraces the *chasseurs*, the *hussars*, and the *lancers*. The chasseurs and the hussars have, however, the same kind of horses, the same weapons, the same methods of combat; they are, therefore, but varieties of the same arm. They are employed to give security to the army, by forming advance-guards, flanking marches, protecting evolutions, masking reconnoissances, and covering retreats. These various duties, at all times necessary, are those for which their light and agile horses especially fit them. The lancers, besides rendering similar services, are especially useful against confused masses, and in pursuits. At the present day there is no longer any irregular cavalry either in France or in other nations. Austria has consolidated her Hungarians and Croats, who now fight in regular formations and in line: even Russia has begun to systematize the Cossacks.*

---

* We may here quote a singular remark of Count Heraclius de Polignac, who had been a colonel in the Russian service. This officer has said: "The Cossacks have great military knowledge, ride excellent horses, and understand the art of defending themselves; but they have not that *élan*, that ardor of attack, which is almost always crowned with success. The Cossacks charge boldly only upon fugitives, or when they are sure of being at least ten to one." (See the preface to his translation of General Davidoff's *Essay on Partisan Warfare*, 1841.)

2. Armament.—The use to which cavalry is applied necessitates special kinds of dress and armament. The jacket, wide trowsers, and the long sabre are proper for all kinds of cavalry. The helmet is indispensable to the heavy cavalry and dragoons; and the cuirass (of the model of 1826, which is proof against musket balls at the distance of 40 yards) is also necessary to the heavy cavalry. The lance is an excellent arm, and both the light and the mixed cavalry of several foreign nations are now wholly armed with it; its use is indeed spreading, and may occasion modifications in the armament of infantry. Fire-arms are useful to cavalry only when serving on detachments and as skirmishers.

3. Numerical Data.—The numerical relation of the cavalry to the infantry has been very variable. It depends upon the character of a people, and the facilities for the supply of horses which the country affords. As a general rule, however, we may say that when the army is to operate in a level country, the number of its cavalry should be one fifth that of its infantry; but only one tenth when in mountainous regions. The weight carried by cavalry horses in France is as follows:

	Cuirassiers.	Chasseurs and Hussars.
Horseman, about,	176 pounds.	143 pounds.
Horseman's arms,	32 "	18 "
Horseman's equipment,	24 "	24 "
Horse equipment,	51 "	40 "
Spare shoes,	4 "	4 "
Utensils, 2 days' provisions, 2 rations oats,	22 "	22 "
Total,	309 "	251 "

The horse of a carabinier carries about $3\frac{3}{10}$ lbs. more than that of a cuirassier, and the horse of a dragoon 22 lbs. more than that of a chasseur or a hussar. All these numbers will be increased some 6 or 8 lbs. in wet weather, on account of the increase in weight of the horseman's cloak; and the same increase is to be allowed when the cavalry is obliged to carry hay or straw in addition to the oats included in the preceding table.

A horse travels, in a minute:

At a walk, about	110 to 120	yards
At a trot, "	220 " 240	"
At a gallop, "	330 " 380	"

If we take the first of these numbers for each gait, we see that the trot is about twice, and the gallop about three times as fast as a walk.

When the horses are in a body, they have less freedom of movement, and accidents of the ground impede them more; consequently, a column of cavalry will not march as rapidly as a single horse. With the weight above given, a column can make as much as $3\frac{3}{4}$ miles per hour at a walk, and $7\frac{1}{2}$ miles per hour at a long trot.

4. Tactical Unit.—The tactical unit of cavalry is the squadron, which, being composed of a much smaller force than the battalion, seldom fights separately, as the latter does. The French squadron is usually composed of 4 platoons, forming together 48 files. The following is its figure in order of battle:

SQUADRON OF CAVALRY IN ORDER OF BATTLE.

2d L.　　　2d S. L.　C. C.　1st S. L.　　　1st L.

2d C.

The shaded spaces represent the non-commissioned officers. We see by this figure that the captain commanding the squadron is in the centre, the crupper of his horse one yard in front of the heads of the horses of the first rank. The second captain is three yards in the rear of the centre of the squadron; he is charged with the alignment of the second rank, and of the file-closers. The 1st lieutenant commands the 1st platoon; the 2d lieutenant the 4th platoon; the 1st sub-lieutenant, the 2d platoon; the 2d sub-lieutenant, the 3d platoon. Each of these officers is placed in front of the centre of his platoon, the crupper of his horse at a distance of one yard in front of the heads of the horses of the first rank.

Each horse occupies 1 metre (39 inches) in breadth, and 3 metres (nearly 10 feet) in depth. The front of the squadron, therefore, occupies a space of 52 yards, and that of a platoon 13 yards. The two ranks are at a distance of one yard, measured from the heads of the horses of the second rank to the cruppers of the horses of the first.

The oldest troops in each platoon are placed in the front rank, and from right to left in each rank.

The minimum effective force of a squadron is 48 files; the maximum is 64 files—a number which admits of easy subdivision. Within the limits of 48 and 64 files, the squadron combines all the conditions requisite for manœuvring and fighting with order and facility. Whatever may be its effective force, the squadron is always divided into four platoons. When several squadrons are drawn up in line, the intervals between them are each equal to one fourth of the front of one of them.

The squadron is now formed in two ranks. Only the front rank can strike the enemy; nevertheless the rear rank has its use, and should be preserved: 1st, because it supports the front rank, and increases its moral force; 2d, because it fills the voids occasioned in the front rank; 3d, because it fights as well as the front rank in case of a *mêlée*—a rare case, in which it is well to have as large a number of horsemen as possible gathered upon the same point; 4th, and finally, because it compels the front rank to march more correctly. It is only in exceptional cases, therefore, that cavalry may be drawn up in a single line, and then there should be some full files on the flanks of the squadrons; it may be done as a ruse, to deceive the enemy as to its real force; but even then, to do it safely, there should be no danger to be apprehended from the attack of vigorous cavalry. The formation in three ranks has been abandoned, because it did not allow the middle rank sufficient freedom and quickness of movement, and disorder was not so easily remedied.

5. Manœuvres.—As the length occupied by the horse is three times his breadth, the horseman cannot make a *pivot*-turn in his place in the rank, as the foot soldier can, for he is wedged in the rank; and we shall presently see why it should be so. In order to bring a troop of cavalry promptly by the flank, and with a depth of column equal to the front in line, it was necessary to devise the movement called the *movement by fours*, which is executed either to the right or the left, and gives a front of 8 horsemen. In this movement, the object of which is to gain ground to the right (or left), at the command "*To the right (or left) by fours*," each group of 4 men, in each rank, wheels by itself upon a fixed pivot. The move-

MOVEMENT BY FOURS.

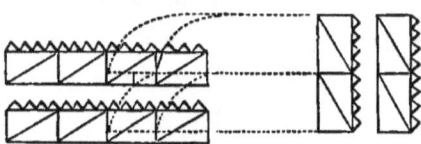

ment being completed, the four horses of the rear rank in each group of four files are found at the right of those of the front rank.

Cavalry also breaks by fours in making an advance diagonally. These oblique marches, and the movements by fours, were much in vogue in the last century, and Marshal Saxe set a high value upon them; but they are no longer employed, except in the elementary instruction of the platoon and the squadron; in actual manœuvres, movements by platoons take their place. The platoons are, then, frequently required to wheel; the consequence of which is, that the horses on the flanks, always going at a quicker gait, are more fatigued than in the movements by fours; but, on the other hand, in the movements by fours there are, in a squadron of 48 files, 24 pivots and 24 flanks, which very much increases the liability to disorder, and also requires better trained horsemen.

Cavalry, not making use of their fire-arms, cannot have any *lateral* action, like that of infantry. In order to defend themselves, they must be able to post themselves facing the enemy, and at a sufficient distance to give full scope to the horse in charging; and this is the reason why changing the front is for them a frequent and indispensable evolution. These changes of front are, like the other manœuvres of cavalry, effected by means of the movement by platoons; but as the obstacles of the ground or an unforeseen attack may often paralyze the manœuvre, it is prudent to cover the flanks of cavalry.

The ordinary gait in manœuvres is the trot; but the horsemen should also be able to execute them all at a gallop.

6. Mode of Action.—The horseman incurs less danger in war than the foot soldier. He therefore gains but little training in the field except in the way of confidence in himself; consequently, he must be very carefully instructed in time of peace. This instruction is always indispensable, and is to be continued whenever practicable; for the great object of cavalry is to act with *ensemble* and precision. Besides, the horses are to be trained to the sound of war; for, notwithstanding the assertion of poets of all ages, they are easily frightened and not fond of combats.*

The mode of action of cavalry fighting in a body consists in actual collision, the effect of which is prepared by a charge. The combination of horse and rider does not form a perfectly dense body; but we may nevertheless consider the intensity of the collision of a line of cavalry as proportional to its mass and its velocity. Hence, to increase its force, the velocity must be accelerated as much as possible, and its mass increased by forming the troop into a united and compact whole, by the adhesion and alignment of the horsemen.

The whole secret of the instruction of cavalry will therefore be to teach them *to gallop in close order and well aligned*, even under the fire of the enemy.

7. Charge.—The decisive action of cavalry, the charge, is employed either at the commencement or at the end of a battle, and as much as possible on the flanks of the infantry, chiefly when the latter has become engaged. At the favorable moment, and at 300 yards from the opposing line, the commandant orders sabres to be drawn, and puts his troop in motion at a trot, to bring the horses by degrees to their work, and to enable the horsemen to adjust their alignment; at 150 yards, he orders the ordinary gallop, and at 60 yards the full charging gallop. The horsemen should

---

* This is the observation of Mottin de la Balme. See his *Tactique pour la cavalerie*, p. 180 to 184.

remain united and masters of their movements, notwithstanding their rapid motion. Thus the progressive acceleration of gait is an important feature in the charge, and necessary to be observed, if we would not quickly ruin the cavalry; nevertheless, in case of surprise, when an enemy unexpectedly debouches from an ambuscade, the charge may be begun at a gallop, in order to regain a part of the advantage lost by the omission of the first movement.

In order to make the soldier charge vigorously, he must be convinced that his officers mean to persevere in the charge to the last, and that, if it fails at first, they will lead him again and again to the combat, until it succeeds; otherwise there will be indecision and weakness of action. In this respect, the French cavalry is preëminent; for, according to reliable testimony, "it is the best in the world for combat, and always charges à fond."* To this, Marshal Marmont, in his *Mémoires*,† adds: "Les Allemands nous sont supérieurs pour l'ordre et l'esprit de conservation; mais pour l'emploi ils sont loin de nous: la cavalerie française, à égalité de force, a toujours battu la cavalerie étrangère."

During the charge, the horseman should not fire, for firing makes the horses restive, and produces but little effect upon the adversary. As for his arms *de main*, the lance may serve for the moment of rencontre, and the sabre will be useful after the collision, during the very short period of the *mêlée*. The van-

---

* Marmont, *Esprit des institutions militaires*, p. 48.
† Tome i., p. 221.

quished party, however, quickly betake themselves to flight, and there are usually very few men killed or wounded in a charge.

Velocity of movement and close adhesion of the horsemen stirrup to stirrup, are the two essential elements of a good charge, to which the officers should especially direct their attention—the more, since the men, to avoid being pressed in the rank, are apt to spread themselves. After all the watchfulness of the officers, and their own example, a charge not unfrequently fails from a very slight cause, as a panic may be produced in a body of troops going at full speed, by the most trifling circumstance: for example, the noise of a ball striking the cuirass of a horseman and throwing him off, may suffice to produce a failure in a charge. On this account, cavalry should be drawn up in two lines, at from 300 to 400 yards apart. As far as possible, the flanks of the second line should extend beyond those of the first. With this arrangement, if the first line fails in its charge, it will rally behind the second, and the latter will charge in turn; observing, however, that, to avoid all disorder occasioned by the scattering and retreat of the first line, the second line is to be formed in columns by platoons, so as to present intervals sufficiently great for the escape of the fugitives; which produces the following figure: *

---

* This figure represents the charge in *parallel order*. The charge in *oblique order* is executed according to the same principles, and is to be preferred when the line of the enemy is extended, in order to compensate this advantage by the refusal of one wing.

For want of a second line of cavalry, the troop which fails in a charge, will rally behind a line of infantry, which will be suddenly unmasked, to arrest

FORMATION FOR THE CHARGE.

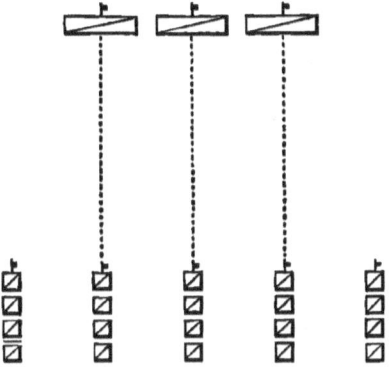

the enemy by its fire, or behind an obstacle; but always beyond the range of the enemy, for the neglect of this precaution might expose it to certain destruction.

If the charge succeeds, the success must be completed by a pursuit. In this pursuit, the victors constantly endeavor to gain one of the flanks of the vanquished party, in order to take them on their weak point; or if some obstacle prevents this, they try to get between the columns of the enemy, and to fight them in detail: but care must be taken to guard against retaliative operations, coming from ambuscades, the troops of the second line, and the reserves of the enemy.

In the charge, the officers retain their respective places in line, except the commanding officer, who goes to any point at which he judges his presence to be most necessary to insure success.

Against artillery, cavalry charges *as foragers*. By this term we designate a dispersive charge, by means of which the scattered horsemen reach their point of destination more quickly, and suffer less from the projectiles of the artillery. Whilst the platoons which arrive first repel and keep in check the troops which protect the artillery, some of the horsemen throw themselves upon the pieces, carry them off, or spike them, and break or carry away the implements, especially the rammers.

We will add that, against the Arabs, the charge as foragers should always be used.*

8. Formations.—Cavalry employs four formations—*order in line, order in column, order in echelons, order in square.*

Its orders of attack are—in line, in column, and in echelons. It attacks cavalry in line: it attacks infantry† in echelons or in column: in echelons, when the infantry is deployed, and cannot be turned; in column, when the infantry is formed in column or in square; ‡ the column of cavalry is in that case a column by squadrons at double distance. The attack in echelons

---

* In the French army of Algiers, the *Spahis* form the light cavalry, and the *Chasseurs d'Afrique* the cavalry of the line.

† Cavalry has beaten infantry in several battles, particularly at Cerisoles (1544), at Rocroy (1643), at Fehrbellin (1675).

‡ In the rain, cavalry has the advantage of infantry, as the fire of the latter is impaired: example, the battle of Dresden (1813). The use of percussion arms at the present day lessens this advantage.

is well suited to cavalry in this, that it allows the charge to be renewed on several points, and facilitates the outflanking of the enemy. Moreover, the mutual protection of the echelons is the more efficacious, because cavalry protects the ground on its front, within charging distance, better than the ground it occupies; and the successive charges of the echelons succeed pretty well against infantry by harassing them, and causing them to throw away their fire precipitately. The attack in columns against a square of infantry is directed against one side of the square, if a small one, or against two angles adjacent to the same side, if the square is of considerable size. In all cases, with one or two columns, four or five horsemen thrown forward are sufficient to make a *breach* by means of their dead horses; and having once gained entrance by this breach into the interior of the square, the horsemen who follow sweep down the third rank, and, aiming at the eyes of the foot soldiers, compel them to raise their guns, thus rendering their fire harmless.

It would seem that cavalry should have no formation for defence, since we have seen that it should never allow itself to be attacked. Nevertheless, in an exceptional case, it may be drawn up for defence, and should then be formed in squares. Heavy and even mixed cavalry, thus formed, may, in case of need, receive the attack of light cavalry. Thus, in 1813, at Juterbogk, the division of dragoons of General Defrance formed a square against the Cossacks. The emperor Napoleon I. without doubt approved of this method of combat, for he seldom had a regiment of cavalry manœuvred in his presence without ordering the formation in square.

The marching formation of cavalry is the column by platoons. A detachment on a march should generally keep the left side of the road, because, in case of attack, each horseman then presents his strong side—the right—to the enemy.

The checker-formation, formerly much used in retreat, has been abandoned by cavalry, on account of the extreme difficulty, if not impossibility, in a retrograde movement, of keeping the squadrons of the second line opposite to the intervals of the first.

9. Eclaireurs.—By this name are designated the horsemen scattered in front, in rear, and on the flanks of a troop, to cover its movements or its position. They are the skirmishers of the cavalry.

They should be selected from the troops who are armed with guns or carbines. Their principal duties are to scour the country, reconnoitre the enemy, cover the preparations for a charge, escort convoys, support the infantry skirmishers, etc. A body of cavalry, in retreat, may also throw out a screen of skirmishers, behind which the broken squadrons may rally. Good results will be obtained by combining the action of these *éclaireurs* with the skirmishers of the infantry, according to the nature of the ground.

The French regulations with regard to the evolutions of the cavalry, fixes the number of éclaireurs at one fourth the number of the troop from which they are detailed.

CHAPTER FIFTH.

HISTORY OF ARTILLERY.

The history of artillery presents this particular interest: that it is connected with the highest efforts and most notable progress of human genius.

The motive force of the projectile-machines of antiquity, of which the *balista*, the *onager*, and the *catapulta* are best known, were either weights, or springs made of cords of hide or sinew, raised or stretched by a windlass or levers, and suddenly abandoned to the effect of gravity or elasticity.

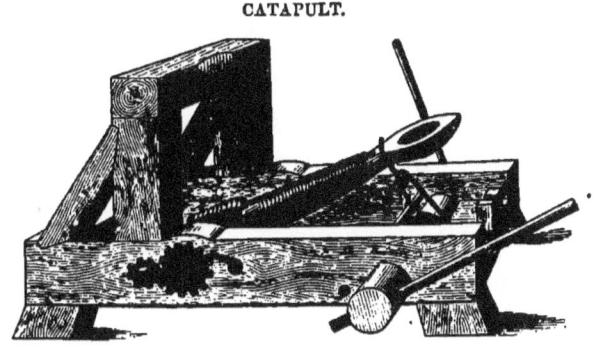

CATAPULT.

These machines, constructed almost wholly of wood, carried upwards of 1,000 yards, and the strongest threw projectiles weighing from 600 to 700 pounds. Besides stones, they threw arrows, beams, red-hot balls, and fire-pots.

As they were transported with armies, they corresponded to our field pieces. The Greeks, excepting Alexander the Great and his successors, made but little use of them. The Romans, in the time of the Republic, employed them only for the defence of their camps; under the Empire, they ventured to take them with their armies. These machines multiplied as the courage and military skill of the Romans declined, and in the legions of the Lower Empire there were even as many as 11 machines to 1,000 men. Thus, also, Frederic II. and Napoleon I., at the close of their reigns, increased the number of their pieces of artillery in the armies which were composed of young soldiers. This coincidence proves, that, from the introduction of projectile machines, the number of them required has always been the greater the poorer the troops.

The ancient machines were put *hors du combat* by setting them on fire, or else by cutting the cords and springs—a manœuvre corresponding to our spiking of guns.

The first kings of France took into their service the projectile machines captured from the enemies' legions, but their people were ignorant of the art of using them, and considered their employment as dishonorable, for which double reason balistics were of little service to them, and began to decline under their successors. This decline stopped under the reign of Charlemagne; but after this great emperor, it continued, and the balistic art soon perished, with all the arts, in the midst of the feudal system. During the Crusades, both parties made use of projectile machines of the ancient kind. Philip Augustus brought them back to France (1191). They were perfected in the thirteenth century, and the onager and catapult reappeared, under the names of *perrière* and *mangonneau*.

Several of these machines were of enormous dimensions, and required a great quantity of wood in their construction; moreover, if they threw very large masses they could not give them great velocity; but notwithstanding these inconveniences, they were preserved for a long time after the invention and use of the first cannon, with which they competed during nearly two centuries.

Many persons still attribute the invention of gunpowder to that celebrated English monk Roger Bacon, who astonished the world by his great scientific discoveries in the thirteenth century; nevertheless, powder—that is, the mixture of saltpetre, sulphur, and charcoal—was known, several centuries before our era, to the Chinese, who employed it in the manufacture of various fire-works, which they put into tubes, and thus formed what we should now call fuses. The knowledge of powder was gradually transmitted to the people of Asia, through India and Persia, and at last to the Arabs, who communicated it to the Greeks of the Lower Empire; and a recent opinion is, that the famous Greek-fire of the last-mentioned people, was nothing more than an incendiary composition made of gunpowder. The invasions of the Arabs, and especially the Crusades, introduced a knowledge of gunpowder to the people of western Europe; and the great number of European claimants to the invention of this agent of war (the English *Roger Bacon*, the German *Albertus Magnus, Berthold Schwartz, Constantin Anklitzen*, etc.), evidently indicates that the epoch was ripe for the invention: that is, this invention was but the reproduction of a thing already in existence, but of which only confused and vague ideas were entertained, diffused throughout Europe by the crusaders returning to their homes.

But if Europe can no longer lay claim to the invention of gunpowder, she is still justly entitled to that of fire-arms, with which neither the Chinese, nor the Indians, nor the Persians, nor the Arabs were acquainted before ourselves; these ancient people being indeed acquainted with powder, but ignorant of the fact that it could be used to project heavy masses to a distance. This point seems now to be established in favor of our science.

The obscurity of the chronicles of the middle ages, and the confusion of names, make it difficult to fix the precise epoch when the projectile property of powder was discovered, and when the first cannon were introduced. It appears, however, that their employment in war does not go back beyond the fourteenth century. In fact, the earliest mention of cannon appears to be that of instruments in the form of funnels, or vases, used by the Genoese in 1319.

The first field artillery differed little from the portable fire-arms, and was frequently mounted upon stationary frames, for which wheels were afterward substituted.

The cannon called *vases* were, from their form, capable of throwing large stones; they soon received the name of *bombards*. The annexed figure shows the nature of their construction.

BOMBARD.

Bombards soon increased their proportions, and at the end of the fourteenth century must have obtained remarkable length and weight; for we find mention of one 50 feet long, and of another weighing 2,000 pounds.

The ancient machines could not contend against bombards; the smallest ball caused their fragile frames to fly to pieces. They were supplanted by pieces of ordnance, which, from the year 1376, were employed to open breaches, and thenceforth were exclusively used (with some rare exceptions) in sieges and on fields of battle.

The term *artillery* existed before the invention of fire-arms. It designated all the arms fabricated by the *artillier* (original form of the word *artilleur*),* namely, balistic engines, bows, arrows, lances, darts, shields,

---

* The old French verb *artiller* signifies to *fashion by art*, and had nearly its equivalent in the old English verb *to artilize*, while *artillier* was nearly equivalent to *artisan;* but its modern form, *artilleur*, is restricted to the signification of *artillerist.—Tr.*

etc. Masters of artillery commanded the *artilliers*. These masters of artillery were charged with the fabrication as well as the distribution to the army, of the new and the old artillery; they consequently also made fire-arms, pieces of ordnance, powder, balls, bullets, and had under their orders soldiers called *cannoniers*, instituted about 1411, for manœuvring and serving cannon.

The first masters of artillery were subordinate to the grand master of the crossbowmen, to whom they rendered direct account of the matters intrusted to their charge. But under Charles VII. the master-general of the artillery, who was chief of this branch of service, succeeded in making his office independent; and from that time its prerogatives went on increasing daily.

The first field artillery, considered, so to speak, as an *obstacle*, was scattered about the army, and interspersed among the wagons; it was soon separated from the baggage and placed on the front or flanks. Cannon, in those days, produced an especial effect upon the spirit of the troops by the noise of their discharges; they increased the importance of defensive positions, and were employed in secondary operations; but, being difficult to manœuvre and slow to load, they could be used but imperfectly in an open country.

Louis XI., about 1475, distributed among three the duties of master-general of artillery; and profiting by the experience of his father, whose artillery had rendered him important aid in the reconquest of his kingdom from the English, he maintained a large amount of artillery. During his reign, twelve pieces of the caliber 45 were cast, which were celebrated under the name of the *twelve peers of France.** One of these pieces was taken at the battle of Montlhéri (1465).

Charles VIII., in 1493, reëstablished a single master-general of the artillery. His expedition into Italy exhibits the first important employment of artillery in a campaign. All the powers, following the French example, set about improving their artillery. The definite foundation of the French artillery dates from this epoch. Charles VIII. left France with about 100 cannon of mean caliber; at Sarzanne his park of artillery was augmented by about 40 large pieces. It was already understood how to place these pieces so as to take the enemy's troops obliquely; nevertheless, in this expedition, artillery played a more important part against fortresses than in the open country; it was fired with precision.

Under Louis XII., artillery of lighter construction was introduced, in order to be a less hinderance to the march of an army. The small calibers became sufficiently portable to take advantageous positions during the combat, to compel the enemy to keep at a distance, and thus to complicate his movements. This monarch established two masters-general of artillery, one in France and one in Italy.

At this epoch the infantry was often made to lie down on the ground, to be less exposed to the balls. The Swiss, in one battle, endeavored to seize

---

* This name recalls the *twelve apostles*, which Charles V. had cast at Malaga for his expedition against Tunis.

upon the artillery of their adversaries, by advancing as skirmishers against the batteries. Under Francis I. the French artillery was increased and systematized; and in its outfit the use of stout horses was made imperative. At Marignan (1515), our cannon gave us the victory. At Pavia (1525), Francis I., after the success of his right, thinking to surprise the army of the enemy, advanced at the head of his gensdarmery, *thus masking the fire of his pieces.* This false manœuvre caused his defeat. At Cerisole (1544), French pieces, by having better horses, arrived at their place on the field of battle as soon as the cavalry. Finally, let us observe that in the sixteenth century, it was artillery that arrested the progress of the Turks, and thus protected European civilization. From a military point of view, we may say that the increase of fire-arms complicated the art of war only for mediocre minds, while making it more simple for great captains.

In 1543, Francis I. gave to the master-general of his artillery the title of *grand master* and *captain-general of the artillery.* The office of grand master continued without change during the subsequent reigns. In 1599, Henry IV. conferred it upon Sully, in whose hands it acquired increased importance; and two years later, in behalf of this celebrated minister, he erected it into an office of the crown. This office lasted until 1755, when it disappeared. It has since been temporarily reëstablished, at several epochs, but with diminished prerogatives, under the name of *first inspector-general of artillery.*

The first cannon were only combinations of large

bars and iron hoops. From the fifteenth and the sixteenth centuries they were cast of iron, of copper, and of bronze. The balls employed were also successively of stone, lead, iron, and bronze. As to the guard of the pieces,—as much importance was attached to their preservation, they were entrusted to detachments of the best infantry, that is, to the Swiss, and for want of them, to the lansquenets (German foot soldiers).

Henry II. adopted five calibers for his ordnance, varying from 1 to 33 pounds; Henry IV. added a sixth caliber of ¾ of a pound, and collected at the arsenal of Paris as many as 100 pieces of ordnance—a large number for that epoch, which is indicative of the projects of conquest entertained by him at the time of his assassination. The artillery of Henry IV., like that of Henry II., had no limbers; but the cannon of 33 pounds caliber had a four-wheeled carriage, and spare carriages for all the large pieces accompanied the train. In 1609, Henry IV., reviving the edicts of Charles IX., forbade the casting of any piece approaching to the six calibers which he had just adopted.

In the battles of this monarch, the artillery, placed at the extremities of a crescent, endeavored to take the enemy obliquely, and to flank the whole line of battle, keeping itself upon the defensive.

About the middle of the sixteenth century we find the artillery of Protestant Germany possessing great lightness, and firing with extraordinary rapidity. That of Prussia also possessed a good and powerful organization, and later served as a model to Gribeauval.

Gustavus Adolphus reduced the weight of artillery,

accelerated and improved its fire, and adopted the calibers 3, 4, 6, 12, 16, and 30. His ordnance was of bronze, of cast iron, and of sheet iron bound with leather thongs. This sovereign employed it especially in attacking, whereas it had been before used chiefly for defence. He divided the artillery on marches, and grouped it in large batteries on the field of battle, placing these batteries on the flanks and in the centre of his lines. He always carried with him a large number of pieces: at the crossing of the Lech (1631), he had 72 of large caliber.

In 1634, Louis XIII. added two new calibers to those existing in France under Henry IV., the 24 and the 12. In the same year bombs were brought into use by the French, who threw the first missiles of this kind at the siege of Lamothe, in Lorraine. From that time, in order to make artillery lighter, the larger calibers began to be left in the rear, and only field pieces, drawn by four or six horses, were carried with the army.

Under Louis XIV., Vauban invented ricochet firing (1688), and specially employed cannon instead of the mine to make breaches. The invention of *carcasses*, an incendiary projectile of ellipsoidal form, belongs also to this period: the French used them for the first time in 1672. In the preceding year, the king had taken from the Swiss the guarding of the artillery, and replaced them by the regiment of *fusiliers of the king*, created for that service. The matchlock was still the ordinary arm of the infantry, and the new name of this regiment was derived from the fact that the soldiers who composed it were the first who were armed with the new muskets (*fusils*) with bayonets. Upon its reorganization, in 1693, the regiment of fusiliers of the king took the name of *Royal Artillery;* and this is the proper date of the organization of the artillery corps. But though the great monarch instituted, as we have said, the first permanent corps of artillery, and gave great extension to the *matériel* of this arm, no great improvement was made under his reign: in fact, they persisted in employing the same kind of artillery in sieges and on the battle field, without considering that the purpose of this arm is quite different in these two cases. Under Louis XIV., the ordnance generally used consisted of long pieces of the calibers 36, 24, 16, 12, 8 and 4.

During the reign of this monarch, the number of pieces of ordnance in the army was increased, as well as the effective force of the troops. The French had at Fleurus (1690) 100 pieces; at Malplaquet, 200. In this last battle (1709) a battery of 50 cannon, placed on the French right and loaded with grape shot, put 2,000 of the enemy *hors du combat* in a single discharge. By his large masses of artillery, Louis XIV. silenced Spain and Holland, and made himself master of Upper Burgundy and Alsace. In the middle period of his wars, his artillery rendered him good service in battles as well as sieges. At the end of his reign, the artillery, as well as the other corps of his armies, was exhausted. Turenne still placed his artillery in advance of his lines: after him, care was taken to distribute it among the several divisions.

In 1732, Louis XV. adopted the artillery system of Lieutenant-general Vallière, and decreed that the calibers 24, 16, 12, 8 and 4, should be exclusively employed in the French armies; the 24 and the 16 principally for sieges: the others indifferently, either for sieges or for battles.

We owe to Frederic II. the introduction of horse artillery (so useful for accompanying the movements of cavalry), and also the use of howitzers in the field. This monarch improved the tactics of artillery, and instead of distributing it on the whole front of his line of battle, as was formerly done, he combined it in large masses. He was indebted to this system for several of his successes. We see him fighting at Czaslaw (1742) with 106 cannon and 3 howitzers; at Zorndorf (1758) with 117 pieces of ordnance; at Torgan (1760) with 244 pieces. These are large numbers, considering the effective force of his armies.

Vaquette de Gribeauval, a celebrated French general, who fought for Maria Theresa against Frederic II., and distinguished himself at the defence of Schweidnitz in 1762, was inspector-general of artillery, and carried the science of this arm to a high degree of perfection. His system of field artillery was adopted in France in 1765, and soon after by all Europe; and, with some modifications, is still followed.

In this system, the pieces, reduced in length and only of about one half the weight of the old ones, are mounted on carriages which are at once solid and light. The different calibers are the 12, the 8, and the 4; and the 1 was promptly suppressed. To these must be added a howitzer of 6 inches for field service.

It is to Gribeauval that we owe the use of the *hausse*, by which cannon can be pointed both promptly and with precision. This illustrious man changed scarcely anything in siege pieces, but he improved their accessories; he invented the garrison carriage, the use of which renders embrasures unnecessary, and the coast carriage, by means of which the movement of ships can be followed while pointing. He fixed the calibers of mortars at 12, 10 and 8 inches; that of stone mortars at 15 inches; and for these different pieces he introduced cast-iron carriages.

He divided the *personnel* of the arm in a happy manner, by establishing as the unit of artillery force, the battery of 8 pieces served by one company of cannoniers.

In the year 1801, the First Consul created battalions of the train, to convey the materiel of the artillery—a service formerly performed by contractors, to the great inconvenience of the army.

Under the Empire, the personnel of the artillery was raised to 60,000 men. *Napoleon employed this arm in large masses:* thus, at the battle of Wagram, 100 pieces were rapidly moved to occupy momentarily a portion of the line of battle. This particular circumstance taught us the necessity of training a mass of pieces to manœuvre with ensemble and promptness; and consequently, during the ensuing peace, attention was paid to drawing up manœuvres of one or several batteries. The methods which were developed had a happy influence upon the last battles of the imperial period. It is hardly necessary to say that Napoleon I. placed his artillery in order of battle as we place it at the present day.

Finally, in 1829, the "Committee of Artillery," taking the English models, adopted a new *matériel* of artillery, called the *new system*. At the present time, the siege and other calibers are 24, 16, 12 and 8; the last two, the 12 and the 8, are those of which field batteries are exclusively composed; for the new carriages, having great mobility, enable us to carry cannon of powerful effect to the field of battle. The new howitzers have the length of cannon; those of the field are of the caliber 24 and of 6 inches; those for siege, 8 inches. Mountain artillery consists only of howitzers of the caliber 12. The mortars have a conical chamber, and their calibers are 12, 10, and 8 inches; the stone mortars have a caliber of 15 inches.

The battery is now reduced to six pieces, with their accessories; of these six pieces, four are cannon and two howitzers.

Several arrangements observed in the construction of the carriages and limbers, give the new system great mobility. It also possesses remarkable simplicity; for it contains but two kinds of carriages, one for the cannon of 12 and the howitzer of 6 inches, the other for the cannon of 8 and the howitzer of 24; moreover, the limber of the caisson is the same as that of the piece, so that the carriage can be refurnished by a simple exchange of limber. The wheels are also of the same size, and can be interchanged.

Another advantage of the new system is that the cannoniers can sit upon the ammunition-chests, and thus be carried with the piece. In consequence of this improvement, the foot batteries manœuvre, in case of need, with the same rapidity as the horse batteries, and the artillery can conform itself to all the movements of the infantry and of the cavalry.

The present French system is sometimes called the "*Système Valée*," after the general officer, since a marshal of France, who is its author, and had already proved its merits at the camp of Saint-Omer (Sept., 1827).

This system is now modified, in its *matériel*, by the adoption of the 12-pounder cannon-howitzer (Napoleon-gun); and in its *personnel*, by the organization of 1854, in which existing defects are corrected, and two important principles established:

1st. The division of the artillery arm into three distinct branches: *light* artillery, the cannoniers riding on horseback; *line* artillery, they being mounted on the ammunition-chests; and *reserve* artillery, where they are on foot. Each is thus enabled to perform its appropriate functions, the first having to manœuvre with the cavalry, the second with the divisions of infantry, and the last to serve in the attack and defence of fortified places. In preceding organizations, the artillery-men were frequently diverted from their special instruction to acquire a knowledge of horsemanship.

2d. The artillery train-corps was entirely suppressed and absorbed in the foot regiments, forming park-batteries.

CHAPTER SIXTH.

ARTILLERY FORMATION AND TACTICS.

1. Purpose of Artillery.—The purpose of artillery is to *destroy*, either the troops of the enemy, opposing artillery, or obstacles; and by such destruction to facilitate the attack of infantry or cavalry. To accomplish this purpose in a decisive manner, artillery should act in large masses; for if it operate against a line of foot soldiers, it will by this means alone be able to make· large breaches, which will divide the line into several detached groups, which it will afterward be easy to assail and to beat in detail. There are, however, cases where isolated discharges produce a useful moral effect upon the enemy; as, for example, when a ball carries off some officer, or simply a bearer of orders.

To accomplish its mission, the artillery must have recourse to different means, according to the nature of the object to be destroyed; hence there are two kinds of ordnance—field pieces and siege guns. But in a broken and hilly country, even the first, which are the lightest, are yet too heavy to be transported; and hence there is a third kind of artillery—*mountain artillery*, carried on the backs of mules; whereas the field and siege guns are placed on carriages drawn by horses.

We have just spoken of the transportation of artillery: this is indispensable, not only on the march, but upon the battle field; for, at the present time, this arm acts not only by its fire, but also by its movements; while, in former days, it was thought that the purpose of artillery was only to fire from a fixed point.

It is evident that the different portions of the army cannot all use the same calibers, since mobility depends upon the weight of the balls. Hence the division of field artillery attached to an army, into *division-batteries* and *reserve-batteries*—the former composed of light artillery, attached to divisions, and always in action; the latter composed of heavy artillery, forming part of the reserve, and, like it, acting only at the decisive moment, or at the last extremity.

Besides the general service of guns, and the construction of all batteries, the corps of French artillery is also charged in the field with: 1st, the furnishing of arms and munitions of war to the army; 2d, the repair of arms, which repairs are entrusted to the companies of armorers; 3d, the construction and placing of movable bridges, and crossing streams by boats.

The artillery, however, is not a self-sustaining arm; it needs immediate protection to accomplish its various objects, and especially when it is engaged in firing, or in the construction either of a battery or a bridge. In fact, if the artillery were not supported by troops of infantry or cavalry, the artillerists would be obliged, in case of attack, to abandon their special functions and convert themselves temporarily into foot soldiers, or into cavalry (according as they were on foot or mounted), to repel the enemy; which would often be injurious to the interests of the whole, by interfering with their special duty at the most critical moment. But if the artillery cannot act with security except under the ægis of the other arms, it renders them, in return, the most important service; and we may confidently assert that it now constitutes an indispensable accessory in the composition of armies.

2. Numerical Data.—The number of pieces of ordnance of an army depends upon the quantity and quality of the troops which compose it. It is usually fixed by stating the number for every 1,000 men. The experience of our later wars has demonstrated that we could adopt two pieces of ordnance to 1,000 infantry; but this number must be regarded as a *minimum** adapted to the best troops—for, the more experienced and inured the soldiers, the less their need of support. In the generality of cases, three pieces to 1,000 men is a more suitable proportion. Foreign nations have often gone beyond this number; the Prussians, for example, have employed four pieces of ord-

---

* A minimum, that is, for the continent of Europe: for, against feeble troops, we come down to a lower figure; thus, in 1830, in the expedition which conquered Algiers, there was scarcely one piece of ordnance to 1,000 men.

nance, and the Russians even as many as seven, to every 1,000 men.

As to the cavalry, it is usual to support it by twice as many pieces as would be used for the same number of infantry.

Artillery being always an impediment to long expeditions, it is proper, in fixing its amount, to take into account its weight in reference to the nature of the ground on which it may have to act; especially as it will be preferable to take a smaller number of pieces than to be reduced to the dire necessity of abandoning some of them to facilitate the march.

The supply of ammunition carried by the artillery, is 200 rounds for each piece of ordnance, and 50 cartridges for each infantry soldier.

Each piece, or caisson, drawn by six horses, as in France, occupies 13 metres (14 yards) of depth in file. The limber, with six horses, occupies but 10 metres. The depth of the piece in battery, including the handspike, is 5 metres; the front of each piece and carriage is 2 metres.

3. Tactical Unit.—A *battery* is the tactical unit of artillery. In France a field battery consists of six pieces,* which, with the accessories and the cannoniers necessary to manœuvre it, produces an effective of 30 carriages and wagons, 200 men, and 200 horses, suffi-

---

* The field battery, composed of four cannon and two howitzers, forms now the exception; there are no longer any such, except in the reserve (where they are of four cannon of the 12 caliber, and two howitzers of 16 centimetres), and not even all the batteries of the reserve have this composition.

cient to form a single command. The personnel of this battery is now composed of homogeneous elements, inasmuch as the artillerists who serve the guns and the drivers who conduct them have the same rank.

Some foreign powers compose their batteries of eight pieces, six cannon and two howitzers; others, again, attach to their armies special batteries of howitzers. In France they have just adopted, for field artillery, as the principal kind of ordnance, howitzer-cannon of the calibre 12 (light 12-pounder), which throw either balls or shells,—thus affording the advantage, that the *six* pieces composing a battery may *all* fire at the same time either balls or shells, as required. These howitzer-guns were proposed by the Emperor in 1849.*

The French field-battery is divided into three sections of two pieces each; † the 1st lieutenant commands the right section, the 2d lieutenant the left section, and the adjutant the centre section.

The mountain-battery is composed of six howitzers of the calibre 12, divided into three sections; but more frequently mountain artillery is organized simply in sections of two howitzers, each section requiring 22 mules for its transportation: this mode is followed in Algiers.

4. **Formations.**—The field artillery has no *defensive* formations. In manœuvring and combating, it

* The new system of field artillery which they constitute has been explained and defended by Colonel Favé, in two pamphlets, published in 1850 and 1851.

† In the battery of 4 cannon and 2 howitzers, the 2 howitzers form a section.

has three different formations: *in column, in line*, and *in battery*. We will point out the distinctive features of these formations for a French foot battery.

1st. *Formation in Column.*—This formation is that in which the battery, formed in sections, has its carriages drawn up in two files, each piece being followed or preceded by its caisson. For a foot battery the interval between the files is as much as 12 metres; the distance between two carriages of a file is 1 metre. The annexed figure shows the position of each carriage and each officer, non-commissioned officer, and of the cannoniers in this formation. The letter *c* designates the captain commanding; the letter *l* the lieutenant, commanding a flank section; the letters *ad* the adjutant, commanding the centre section; *mc* the chief quartermaster, commanding the line of caissons; *m* assistant-quartermasters, chiefs of pieces; *a* artificers, chiefs of caissons; *t* the trumpeter. A foot battery in column by sections occupies 16 metres of front and 83 metres in depth. The artillery, like the other arms, employs the formation in column for manœuvre, especially when prolonged. It is used equally for attack and march.

In the march in column, each carriage should carefully preserve its interval and distance. The *column of attack* is formed upon the centre section taken as the head of the column, the two other sections being each *in column by piece*, behind one of the pieces of the centre section; a formation which facilitates the deployment of this column by a *forward into line*. It is evident that, for the purpose of passing over a narrow road, the whole battery may be formed in column of pieces.

2d. *Formation in Line.*—In this formation the carriages are arranged upon two parallel lines, the

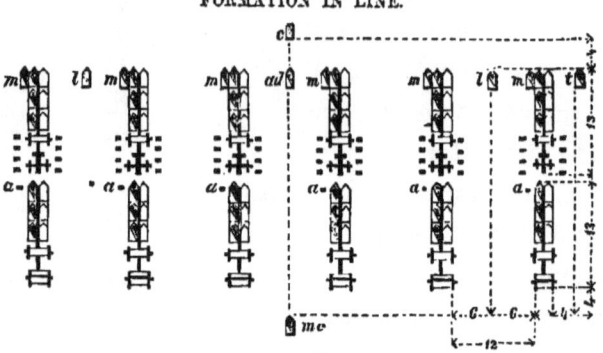

FORMATION IN LINE.

pieces, limbered up, forming one line; and the caissons, each following or in front of its own piece, forming the second line. The horses of all the carriages face in the same direction. For a foot battery, the interval between the carriages is 12 metres; the distance between the lines is 1 metre, as in the above figure, in which the reference letters have the same signification as in the figure on page 153. This formation is especially an order of review;* yet it may be used for advancing a few hundred paces, when the ground is sufficiently clear to permit the passage of a body, which, though but a single battery, presents a front of 72 metres and a depth of 27 metres.

3d. *Formation in Battery.*—This formation is that in which the pieces in line are prepared to fire; the pieces, their limbers, and the caissons remain turned toward the enemy, and are formed on three parallel lines. For a foot battery, the interval between the pieces is 12 metres; the distance between the line of pieces and the line of limbers is 6 metres, and the distance between the latter and the line of caissons is 10 metres. The following figure illustrates this formation,

FORMATION IN BATTERY.

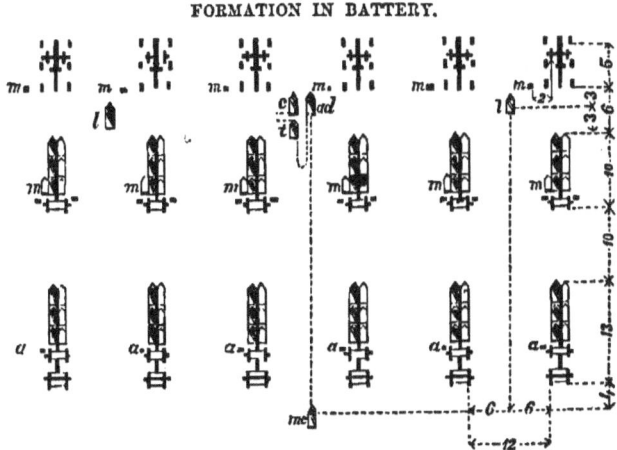

* On reviews and parades, the order is modified by throwing back the caissons to the distance of 15 metres from the pieces, and grouping the cannoniers in a small detachment at a distance of 6 metres in rear of the muzzle of the pieces.

which occupies 72 metres of front, and 44 in depth. The letters have the same signification as before. This is the true formation of the artillery for combat. After the firing has commenced, the battery can be carried, in parts and successively, to more advanced positions—a movement usually executed by half-batteries, the right half-battery firing while the other half marches, and reciprocally. In the particular case where a battery, fully formed in the order in battery, retires while firing, the limbers and caissons, after the first retrograde movement, should remain with their backs to the enemy, in order to continue the movement more readily.

5. **Manœuvres.**—To pass from one to the other of the preceding formations, the artillery necessarily makes use of *manœuvres:* moreover, it is proper for it to be able to manœuvre, in order to participate in the transformations to which the contingencies of battle may give rise in the tactical disposition of the troops which it supports; and this, both for foot and horse batteries.

What shall be the character of the manœuvres of artillery? This arm is complex; it embraces men, horses, carriages: consequently great precision of movement cannot be exacted of it. All that can be required is, that it shall manœuvre promptly; and, when the manœuvre is completed, that it fire quickly upon the enemy. It will therefore manœuvre rather like cavalry than like infantry; and, even thus, the presence of carriages must render the movements somewhat disjointed. This slight inconvenience will be made to disappear rather by skill in manœuvring than by quickness of motion; for artillery does not admit of a faster gait than a trot in its movements. It is evident, indeed, that if it were manœuvred at a gallop, the horses, harnessed to such heavy carriages, would soon be ruined; nevertheless, in a critical moment, a battery may, by way of exception and for a short time only, effect a movement at the gallop.

As we have just remarked, artillery manœuvres somewhat after the manner of cavalry; consequently it employs for the most part oblique movements and wheeling, which are adapted to combatants who cannot follow the compact and right-angled movements of infantry. This will be readily seen from some examples.

1st. The battery being in column, either at a halt or marching, to form it in line upon the head of the column while gaining ground to the left, the command is to be given to the two rear sections—*left oblique* —which oblique movement they continue until, by resuming a direct march, they will be severally at their proper interval from the next section on the side toward the guide; and then they continue their march on a line parallel to the axis of the column until they reach the front of the section at the head of the column. If they wish to gain ground to the right, the formation in line is effected in an analogous manner by a *right oblique.** The choice of the

* The "*right oblique (or left)*" is performed by artillery at an angle of 45 degrees; it is, therefore, in reality, a half turn to the right (or left).

side on which it will be most advantageous to form is to be determined by the ground alone; for, as artillery now makes no account of inversions in its manœuvres, it is a matter of indifference whether the two rear sections are carried to the right or to the left of the leading section of a column.

2d. To form the column of attack upon the centre, the battery being in line at a halt, the centre section advances; when it has left sufficient space the right section *obliques to the left*, and comes up in column by piece in rear of the right file of the centre section; while the left section *obliques to the right*, forms in column by pieces, and takes up its position behind the left file of the centre section. The formation of the column of attack is formed in an analogous manner, if the battery, instead of being at a halt, is marching in line.

3d. The column being in march, the formation in line *to* the right or *to* the left is effected by a wheel to the right or to the left, performed simultaneously by all the sections. To form line *on* the left or right the movement is analogous, except that it is performed first by the leading section, which halts when it has fully completed its wheel, the other sections wheeling successively when opposite their proper places in the line to be formed, upon which they halt and dress upon the leading section already on the line.

4th. The battery being in line at a halt, or marching in line, may effect a change of front to a line making a greater or less angle with the former front, by means of a *wheel in line*, which is executed by the pivot-carriage moving at a walk while the others proceed at a trot. It is likewise by wheels in line, followed by march in line, executed by each battery separately and in parallels, that in evolutions of several batteries combined, changes of front upon one flank are effected, the other flank being thrown forward or to the rear.

The evolutions of several batteries, of which we have just spoken, present some analogy to the evolutions of the line of several battalions, taking into account the essential differences of constitution which distinguish the artillery from the infantry.

In the manœuvres of artillery there are neither general nor particular guides; the direction of the column or of the line, in march, or while being formed, is intrusted to the chief of the piece upon which the formation is made. Since the adoption of the new *materiel*, but one mode of wheeling is admitted in the movements of artillery, which is that of infantry on the side of the guide, and is always executed upon a *moving pivot*, the pivot-piece describing an arc of a circle, to clear the ground where the movement begins. We must also remark that *countermarches* and *abouts* of carriages are always made to the left, because the drivers ride on the near horses.

6. Positions.—The term *battery* is used not only to designate the unit of force of artillery, but also any collection of several pieces upon any determined point of the field of battle. The choice of positions to be given to the batteries is not indifferent, for the skill of the gunner would be paralyzed by a bad location.

An open ground, with the flanks supported, and slightly overlooking the position occupied by the enemy, offers an eligible site for a battery. The soil should be solid, but not stony; for the smallest projectiles of the enemy striking the stones would produce flying fragments quite injurious to those serving the pieces. The position should also afford commodious and safe exits, not only for the offensive, but also for retreat—for which prudence requires that we should always be prepared. As much as possible, the artillery should be posted so as to *see without being seen*, by concealing it behind some obstacle, provided always that this obstacle does not interfere with the certainty and facility of its firing, or with the convenience of exit.

The position having been determined upon, the direction of the line of fire of the pieces is to be fixed more or less obliquely with respect to the front of the enemy, so as to produce the greatest damage possible in his ranks by the angle under which the balls will reach them. Hence the different names given to batteries. Thus a *direct battery* is one which strikes the front of the enemy perpendicularly, which is destructive in proportion to the *depth* of the opposing force; an *oblique battery* is that whose line of fire is oblique to the front of the enemy; a *reverse battery* is that which plays upon the rear of a body of troops already exposed to direct fire—a difficult position to take, but one which is exceedingly harassing to the force thus menaced; an *enfilading battery*, that which fires on the flank in the direction of the prolongation of the enemy's line—a battery which light artillery can easily establish when the enemy offer their flank and thus expose themselves to this most murderous fire, which not unfrequently occurs in manœuvring; a *cross battery*, one whose pieces firing obliquely, cross their fire; or, by extension, one which crosses its fire with another—a very destructive kind of battery, as it concentrates a large number of projectiles upon the same point.

When speaking of the purpose for which artillery is destined, we subdivided field artillery into division-batteries and reserve-batteries. The former, also called artillery of the line, because it is permanently attached to the line, are active from the first to the last moment of the combat; the latter, destined to sustain the feebler portions of the line, act but temporarily. Hence they have two very different kinds of position in battle. The division-batteries are placed (say 150 or 200 yards) in advance of the first line of troops, or behind the extreme flanks of the lines. The reserve-batteries, in the mean time, keep out of reach of the enemy's fire, ready to throw themselves quickly upon any points that may be menaced, or to accompany an attacking force. In battle, moreover, care must be taken to post the caissons in a strong and well-sheltered place, as they are constantly needed, and their preservation is of the first importance.

11

CHAPTER SEVENTH.

HISTORY OF ENGINEERS.

THE history of the engineer arm, as constituted at the present day with a staff and troops, may be comprised in a small compass, for it is not of ancient origin.

In the sixteenth century, after the invention of bastioned fortifications, the Italian engineers, reputed the most skilful, were spread over all Europe; Catherine de Medicis employed several in the French service. At the close of the civil war which marked the end of the dynasty of the Valois, Sully, having been made superintendent of fortifications, undertook to repair the French fortified places then in ruins, and to consolidate the engineers charged with these works, calling them *ingénieurs ordinaires du roi* (this about 1602).

Until 1690, these engineers held their rank in the arms or staffs of which they were a part. After that date, being charged with the coast defences as well as those of the interior of the kingdom, and placed under the immediate orders of the Minister of War, they formed a wholly military corps, and served at the fortifications, or with armies in the field, according to circumstances. Under Louis XIV., a prince who delighted in the war of sieges, their corps was increased; and from 55 officers in 1688, it grew to 600 in 1697—a number which it has never since attained.*

Under Louis XV., from 1755 to 1758, the corps of engineers was, for the time, united to the staff of the artillery. In the year 1758, when the two corps were again separated, the military engineers adopted a uniform, consisting of a blue coat faced with black velvet; and from that time, the black velvet has remained the characteristic feature of the French engineer dress. In 1762, the number of engineers was fixed at 400, and has since varied but little, being sometimes greater and sometimes less. In 1776 this

---

* Under the direction of Vauban, the corps of French engineers rendered eminent services in the long wars of this period, and won in Europe such a preëminence, that everywhere its usages, its regulations, its *tracés* or forms of fortifications, and its methods of attack, were followed and imitated. It was to reward the whole corps, in the person of its real chief, both by rank and merit, that the great king gave the bâton of marshal to Vauban.

The science of the Attack and Defence of Places made prodigious advances under this distinguished engineer, who invented *parallels, trench-cavaliers,* and *ricochet-firing*. The art of fortifying places felt the power of his skilful hand; the demi-lune was enlarged, the bastion perfected, the redoubt of the demi-lune invented, the tenaille given a more advantageous form, water made useful in defence, and fortifications were admirably conformed or adapted to the ground.

The great increase of armies made a resort to field fortifications indispensable; immense lines were constructed, supported by rivers or the sea, to protect entire countries; but the great extent of these lines rendered them weak, for it was impossible to guard them everywhere; hence they were almost always forced, and consequently fell into discredit.—*Tr.*

corps received the official designation of *Corps Royal du Génie*. Soon after the employés charged with the care of buildings, fortifications, magazines, dams, etc., received the name of *gardes du génie.**

* Few changes took place in the French engineers until the Revolution, when, in common with the other branches of the service, they lost many valuable officers by emigration, among them Bousmard, the author of an able work on fortifications.

The number of officers was kept up to 310 in 1791, 450 in 1795, and 371 in 1802, by introduction of engineers from other corps—the *ponts et chaussées*, etc.

During the reign of the great Napoleon, the officers of engineers, who had, in Germany, more the duty of staff officers than continually making a war of sieges, found in Spain the opportunity of devoting themselves anew to the art of attacking places.

The engineer arm had a staff of nearly the same strength as in 1802, having at its head a first inspector-general of the arm, who was a grand officer of the Empire.

In 1813, when France was constrained, after twenty years of a glorious offensive war, to defend the ancient frontiers of the monarchy, the staff of engineers, distributed in a great number of fortified places, which she still occupied in Europe, was found too small to satisfy the wants of the service. She was consequently obliged (without incorporating them in the *corps du génie*) to employ a large number of engineers of *ponts et chaussées*, and even surveyors.

In the engineers, as in the artillery, the general officers present at Paris formed, under the orders of the first inspector-general, a *consulting committee*, called to give its advice upon the different branches of the service of the engineer arm: the influence of these committees was then less than it has been since.

From 1840 to 1846, Louis Philippe, at an expense of 140,000,000 francs, caused to be constructed the fortifications of Paris, consisting of a continuous bastioned *enceinte*, or line, and a chain of detached forts, the perimeter of the whole of these stupendous works being nearly forty miles. They were designed to defend the capital, and modify the plan of attack against France. The entire works were skilfully constructed by the *corps du génie*, under the direction of Marshal Dode de la Brunerie.

From the first to the second Empire, the number of engineers of the

As to the troops of engineers in France, the creation of *sappers*, called for by Vauban, dates from 1671; the first company of *miners* was raised two years later. In 1695 there existed one company of sappers and three companies of miners.

Vauban commanded the company of sappers. Mesgrigny, who died after seventy-two years of service; Goulon, subsequently chief of the corps of military engineers of the Empire; and Esprit, a brave officer, who fell at the siege of Barcelona in 1697, commanded the three companies of miners, which remained at first independent, and were not all finally attached to the artillery until 1705.* The sappers and miners, from their creation until the Revolution, constituted at one time a part of the artillery, at another a part of the engineers. Thus, from 1759 to 1761, when there existed six companies of miners, each consisting of 6 officers and 60 men, these companies were under the orders of the engineers. It was the Convention that really established the troops of engineers; for, in 1793, it took the sappers and miners from the artillery, to assign them to the engineers. In the following year, the officers of engineers had under their orders twelve battalions of sappers, six companies of miners, and two companies of *aëronauts (aërostiers)*. The troops of engineers remained throughout the reign of Napoleon I., organized in battalions.† At the restoration they formed three regi-

---

staff has steadily increased, until Napoleon III., in 1855, fixed them at 460, of which 160 were superior officers, and 300 captains or lieutenants.—*Tr.*

* Allent, *Histoire du corps impérial du génie*, 1st part, 1805, p. 368.

† Of engineer troops in the French army there were, in 1812: two bat-

ments. At present these troops also include two companies of workmen, and three companies of sapper-drivers; one of the latter companies is attached to each regiment.*

talions of miners; five battalions of sappers; one battalion of Walcheren sappers, created in 1811; two battalions of Spanish sappers, created in 1811; two battalions of the engineer train; and two companies of artificers.

The battalions of French sappers and miners had each nine companies, the other battalions four companies, and the battalions of the train seven companies, of which one remained in dépôt. The battalions of Spanish sappers were formed by Napoleon, who utilized everything, of mechanics selected from the Spanish prisoners. These battalions wore a white uniform, the others sky-blue, to distinguish them from the national sappers, and served till 1814 with fidelity and bravery. The two companies of artificers were attached, one to the arsenal of engineers of Metz, and the other to the arsenal of engineers at Allessandria.—*Tr.*

* In striking contrast with the ample numbers of officers and troops of engineers in the French service, is the meagre Corps of Engineers of the United States, now engaged in the most gigantic revolution on the page of history. It numbers but three companies of sappers, miners and pontoniers, and fifty officers, of which latter more than one half are unavailable as engineers in the field, being engaged in the construction of one vast line of Atlantic, Pacific and Lake coast-defences, on duty at the Military Academy and Engineer Bureau, or serving with volunteers as generals and colonels. Recently, as the Chief Engineer of the Department of the Mississippi, in which 150,000 men were in active campaign, I had not one regular engineer soldier, and but a single officer of the Corps of Engineers to assist in directing the varied operations of that service, extending over the States of Missouri, Kentucky and Tennessee, and parts of Arkansas, Mississippi and Alabama.—*Tr.*

CHAPTER EIGHTH.

FUNCTIONS OF THE ENGINEERS.

The engineers, on account of the important services they rendered in the great continental wars of the French Republic and Empire, and by the extension given to their personnel, may be considered as a fourth arm. The general functions of this accessory arm are now exclusively military, and are fixed by the regulations of the French army as follows:

1st. All the works of permanent fortification; that is, the construction and repairs of fortified places and military posts.

2d. The construction and repairs of all military edifices, such as infantry barracks, quarters for cavalry, guard houses, cisterns, hospitals, workshops, bakehouses, magazines and stables. The artillery is still charged with the buildings destined for its special service: nevertheless, the engineers construct the powder magazines situated in the interior of works of fortification, and when finished, turn them over to the artillery.

3d. The construction of field fortifications, which

the generals in chief or generals of division think proper to put up in the field, such as breastworks, trenches, redoubts, small forts, block-houses, lunettes, flèches, têtes-de-pont, intrenched lines and camps, and dykes. The engineers also construct ovens for baking bread in campaign.

4th. The construction, reëstablishment and destruction of roads, in campaign; the opening of certain thoroughfares: in a word, the various works which in war may facilitate the march of columns.

5th. The construction, in campaign, of raft-bridges, and bridges with fixed supports which can be improvised with the materials drawn from the country; such as trestle-bridges, pile-bridges, bridges of trees, draw-bridges; in short, the construction of bridges for which it is necessary to saw, hew, and frame wood.

6th. The various works required in the defence or attack of places, and the reconnoissances connected with these works.

These functions appertain to them in times of peace as well as war. In peace, the engineers have their works executed by contract by workmen drawn from various localities: for their execution in time of war, they have under their orders military workmen,* organized and trained in advance—namely, the sappers and miners; and are also frequently aided by auxiliary laborers taken from the other arms, principally from the infantry.

* The engineer soldiers are chiefly recruited from artificers of wood and iron, such as carpenters, joiners, wheelwrights, and blacksmiths; from masons and builders; and from miners and quarry-men.

In campaign, there is attached to each division of infantry, one company of sappers, which, upon the war-footing, numbers from 120 to 150 men. In the engineer arm, then, the unit of force is a company, attended by a four-horse wagon and its drivers. This wagon carries *spare* tools, to replace those carried by the men, when these are worn out or damaged. Each sapper, besides his sword, which may be of some service to him in cutting and trimming light wood, is also kept supplied with one tool, as a part of his equipment—either a shovel, a pick, or an axe with a very short handle, which is placed in a sheath passing through the knapsack, as shown in the annexed cut. In a company of 120 sappers, there should be 40 picks, 40 shovels, 30 axes, and 10 bill-hooks.

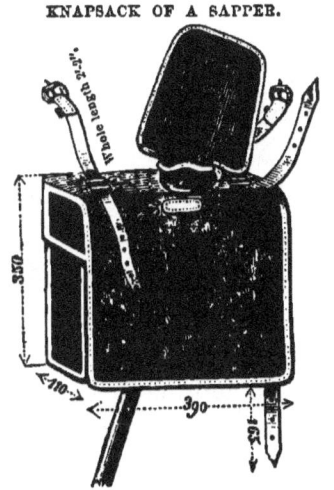

KNAPSACK OF A SAPPER.

The companies of miners carry special tools, useful in working mines. They usually march with the engineer train accompanying the army, which, with its heavy auxiliary materials, travels in the rear, carrying sappers' and miners' tools, cuirasses, helmets, sap-hooks and sap-forks, utensils for bridges, a pile-driver and its appurtenances, two or three travelling forges, and various articles of equipment and re-supply.

The sappers and miners are drilled as foot soldiers

in all the manœuvres of infantry,* and in gymnastic practice. They form, in case of need, excellent infantry for disputing a post and fighting in the midst of obstacles; but, not to divert them from their specialty, they are rarely employed as foot soldiers, and they usually brave death with their implements in hand, if the enemy falls upon them while they are engaged in opening a road, constructing a bridge, or erecting a field-work.

We will close this chapter with a single observation. In France the engineer corps is charged with the construction of those bridges only which require the use of tools for working wood; other bridges, chiefly those which are constructed with supports prepared in advance and transported with the army, such as bridges of boats or pontons, are intrusted to the artillery, which is the arm best supplied with conveyances. The case is different with the other great powers; in Prussia, in Spain, and in the United States, the pontonniers are a part of the engineer corps; in Austria and Russia they form a separate and distinct corps. Several French authors have expressed the opinion that it would be advantageous in France to annex the pontonniers to the engineer arm.

* The engineer troops have retained the old equipment, and are armed with the musket of the voltigeurs. The total weight of the armament and equipment carried by a man amounts to about 45 pounds.

PART SECOND.

COMBINATION OF THE ARMS.

CHAPTER FIRST.

ORGANIZATION OF ACTIVE ARMIES.

THUS far we have considered the several arms separately, as they are constituted and instructed in time of peace; but in war it is manifest that, in order to afford each other mutual support, they must be *combined*, and must operate under the orders of one and the same chief, who will direct their common action in the way which promises the most certain victory. Let us, then, see how they are to be united under one head, or in what manner they are to be grouped to constitute an army.

1. Principles of Organization.—The unit of force of each of the three arms which fight in line—the battalion, the squadron, and the battery—may enter directly into the composition of a brigade, and then there is no intermediate commander between the general of the brigade and the commandant of the battalion, the squadron or the battery. With reference exclusively to its application in war, this is evidently a practicable organization, and, in fact, it is that which exists in the federal army of Switzerland. But in most countries, and especially in France, we have combined together, in order to centralize the administration and instruction, and also to keep alive discipline, many units of force into *regiments*. In the same manner, in the organization of active armies, brigades are composed of a certain number of regiments—two at least.

Above the brigade comes the fraction of the army called a *division*, which includes troops of the various arms, in the proportion required by circumstances; and usually consists of either two or three brigades, either of infantry or of cavalry.

The division is to be regarded as the essential component fraction of an active army; and accordingly, the French regulations respecting campaign service declare that, " *The division is the fundamental element in the constitution of every army.*" A division, in fact, is a sufficiently large body to form a first separate command in which the generalship of the officer may be tested and his qualifications for a chief command may be proved; it does not require an expensive staff; and is, in short, the force best adapted to the scale of promotion which it is desirable to preserve in the hierarchy of the general officers. Frequently, the combination of several divisions forms an army, commanded by a general-in-chief, without having larger permanent fractions; and, in this case, the chief of the army transmits his orders directly to the generals of division. We say *permanent* fractions, for there may exist *temporary* ones, under the names *wing, centre, reserve;* thus, supposing an army to be composed of eight divisions, it may be drawn up upon a line containing six divisions (two in the centre, and two on each wing), with a reserve of two divisions; and then each of the wings, as also the centre or the reserve, will form a fraction larger than a division. These temporary fractions depend upon the general-in-chief, who can vary their amount according to the number of troops at his disposition; and for this reason their command, equally temporary and variable, is assigned at his discretion.

The case is different with *corps d'armée.* These are permanent fractions, established in the organization of an army, commanded by generals appointed by the sovereign at the same time with the general-in-chief. As a general rule, it is more advantageous to compose the army solely of divisions; but, in certain cases, we should resort to the organization in *corps d'armée;* for example, 1st, when the force of the army is so great that, in marching in a single column, there would be an interval of several miles between the front and rear; 2d, when the resources of the country, which is the scene of warfare, are not sufficient to maintain the army in a single body; 3d, when circumstances render it necessary to make a diversion, to succor an ally, or to operate eccentrically; in a word, to act separately, although in the same theatre of operations.

Thus we perceive that an army may contain the

following fractions, taken in the order of their importance: the *corps d'armée*, the wings, the centre, the reserve, the divisions and the brigades. There are also the parks and accessories. Let us stop for a moment to consider each of these fractions.

A *corps d'armée* is required to act independently; it must therefore be self-sustaining, at least for a certain time. It is to be constituted in a manner to give it a maximum of force; that is, in its formation it should embrace all the arms, each proportioned to the nature of the theatre of war, and the kind of enemy to be met. *Corps d'armée* composed of a single arm are an exception. Nevertheless, under the Empire, *corps d'armée* existed composed entirely of cavalry. These did not conform to the condition of maximum of force, but they were able to retire or to fight according to circumstances; and when they fought, they possessed the advantage of a large mass, well suited to overwhelm the enemy at the close of an action; and this is the reason why Napoleon often employed them: but he finally discovered that beyond twenty-four squadrons, a body of cavalry loses the qualities which constitute the chief excellence of that arm, namely, the power of command, opportuneness of movement, celerity, and precision in execution.* Let us return to the ordinary *corps d'armée*, which are principally composed of infantry, with some cavalry and a little artillery. The force of each corps should be at least two divisions; but two divisions are ill

---

* Prévoil, *Commentaires du projet d'ordonnance sur le service en campagne*, p. 14.

adapted to tactical formations, and three divisions give an order of battle upon a single line; hence four divisions will be the most suitable number. For, with this number, a corps may be drawn up in order of battle with a centre, two wings, and a reserve, each of these fractions being determinate and complete, under the orders of a chief, with whom it is already acquainted; and, thus formed, the *corps d'armée* will maintain a stout resistance, in conformity with the rules of tactics. Moreover, four divisions are well suited to the formation in checker-form. Beyond four divisions

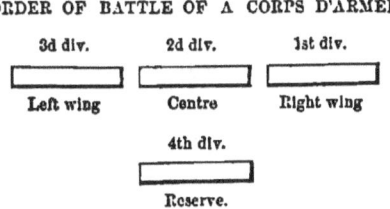

the command becomes too unwieldy, and many details escape the notice of the chief. Under the Empire the *corps d'armée* were rarely formed of a greater number.

As to the division, if it be composed of three brigades, it will have an independent reserve not taken

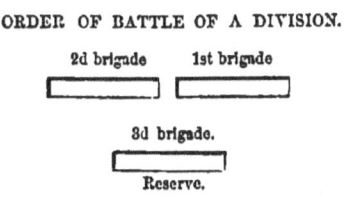

out of its line of battle, and its tactical formation will remain complete; and this composition, therefore, should be adopted whenever it is called upon to act separately, or when the army does not contain any *corps d'armée*. Some authors have proposed to constitute the divisions unequally, in order to deceive the enemy as to the force of the army, making it necessary for them to observe each division individually, in order to judge of the force; but this trifling ruse goes a very little way, and it is, moreover, wiser to realize it by withdrawing some troops out of line and successively annexing them to one or another of the divisions.

If the army is divided into *corps d'armée*, a centre or a wing will contain one or more of these corps; and one or more divisions, if the army is subdivided only into divisions. The reserve will also embrace one or more *corps d'armée*, or one or more divisions, according to circumstances. In order that it may not be a delusive support, by being too feeble, nor exhaust the army by being too numerous, it is now universally agreed to form it at least of one fifth or at most of one third of the whole army. The reserve plays a most important part: placed out of reach of the enemy's artillery, it remains fresh until the moment when the general-in-chief thinks proper to bring it into action to strike a decisive blow; and history proves that victory usually declares for those who succeed in being the last to bring their reserve into play. Nevertheless, it must not be inferred that it is best to keep them indefinitely intact; for, if the opportune moment for their employment is allowed to pass,* they often prove useless. Besides the offensive

---

* Marshal Marmont observes that Napoleon brought up his reserve

part they may take in deciding a victory, the reserves also have a defensive part to perform, in protecting the flanks and rear of the army, and serving as a rallying point, behind which the beaten troops may reform, either for the purpose of making a second attack, or of retiring in good order. The reserves will embrace the heavy cavalry and the pieces of large caliber. If composed of infantry, they should be the most veteran troops; for the effect of a *last argument* cannot be too certain. Napoleon usually employed a *corps d'armée* as a reserve; he also had for this purpose the Imperial Guard and the *Oudinot* grenadiers. The practice of taking away the companies of grenadiers and voltigeurs from the regiments of infantry, to form them into battalions of select soldiers, is objectionable, as it enervates these regiments, by taking away their best soldiers; and on this point the ordinance upon campaign service directs that: "The select companies be not drawn away from their regiments, except during the time when the latter are not in line, and then only for operations of brief duration." Notwithstanding this prohibition, it is probable that, in the case of a continental war, France would be obliged to return to the use of battalions of grenadiers, though the Imperial Guard has again been reëstablished in her army; because solid reserves are imperatively necessary in the field.

too late at Moscow and at Waterloo, thus violating his own favorite maxim: "Those who keep their troops fresh for the day after a battle, are almost always beaten." (*Esprit des institutions militaires*, p. 29, et *Mémoires*, t. viii. p. 143.)

According to the regulations, brigades are formed of at least two regiments; there appears to be no reason for forming them of more than three regiments. Besides brigades composed of a single arm, either infantry or cavalry, the regulations permit the formation of mixed brigades, of infantry and light cavalry, more specially destined for the service of advanced-guards.

There are various appendages belonging to and following armies; such as the parks of artillery, bridge trains, engineer-parks, ambulances, and wagons for the transportation of hospital stores, provisions, clothing, &c., the latter belonging to the service or drawn from the country by requisition. An army is also accompanied by a special reserve of heavy cavalry; but a *corps d'armée* does not have this great accessory. For its supply, the army also possesses large and small dépôts. The former are established at places so far from the scene of active operations as not to be subject to frequent removal; the latter exist with the army itself, and embrace, as far as possible, the establishments for convalescents and the hospitals, and occupy positions where they may serve as halting places and points of reunion for the detachments rejoining the army; so that any disposable men may be added to these detachments, and those may be taken out of them who have become disabled for continued service.

2. Commands.—The command of an army or of a *corps d'armée* in the French service, devolves either upon a marshal or a general of division, who receives from the Emperor a temporary commission as *commandant-in-chief* in the first case, or *commandant of* (a particular) *corps d'armée* in the latter. The chief of the army designates the commandant of each wing, of the centre, and of the reserve, whose functions, being temporary, and conferring but transitory honors, should be confined to the direction of the troops in their movements and upon the field of battle. This temporary command is given to a general of division, the principal tactical fraction* being, however, reserved to the commandant-in-chief. Every division is commanded by a general of division; every brigade by a general of brigade. Usually, the distribution of the general officers is made by the Minister of War at the time of the composition of the army. In the field, where many commands become vacant, it would often produce too great delay to wait for the orders of the Minister to provide for them; and it would be imprudent to fill them by appointments according to seniority, as was still done in the time of Louis XIV., until the ordinance of February 1, 1703,† notwithstanding the example of Turenne and Catinat, who, as generals-in-chief, understood the necessity of breaking through the custom. Hence the fifth article of the ordinance of

---

* We may distinguish the fractions of an army as *tactical fractions* and *fractions of organization*. Each wing, as well as the centre, is a tactical fraction; each *corps d'armée*, each division, each brigade, is a fraction of organization; the reserve is at once a tactical fraction and a fraction of organization.

† By this ordinance, Louis XIV. "wills and requires that the general of each army shall choose from among the lieutenant-generals therein serving, *those whom he may judge fit* for the command of the two wings of cavalry, and those who should command the corps of infantry."

May 3, 1832, in relation to service in the field, authorizes the commandant-in-chief of the army to effect, *during the course of the campaign,* the changes which losses or the good of the service render necessary.

The functions of the commandant-in-chief are facilitated by the existence of the various fractions of the army, since he communicates only with the generals who command those fractions; and consequently has more time and greater latitude for combining his plan of operations. Nevertheless, he would not be equal to the multiplied exigencies and responsibilities of his command (at the present day especially, when a general-in-chief is overburdened with written papers by the somewhat excessive complications of administrative practices), unless he were assisted by a chief of staff, an intendant, a general commanding the artillery, and a general commanding the engineers.

The chief of staff* of an army is either a general of division or a general of brigade. He is assisted by a general of brigade or a colonel of the staff, called *sub-chief of staff.* In a *corps d'armée,* unless its importance requires it, there will be no sub-chief of staff. Officers of the staff corps, of various grades, serve as aids to the chief of staff, whose functions, in the French army, are defined by the eighth article of the ordinance of May 3, 1832, to be as follows:

" 1st. To transmit the orders of the general, and to execute those he receives himself for detached duties, such as the establishment of camps, recon-

---

* If several armies be combined to form one grand army, the chief of staff temporarily takes the title of *major general* in France.

noissances, inspections of posts and all other parts of the service.

"2d. To correspond with the commandants of artillery and engineers, and with the intendants,* in order to keep the general correctly informed of the condition of the various branches of the service.

"3d. To maintain constant correspondence with the different corps, and to have a thorough knowledge of their condition in detail.

"4th. To furnish to the commandant-in-chief and to the Minister of War tabular statements of the strength and position of corps and posts, reports of marches and other operations; in a word, all necessary information."

There is attached to each army and to each *corps d'armée* a military intendant, who has under his orders sub-intendants or deputies, employés of the various administrative services, and troops belonging to the administrative corps. The military intendant makes reports to the commandant-in-chief or to his chief of staff; he centralizes all the details of administration and accounts of the army, and also those of the corps and detachments composing it, except in what relates to the materiel of the artillery and engineers.

In each army, and in each *corps d'armée*, a general officer commands the artillery, and another general officer commands the engineers. Each has under his orders a certain number of officers of his arm, among others a colonel or lieutenant-colonel, chief of staff of

* The military *intendance* of the French army embraces the quartermaster's, subsistence, medical, clothing, and pay departments.—*Tr.*

the arm, and a superior officer as director of the park, together with the number of guards and employés, indicated by the wants of the service. He centralizes all the details relating to the personnel and the matériel of his arm.

The system which exists in each army and in each *corps d'armée*, is reproduced, for the same reason, in each division. To assist him in his command, and to leave him more liberty with respect to military operations, the general of division has near his person a colonel of *état-major*, who is chief of staff of the division, an officer of artillery, an officer of engineers, and a military sub-intendant. The officers of artillery and engineers attached to a division receive the orders of the general with whom they are employed, either directly or through the chief of staff of the division. They should communicate to that general the orders they may receive respecting their specialty from the general or superior officers of their particular arm.

We will add that all the general officers attached to an active army, or to a *corps d'armée* of any kind, have, in addition, a certain number of aides-de-camp and orderly officers, proportioned to their grade.

Among the officers attached to the general headquarters—that is to say, the quarters occupied by the commandant-in-chief—we should mention three in particular: 1st. The *Commandant of the general headquarters*. This is a superior officer of the staff, charged with establishing the quarters, placing the posts and guards, and, in conjunction with the gendarmery,

ORGANIZATION OF ACTIVE ARMIES. 183

preserving order at headquarters. 2d. The *Provost-marshal-general.* This title is given to the commandant of the brigades of gensdarmes attached to the army. His province is to protect the inhabitants of the country from pillage and violence; to maintain good police; to institute proceedings against those suspected of crimes or misdemeanors committed within the precincts of the army, or of *corps d'armée;* to pursue and arrest the offenders; to watch all the non-military persons or camp followers;* to follow the columns on a march and bring up the stragglers. He reports daily to the commandant-in-chief and receives his orders; and every week makes a report of his service to the chief of staff. Besides these duties, which are assigned to him by army regulations, the provost-marshal-general (also the provost of each division), since the promulgation of the *Code de justice militaire,* exercises jurisdiction over the territory occupied by the army (or the division), and assisted by a clerk (a non-commissioned officer or corporal of his arm), decides of himself in all penal cases involving a penalty of not more than six months' imprisonment, or a fine of not more than 200 francs; and in all cases of claims for damages which do not exceed 150 francs.† 3d. The *Wagon-master* of the general headquarters, a superior officer charged with the direction of the equipages following the army, and

---

* The provosts can inflict a fine to the amount of 100 francs. (*Service en campagne,* art. 175.)

† *Code de justice militaire pour l'armée de terre,* du 9 juin 1857, art. 52, 75.

the preservation of order among the wagons and domestics of the staff.

There are also connected with each division a commandant of headquarters, a provost, and a wagon-master—officers of a grade inferior to that of the officers who hold similar positions in the general headquarters.

3. Standing Armies.—In France, active armies are formed only in case of war, or, as exceptions, upon certain points of the national domain, when the security of the interior is in danger. This policy, which is also that of Austria, leaves the enemy uncertain as to the mode of organization which is to be finally adopted in the armies formed to oppose him; and, besides, reserves the power of varying this mode, according to the nature of the war to be undertaken.

Russia and Prussia have adopted a different policy, and, both in peace and in war, keep their troops constantly formed, in *corps d'armée*, divisions, and brigades. Thus the Prussian army, besides the Royal Guards, and the brigades garrisoning Mayence and Luxemburg (fortified places of the Germanic Confederation), consists of eight permanent *corps d'armée*, each embracing two divisions of infantry, two brigades of cavalry, one regiment of artillery, and one battalion of engineers. Under this system, the troops complete their education better, especially with respect to combined manœuvres, become accustomed to the generals who command them, and are eminently qualified to act promptly or to repel an invasion; but they remain a long time in the same garrisons, and this is a positive disadvantage, on account of the habits which the soldiers may there acquire. The troops who frequently travel, as they do in France, and are therefore not accustomed to any fixed garrisons, are, in consequence, more easily mobilized.

CHAPTER SECOND.

MARCHES.

The army being organized, it is next to be transported from the place of its formation to a point more favorable for its action. This requires a *march* of a greater or less number of days.

1. Marches of Concentration.—The march will be of easy and simple execution when it takes place far from the enemy, and is thus performed as a *march of concentration*. The army is then put in motion by small fractions, and moves upon several parallel routes. Each fraction will march in open lines on each side of the road to leave a free circulation; will make a grand halt at about the middle of the march; will travel from six to ten leagues per day, and will observe the most perfect discipline in any town where it may be lodged for the night or receive its daily supplies.

All marches should be performed by day; for a night march, especially from midnight to four o'clock in the morning, gains nothing that is not more than lost by the relatively greater fatigue suffered by the soldiers. The soldier needs *at least* six hours of sleep: to assert the contrary is to utter nonsense.

A march should be conducted slowly, in order to save the strength of the troops. Assuming that there is sufficient time, one hour at least should be allowed for a league, including the short halt necessary after each league, and an additional half to three quarters of an hour should be allowed for the principal halt.

Slowness, and especially uniformity of gait, are equally important for cavalry. When far from the enemy, this arm need not govern its rate of motion by that of the infantry.

2. Marches of Manœuvre.—If the march takes place in presence of the enemy, it assumes the character of a *march of manœuvre*, and requires additional precautions. Its disposition should be based upon the principle of being always in a condition to check and to repel an attack. With this object, instead of proceeding in fractions distributed on each side of a road, the army will still march upon several routes,* but grouped on each route *in column* of one section at least, or one division at most. Each column should be sufficiently strong in front to resist, and should at the same time be so short that the front and rear can support each other. While beyond the circle of activity of the enemy, the column may advance at full distance,† but within this circle, or, so

---

* In order to subsist more easily by requisitions, and also to keep the enemy in uncertainty.

† It is assumed that the column then occupies the same space as in order of battle.

to speak, under the cannon of the enemy, and preparing for combat,* it will gain ground in more compact order.

In a mixed column, the infantry, accompanied by its artillery, march at the head; and the cavalry always in the rear. A different arrangement would compromise the whole column in the case of a strong attack on the front, as was proved in the case of the central column of the French forces at the battle of the Trébbia (June 19, 1799).

The number of columns will often vary, according to the kind of troops, the nature of the ground, and the end to be attained. Their distance will be calculated so as to permit easy communication between them, and also of their reunion; and for this purpose, the chief of one column should know the effective force and the direction of the other columns.†

Notwithstanding this multiplicity of columns they should not habitually reckon upon mutual protection, which their distance and their specific object may prevent; and, besides, prudence dictates that each should rely upon itself for this protection. In this view, we employ the ancient and well known system, the result of experience, of detaching a small portion of the moving force in advance, in rear and upon the flanks of the column, so as to surround it with almost a continuous chain, as mobile as the column itself, and destined to parry the first blows.

---

* The place of combat is usually reached first by the head of the column.

† *Service en campagne*, art. 120.

This covering portion is in preference chosen from the light troops; it embraces an *advance-guard*, a *rear guard*, and *flankers*.

The advance-guard precedes the column. It is of mixed composition, but variable, according to the difficulties of the road and the proximity of the enemy; it scours the country and watches for any attempted attack, whether open or covert, baffles it or restrains it, and, in all cases, gains time for the column to dispose itself for combat. For this purpose the advance-guard also protects itself by an advance-guard or some scouts. It should also open the road or make it practicable, and for this reason a company of sappers often accompanies it. At branch roads, it will be careful to indicate the direction taken by landmarks, in order to avoid all mistakes and to point out the road to belated soldiers and vehicles. In the daytime this is effected by blazing trees or tying bundles of straw to posts along the proper road; but at night, by stationing non-commissioned officers, who are successively relieved.

The commandant of an advance-guard should possess all the qualities required of a chief of detachment. It is his duty to avail himself of all the auxiliary expedients employed in reconnoissances, especially to draw information from the guides, from the inhabitants, and from prisoners; and also to cause prompt reconnoissances to be made by the officers under his orders. He turns all villages, woods, or defiles, through which it might be dangerous to pass; levies contributions upon the villages to keep his troops constantly supplied with subsistence for two or three days; makes his grand halt in a covered place, surrounding it with sentinels posted upon the eminences or on the roads; and is careful during his march not to betray his approach by the noise of trumpet or drum.

The advance-guard will vary in force from one fifth to one tenth of the column. Its distance from the column will be at least equal to the length of the column, so that, even in the most unfavorable case, that is, when the advance-guard is driven back, and does not succeed in retarding the approach of the enemy, the rear of the column may yet have time to rejoin the front, and also to come into line.

The rear-guard closes the march, and is smaller than the advance-guard. Its province is to arrest any adverse detachment, or any suspected individual, prowling in the rear of the column. It frequently protects itself also by an extreme rear-guard. In a forward march, it escorts the baggage, which is always separated from the body of the troops, and brings up the stragglers. In a retreat, it performs the principal and most glorious part: in that case, relieved of the baggage, which then goes on the side farthest from pursuit, it avails itself of the resources of petty warfare, and of the obstacles of the ground, to paralyze the forces of the pursuer. The chief of the rear-guard should possess high qualifications: perhaps he does not need to be as fertile in invention as the chief of the advance-guard, but he certainly requires more energy and coolness. Ney, in the retreat from Russia, immortalized himself as the chief of the rear-guard.

The flankers* march parallel to the column, upon each of its flanks. They scatter themselves in groups of *three*, at 400 or 500 paces from the road, and reconnoitre, while protecting themselves behind the inequalities of the ground, but also exploring every recess and every obstacle. To give warning, they despatch one of their number, and never have recourse to discharging their guns, except in the case of a surprise.

We are now acquainted with the order of march of a separate column: let us return to an assemblage of columns—an army.

This assemblage will be preceded by a general advance-guard, relatively to all the columns; each of these still requires its special advance-guard. There will also be a general rear-guard.

We may deceive the enemy as to the general direction about to be adopted by an army (or by a column), by ordering the preparation of provisions as if for a movement in another direction. This ruse, to which every one may resort, is always effective.

The chief of a column thrown forward for a special purpose in advance of an army, even beyond the general advance-guard, will scatter along his route small posts of cavalry, for the purpose of conveying his messages promptly; and when he despatches an officer upon a mission to the general-in-chief, he should also send after him two others, at intervals of a half hour from each other, as the first might lose his way.†

---

* Do not confound these flankers with the skirmishers, which the advance and rear-guards detach for their own security.

† Letter of Napoleon to Marmont, July 11, 1809.

Marches of manœuvre of an army are executed either by the front or by the flank.

In the first case, the columns remain grouped together, adopt a close formation, and follow parallel routes, in such a manner as not to occupy much more space on the front of the march* than the extent of the front of the army in order of battle; for an attack then presents few dangers, even when it comes from the side.

MARCH OF MANŒUVRE BY THE FRONT.

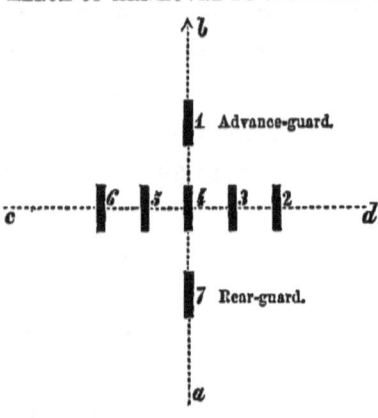

In fact, if this combination of five columns, instead of continuing its march in the direction ab, is suddenly obliged to take the perpendicular direction cd, it still has an advance-guard in the column 2, a rear-guard in the column 6, and two flanking corps, in the columns 1 and 7; and the case would be the same for the directions ba and dc. Thus, with this arrangement, a sudden change in either direction becomes easy, and the possibility of such changes sometimes constitutes the whole secret of marches. The march of the Austro-Russian army under Kutusoff, from Olmutz to Wischau and Austerlitz, in 1805, is an example of this arrangement.

In the second case, in which a march by the flank is vigorously executed in a single and long column,

---

* We call *front of the march* the space between the columns 2 and 6.

either to move along the positions of the enemy or to traverse a narrow and unavoidable route, in order to arrive promptly before a town, or upon the field of battle, the army in movement runs greater danger; since, by the manœuvre itself, it is already in a state of crisis, and in this situation exposes its flank. Nevertheless, these dangers are sometimes voluntarily incurred, principally with a view to gaining time. In this event, besides observing the precaution of forming at full distances, to preserve exactly the intervals, and to conceal the march under the cover of night, or of a fog, it will be best to place on the menaced side, at about 1,000 yards from the column, a flanking corps, marching, as much as possible parallel to it, and possessing its own protecting auxiliaries, namely, an advance-guard, a rear-guard, and flankers. Frederic the Great usually fell upon his enemies by a march by the flank, and he succeeded by this method, because he employed soldiers expert in manœuvres against troops of little mobility; nevertheless, at Kollin (June 18, 1757), a march of this kind, executed under the fire of the Austrians, was fatal to him, in spite of the tenacious energy of his foot soldiers, who returned seven times in succession to the charge.

Whether made by the front or flank, marches of manœuvres must be rapid. Without the celebrated march of Massena's division, running on the 13th of January from Verona to Rivoli, fighting on the 14th by the side of the soldiers of Joubert, returning on the 15th upon Mantua, and fighting on the 16th at Favorita, Bonaparte would not have obtained his two final victories, and so happily terminated the campaign of 1796. Fifteen years later, in the month of April, 1809, during the operations about Ratisbonne, if the army of the Archduke Charles had not been so slow in his offensive operations amidst our scattered forces, and had not taken three days (from the 19th to the 22d of April) to move about six leagues (from Rohr to Eckmühl), the first part of the campaign would have resulted more favorably to his arms.

It is principally when the march of manœuvre is directed against an enemy wholly defeated, and becomes, in consequence, a pursuit, that rapidity becomes indispensable,—provided, be it well understood, that this rapidity is not prejudicial to the strength and prudence which it is essential to preserve in the presence of an energetic though vanquished enemy, capable of turning again and assuming the offensive.

The march of the vanquished party, who is retiring —in a word, the retreat—is also a march of manœuvre. This, indeed, is implied in what we have said. But to constitute a *retreat*, we must not forget that there must be a *series* of retrograde marches. Napoleon, on the eve of the battle of Austerlitz, certainly did not beat a retreat, but he nevertheless made *one* retrograde march, in order to entice the Austrians and Russians upon the battle-field which he had selected and studied! We have above indicated the important parts to be performed by the general, and the particular rear-guards, which, in this case, become the head of the army or of the column.

We will add that, to have any chance of success in

a retreat, we must carefully guard the flanks, as being more vulnerable than in a forward movement; and endeavor to preserve a certain distance in advance of the rear-guard, to gain which the latter will give special battle, as was done by the prince Bagration at Hollabrunn, November 16, 1805.

We will confine our remarks upon marches to these brief hints, as we do not intend to enter upon strategy, which would exceed the limits prescribed for these *Elements*.

CHAPTER THIRD.

BATTLES.

1. Primitive Order of Battle.—After a march designed for the purpose, or in case of a fortuitous renconter, an army meets the enemy and gives him battle. How is it to be disposed for the action? This we are now about to consider, at first from a theoretical point of view, under the most ordinary circumstances, and upon the supposition that the field of combat is perfectly horizontal, and free from all kinds of obstacles.

In preparing for battle, the whole army is drawn up in three distinct masses, destined to take part in the contest at different times—a first line, a second line, and a reserve.

The first line brings on the action. The mission of the second line is to afford the first both moral and material support: moral support, by inspiring confidence by its simple presence; material support, either by offering a rallying point, or by taking its place in the contest. Therefore, from the instant when the first line becomes engaged, we should, in general, avoid withdrawing the troops of the second line from their position, to take them to another; for this would both discourage the combatants, who would no longer feel themselves supported, and would embolden the enemy, who would take the movement for the beginning of a retreat. The duty of the reserve has already been explained.

According to its particular destination, each of the masses of the order of battle will have a distinct formation. The first line will be deployed, for it is necessary that it offer a large front, with the smallest possible intervals; for large intervals would be, in fact, breaches, and would weaken its resistance. The second line will usually be formed in columns by battalions at deploying distance, in which form it will be better prepared to advance to assist the first line. But, if the position of the second line upon the battle-field is such as to expose it to the fire of the enemy's artillery, it will be better to deploy it,* since, when extended upon a front of little depth, it will suffer less from the projectiles. The reserve not being required for immediate combat, should always remain grouped under the hand of the general-in-chief. It will therefore be massed in columns, by brigades, in rear of the second line.

The next question is, at what distance from each other should the three masses of this primitive order of battle be established ?

---

* At the battle of Moscow a brigade of the second line lost 500 men in ten minutes, because it preserved the order in column. (Marbot, *Remarques critiques sur les considérations sur l'art de la guerre*, p. 436.) In similar circumstances, at the battle of Konieh (December 21, 1832), Ibrahim Pacha saved his troops by deploying the second line.

Supposing the field of battle to be wholly free from all obstacles, the local circumstances will be the same upon the whole extent of the front, and the second line should hold itself at a distance of 300 yards in rear of the first. At this distance the fire of the enemy will probably reach it with difficulty, and yet it will be sufficiently near* to give effective support to the first line. The same interval is equally applicable to both infantry and cavalry. If, however, the plateau on which the combat takes place is of such small dimensions that the second line, at a distance of 300 yards from the first, should find itself near the extreme boundary, this distance may be reduced, but not beyond the limit that would bring the line under the fire of the enemy.

As the reserve should remain fresh and intact until the decisive moment, while the lines are engaged, conjointly or separately, it will be posted at 1,000 or 1,200 yards from the second line.

The cavalry should never form the centre of the line of battle, for all their power depends upon movement, and in that position they could neither move forward nor backward without breaking the line. Besides, as they do not make use of their fire-arms, they are not so capable as infantry of standing the fire of the enemy's musketry or cannon without stirring. For these reasons, they are usually placed on the

---

* At the battle of Rio-Secco, or, rather, at the battle known by that name, the Spaniards were beaten, in spite of their bravery, in consequence of having placed their second line 1,400 or 1,500 yards in rear of the first.

flanks, where they have the best opportunity to start quickly (*pendre carrière*),* and to throw themselves in every direction for attacking and turning the enemy's flanks. In this position, too, they serve as a support to the extremities of the line of infantry. As an exception, however, the cavalry may form the centre of a line of battle, when the two bodies of the infantry placed upon the wings are sufficiently near to each other to give adequate protection, by their fire, to the cavalry placed between them, and thus still to keep the different parts of the army united.†

The artillery of the first line will occupy with strong batteries many positions, from 150 to 200 yards in advance of the front, opposite the great intervals of the order of. battle : to increase this distance would expose the artillery to be captured ; to diminish it would render the fire of the artillery dangerous to the infantry posted in its rear. The artillery of the second line will wait in column in rear of the flanks and intervals of this line ; the artillery of the reserve will remain close to the main body of the reserve.

The parks, ambulances, and other accessories, will be posted in a safe place in rear of the reserve, and covered by troops of the rear-guard.

For the facility of command, and the entire inde-

---

* That is, to assume the charging distance of about 300 yards from the point to be attacked.

† Ternay, *Traité de Tactique*, t. i., p. 246. We may add that this may also be done upon a contracted battle-field, when the wings of the position are formed by villages, as at Essling.

pendence of the lines, the troops of the same division will generally form a part of the same line, especially the infantry troops.

Such are the principles according to which an army, whatever its force, is drawn up, according to the *primitive* order of battle; and it is only necessary to add that, if the army contains several divisions, or *corps d'armée*, care must be taken to leave intervals between them, proportioned to their effective force, and the number of cannon to be employed in front of the line of battle.

In the following figure of the primitive order of battle, we give a greater development to the second line than the first, to protect the flanks of the first, both by infantry and cavalry.

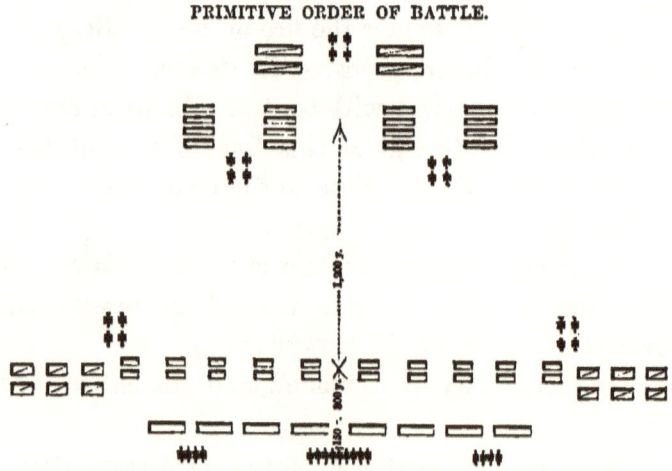

PRIMITIVE ORDER OF BATTLE.

This primitive order of battle is in reality but a diagram to regulate the position and the disposition of the various elements of the army—merely an order of *review*, from which innumerable circumstances in war may often compel us to depart. Accidents of ground, the superiority of the enemy in cavalry or in artillery, the defective composition of the army itself, may force the general-in-chief to adopt a less symmetrical order of battle; but in all cases he must save himself a reserve, and, as far as possible, draw up his forces upon two lines, in addition to the reserve, even when it might be necessary for that purpose to reduce the extent of the front which he presents to the enemy.

2. Orders of Battle.—Whatever the number of lines of an order of battle, it is useful to know the various figures that order may assume, and any good reasons for such dispositions of troops. The forms of these figures will be more readily understood by tracing a single line to represent each of the opposing orders of battle.

The various figures may be reduced to four principal ones:

1st. *Parallel order.*—When the two armies are drawn up parallel to each other upon the whole line.

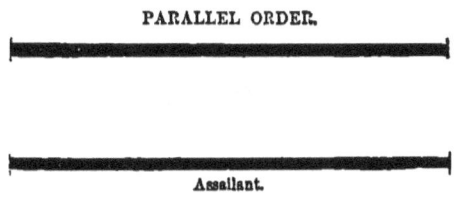

PARALLEL ORDER.

Assailant.

the order is the simplest of all; the assailing army is everywhere equally weak, everywhere equally strong, and there is nothing to indicate the point upon which its first efforts will be directed.

This was the habitual order of battle of the first nations of antiquity, among whom the art of war was not far advanced; but it is used even at the present day, upon the defensive, when the object is to bar the way of an assailant.

Sometimes, in this order, the centre of the assailant is strengthened, and presents a column instead of one or two lines; or a wing may receive an increase of troops, or else have a particular corps perpendicular to, and in front of the line,* forming a *crotchet*, or L. In the latter two cases, the order approximates to the following, and possesses several of its properties.

2d. *Oblique order.*—The assailant advances one wing, the right, for instance, and refuses the other, so that he keeps the whole line of his adversary in check, and yet engages but a small portion of his troops. This is, consequently, the most suitable order for an army of inferior force, which thus has its first reserve in the wing refused.

OBLIQUE ORDER.

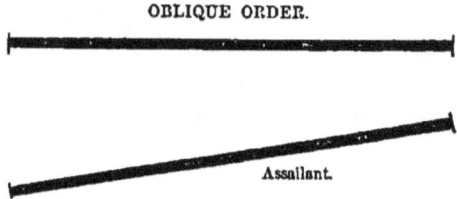

In reality, excepting the case of an attack by the centre, almost every offensive order of battle partakes

* The same order in rear of the line is called a *potence*.

of the nature of the oblique, for it is very rare that one portion of the line does not attack before another.

Epaminondas at Leuctra and at Mantinæa, Cæsar at Pharsalia, Gustavus Adolphus at Leipsic, Frederic at several battles, and especially at Leuthen, Bonaparte at Marengo, employed the oblique order.

If the obliquity of the assailing line is so great as to make this line form a right angle with the front of the adversary, the order of battle takes the name of the *perpendicular order*. This particular case of the oblique order hardly deserves mention, since it must always be of short duration, the interest of the enemy evidently requiring him, in such case, to effect at least a partial change of front.

3d. *Concave order.*—This order may be formed by echelons, as in the following figure, or in a semicircle; but it is better for the march to be by echelons. Its advantage consists in great concentration of fire; but, on the other hand, the flanks are very much exposed, and require to rest firmly upon some obstacle, a river,

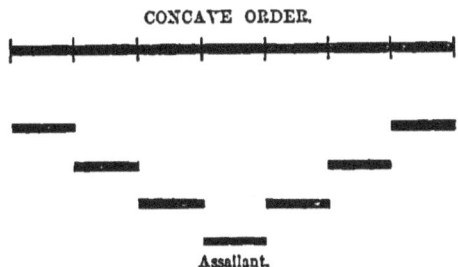

for example, as in the formation adopted by the Archduke Charles, against the French, in the battle of Essling.

In general, this order is rather the result of changes incident to the contest, than of premeditated design.

A successful use of the concave order was made by the famous Hannibal at Cannæ, by the Roman general Narses at Casilinum (A. D. 553) against the Franks, and by the English at Crécy.

4th. *Convex order.*—This order is formed either by echelons on the centre, or in a semicircle. It serves for the defence of a defile or a bridge indispensable to a retreat, or better still to resist a concave formation. Except in these two cases, it is a bad disposition to adopt against an unbroken and compact line, for its flanks are more feeble than in any other order, and if

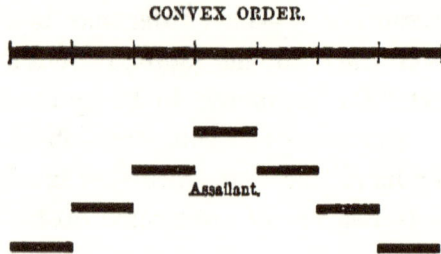

the centre gives way, the defeat of the army is certain. It has no chance of success except against an excessively extended and disjointed line, or against an attack in four or five columns, firing in divergent directions.*

The Turks formed for attack in the convex order, almost in a triangle. After the first shock, the two

---

* The fire of the convex order takes place in diverging lines from the moment that its echelons are so much subdivided and increased in number as to approximate to the semicircular form.

wings formed again and advanced beyond the centre, thereby transforming their order into the concave.

In practice, none of these orders of battle could be assumed with the exactness indicated by the figure. We endeavor to conform to the system indicated as much as possible, taking this system, however, as a mere approximation.

We must not forget that an order of battle, whatever may be its tactical form, its figure, or its name, may be traced *continuously*, or with *intervals*, either in whole or part. With intervals* it possesses little solidity, and gives less fire; and it should never be so formed unless at a sufficient distance from the enemy, or when the cavalry forms the second line and stands ready to charge in the intervals threatened by the enemy. A continuous order has but small intervals, which are indispensable for the movement of the corps which constitute it.

3. Conduct of the Battle.—We have now learned the number of lines in which an army is drawn up for combat, and the figure which its order of battle assumes. There are, however, yet other conditions to be fulfilled to secure a fair chance of success in the struggle.

We fight a battle either to repel an attack and preserve a favorable camp, or voluntarily to strike a decisive blow, conquer a region of country, reach an important city or relieve it, or to terminate the

---

* By intervals are usually meant spaces equal to the front of the full portions, as in the checker-formation.

campaign and secure a peace. After having, from various motives, deferred this great act, we must almost always come to it at last, as the only prompt solution and frequently less costly than the prolongation of the war.

He who wishes to give battle need not have at his disposition a number of troops much superior to that of his adversary; it is sufficient that the character of his soldiers, the ground on which the contest is to take place, the genius of his officers, or any circumstances whatever, afford him some probability of success.

He will, *à priori*, calculate the possible issues of the action, and will place himself so as to augment them if he is victor, and diminish them if he is vanquished. In the former case, the best he can do is to cut the line of operations of the enemy; in the latter, it will be to preserve his own line, and his dépôts.

The general-in-chief will determine upon his order of battle according to the means at his disposal, and the obstacles to be surmounted. He will especially adapt it to the ground, making it weaker where the ground is strong, and *vice versa*, posting light troops in the more irregular portions, and artillery upon the commanding points; each, in short, upon the locality where they can act at once with the greatest facility and the greatest energy. As far as possible, he will have those vulnerable parts of his formation, the flanks, supported by natural obstacles, or he will strengthen them by bodies of troops, principally infantry troops, for cavalry is no longer a protection against a flanking attack from the moment it has been compelled to move at a gallop and to charge from a distance. If he refuses one wing, he will place his heavy artillery there,* in order to keep the opposing wing at a distance and to prevent its advancing sufficiently to destroy the effect of this oblique arrangement by restoring the parallelism of the two orders of battle.

The choice of the point of attack will be determined by principles of strategy, tactics, or character of ground. If the enemy keeps one of his wings in proximity to his lines of communication or to his frontier, strategy requires that the attack should commence upon that wing. Where the enemy is near some dangerous obstacle, which covers him, do not, on any account, attack him on the side nearest that obstacle, but direct your blows beyond, so as to penetrate the lines which face you, and drive him headlong upon the obstacle. There is also another case in which a tactical principle determines the direction of the attack. Suppose the order of battle of the enemy presents a void, or any other defect, then you should doubtless throw yourself upon this weak point, always guarding yourself by small flanking reserves against any traps he may lay for you. Finally, a topographic reason will determine the choice of a point of attack when the enemy occu-

---

* The same recommendation may be offered, though it is not of so much consequence, in the case of a refusal of the centre, in order to prevent the enemy from advancing the middle of his line, and opposing a convex order to a concave order.

pies some elevations,* then aim at the mastery of the highest, and if you succeed, all his other positions must fall. A village or a wood may sometimes perform the same part as such an eminence, and will, for the same reasons, require your special attention.

The general-in-chief most frequently determines his point of attack by a combination of principles: thus, for example, he may be governed by both tactical and topographical reasons. This is a matter of inspiration—of genius—much more than of experience.

When his choice turns upon one of the wings, his object will be, in some cases, to surround his adversary; in others, to take him in flank. An enveloping attack should not be executed by a long circuit, for the corps intrusted with its execution may then get astray, or appear too late. To attempt it upon several sides at once, moreover, divides the army, and makes it weak throughout, an evil of the greatest magnitude in the presence of a bold and active adversary. This was experienced by Alvinzi in 1796, on the day of Rivoli, when one of his two flanking columns, that of Quasdanowich, was unable to debouch upon the plateau, on which were the two divisions of Bonaparte; and the other, that of Lusignan, appeared at the end of the action, when the French were already victorious, and was itself surrounded. If one's whole army is thrown upon the enemy's flank, it amounts to the oblique order pushed to its extreme limits. The enemy usually opposes it by a similar manœuvre, and

* All this information respecting the enemy is obtained by means of a preliminary reconnoissance, called an *offensive* or *open reconnoissance*.

attacks the weakened flank. Nevertheless, such an attack may be greatly favored by local circumstances: thus, when Bonaparte was advancing to attack the Austrians at Arcola, his movement was covered both by the Adige from Verona to Ronco, and by the marshes between the Adige and the Alpon: hence he threw his forces upon the dykes of the marsh, where he had only to fear a resistance in front, and thus placed himself *on the left flank* of Alvinzi. Even if the village of Arcola had yielded to his arms at the commencement of the first day of this triple battle, he would have reached Villa-Nova* and established himself *in rear* of the enemy, who still occupied Caldiero.

Whatever may be the kind of attack, or the point upon which it is directed, we must make our own force at this point superior to that of the enemy. In bringing our forces to the points of attack, we must especially endeavor to cover the preparatory steps, either by some inequalities of the ground, or by a screen of skirmishers, or by false attacks. Perfection consists in not receiving the fire (even partial) of the enemy until the action is engaged, which, however, is not always possible. By concealing our intentions till the last moment, we prevent the enemy from making his first dispositions with certainty.

The attack being arranged, the measures to be taken by each independent portion of the order of battle, in case of failure, are again to be prescribed and

* A hamlet at the intersection of the Alpon with the road from Verona to Vicenza.

explained, and the posts to be occupied successively in the retrograde movement are to be indicated, some as simple points of transit, others as rallying points. The order of the day, often completed by verbal instructions, also exhibits each person's part in the attack, develops and explains the principal manœuvre, sometimes gives the reasons upon which it is based, in order that each general may intelligently perform his part toward the success of the manœuvre, even should circumstances oblige him to depart from his orders, and to make use of the large discretionary powers necessarily intrusted to him.

The general-in-chief now gives the signal, and the action commences. A combat of skirmishers upon the front of nearly the whole line, and especially of the centre, is the necessary prelude. Under the screen formed by these scattered soldiers, the deployment of the first line is completed, if it had not before been effected, and the columns of attack advance. At the moment when the skirmishers, having advanced some 1,000 yards, retire and unmask the front, everything is ready, and the first line comes into play. It begins by fire of artillery, which approximately indicates the distance which usually separates two armies drawn up in order of battle at the beginning of the action;* then fire of musketry follows, as soon as the distance has been sufficiently reduced, either by the regular progress of the attack, or, sometimes, by the mutual advance movements of the two armies. If the firing

---

* Artillery becomes formidable at about 1,200 yards.

throws the enemy into disorder, the opportunity is seized for making a bayonet-charge upon the chosen point of attack. This first charge, resolutely conducted, may succeed: in this case, we must not give way to excitement and momentary enthusiasm, but should re-form our ranks, take breath, and march with ensemble upon the second line. If our first charge fails, we fall back calmly upon our second line, which, in its turn, charges, either alone, or in combination with the unbroken portions of the first line. Now, the fighting must be desperate, especially in the decisive direction; for this struggle of the principal arm decides the fate of the day.

The artillery continues to fire, to assist the charges of the infantry, and its action is kept up throughout the whole contest, so long as no friendly column masks its fire.

The light cavalry skirmishes from the time the first blow is struck, and at the end pursues. The cavalry of the line charges at any propitious moment, but chiefly at the end, to finish the victory, by overthrowing the last masses that make a stand.

If the action of the two lines does not suffice, the general-in-chief* detaches a part, or nearly the

---

* During the action, the general-in-chief occupies some elevated point, with a chart before him, and a telescope in his hand. He is calm and watchful, and gives his orders according to what he sees, and the intelligence brought to him. It is obviously of the first importance that every aide-de-camp should be able to find him readily. The same is true, though in a less degree, of every general officer, who, when he leaves his usual position, should make it known, and take care to indicate how and where he is to be found.

whole of his reserve, at the decisive moment, of which he is the sole judge.*

Success crowning the last vigorous blow, the victor may commence the pursuit without delay, but with circumspection, so long as he is not certain of the total defeat of the enemy; for if one wing on each side is victorious, the party that starts first upon a pursuit will be easily surrounded or taken in flank, and will ultimately lose the battle.

To these various operations, add the more or less complete coöperation of a false attack, as well as the inevitable episodes of corps imprudently engaged or overcome by numbers, which have to be supported, and you have before you a foreshortened picture of the action as carried on by the attacking party, or, to use the common expression, a picture of an *offensive battle*.

The army which *accepts* instead of *offering* battle, and thus fights a *defensive battle*, observes still greater precaution in the choice of its position. This position should be: 1st, somewhat elevated, with respect to that of the attacking party; 2d, firmly supported upon the flanks; 3d, intersected on the front and in the salient parts of the front, by thickets, villages, farms, obstacles easy to occupy and defend, and which divide the attack of the assailant; † 4th, it should allow sufficient freedom of movement among these ob-

---

* We have already treated of the functions of the reserve in the first chapter of this Second Part.

† In the absence of natural obstacles, redoubts are thrown up, as was done by Peter the Great at the battle of Pultowa.

stacles; and, 5th, should offer in the rear several avenues of retreat. If its force is weak, the repelling army forms no second line, except in uncovered and easily accessible places; which, however, be it observed, does not obviate the necessity of stationing the heaviest and most destructive ordnance at the principal point, upon which the assailant will most probably make his strongest demonstration, and which is the key of the position. It keeps a watch upon its flanks, and protects them by battalions *en potence*,* which close the extremities of the lines of infantry, and assure the order of battle independently of the cavalry—an advantageous arrangement adopted by Frederic the Great in his first two battles, at Mollwitz and Czaslaw. Some squadrons specially posted in echelons in the rear of the second line, near the wing, may also, by their sudden appearance, fulfil the same purpose. It is also recommended, as a final means, to extend the second line beyond the first, and the reserve (which, in this case, is placed almost wholly upon the flanks) beyond the second: this renders flanking manœuvres difficult and hazardous undertakings for the enemy.

In defensive battles, the general-in-chief awaits the enemy, and acts by fire of artillery and musketry, everywhere prepared, but not announcing any other intention than that of resisting. The assailant continues his movement, and when his manœuvre is in full tide, the defender redoubles his fire, catches at the least indication of disorder or mistake, and throws

* See note, p. 202.

himself forward to profit by it, with the whole of the troops still remaining fresh. If no such indication of disorder or mistake is presented, he charges only when the first line is too much pressed, taking for that purpose the columns of the second line and a portion of the cavalry.

In actions of this kind, when we do not succeed in repelling the enemy, we resort to squares. If they are well combined and flank each other, they resist a long time, and may defy an enemy who is already fatigued; and, in all cases, they facilitate the defence, inch by inch, of an irregular field of battle, make the retreat more respected, and often serve to gain sufficient time to enable the defeated party to commence this retreat under cover of night. Squares may also serve against an enemy very superior in cavalry: example, the French at the battle of Lutzen (1813).

A flank deprived of support, being uncovered in consequence of the progress of the assailant, may again be established by carrying it against some other obstacle, or even, for entire security, by setting fire to a village in its vicinity. The battle of Warsaw (1656), between the Poles and the Swedo-Brandenburgers, presents such a case on the second day of the contest.

There are circumstances in which an army upon the defensive will change its tactics before or during the contest, and will suddenly assume the offensive. It may be that the commander may resolve upon a desperate blow, to parry an attack which comes before his preparations are completed; or it may be pure audacity on his part. In such case, it is best to attack the assailant upon his flank, with the best troops, or reserves, at the same time exciting the enthusiasm of the soldiers and exalting the courage with which such a resolution inspires them.

Every expedient being exhausted, if you are defeated, abandon the field of battle, beat a retreat, but with order and as slowly as possible. Send off your baggage in advance, under escort: send a force to occupy the defiles through which you must pass. Adopt for your two lines the checker-formation by battalions; for the first line, when fatigued, can then retire through the open spaces of the second, or, still better, the second line may, by a slight movement, be brought in front through the spaces of the first, which slight offensive demonstration is always effective. When both lines are disorganized, they retire and rally beyond the reserve, which should be formed in squares, and stubbornly stand its ground.

The retreat having successfully begun, the line nearest to the enemy turns, from time to time, and makes a stand, seconded by repeated charges of the cavalry upon the flank of the pursuers. In this manner, time is gained until night supervenes; then, favored by darkness, we make a forced march, to put a respectable distance between ourselves and the enemy, and the next day the rear-guard suffices and organizes an obstinate defence.

Here we will terminate our exposition of the mechanism proper of the contest. To dwell longer upon it, in an abstract and didactic manner, would be of little use in the way of instruction. To obtain a just idea of a battle, it is necessary to read a great number of narratives, to know the antecedents and the issues of the day, to possess a detailed plan, upon which we mark the disposition of the troops, and correct or change this disposition according to the views we acquire as we read; in short, we must give ourselves up to systematic and extended research. We must, especially, consider each battle not as an isolated fact, but as the necessary and calculated end of a march, or of a combined strategic movement, or sometimes of a whole campaign; and we must therefore endeavor to trace in it the denouement, more or less happy, of each of the measures taken.

PART THIRD.

MINOR OPERATIONS.

CHAPTER FIRST.

OUTPOSTS.

INTRODUCTION.—In the field, an encamped or cantoned army does not know when it may be attacked; and therefore, that it may not be surprised, it must be at all times prepared for combat. But as keeping constantly upon the *qui vive* would fatigue it too much, a *portion* is charged with the duty of watching over the safety of the whole.

This portion of the army incurs a twofold responsibility: 1st, it must *watch* the enemy, in order to *give notice* of its approach; and 2d, it must then *stop* it, in order to *give time* for making the preparations for combat. That it may fulfil these purposes, it must necessarily be posted in advance of the main body of the troops, on the side toward the adversary: hence the various fractions of this portion are collectively designated by the term *outposts*.

We thus see that outposts perform the same service for an army at rest, as skirmishers and scouts for one upon a march. Outposts take the place of the scouts (*batteurs d'estrade*), employed by the ancients, which would be insufficient with the modern methods of warfare.

The composition of outposts is based upon the character* and force of the adversary; but that army will be the best guarded whose outposts are calculated upon the supposition that the enemy is *the most active*. We must, indeed, consider outposts as the *eyes*, which constantly watch the enemy, and prevent him from approaching unperceived.

It is a fundamental rule that outposts are never to fight merely for the sake of fighting. Thus, on the eve of the battle of Emmendingen, October 18, 1796, a skirmish occurred between the patrols of the outposts, and in this untimely action the Austrians lost the village of Malterdingen, which, notwithstanding their occupation of the heights in the rear, they had a hard struggle to regain on the following day.† A chief of outposts must, then, consider the injurious consequences which might ensue were he to hazard an attack, and will refrain from useless combats. His duty, in fact, consists in covering the army, and not in displaying his courage.

The outposts will have accomplished their end, if

---

* According to Decker, the German, in this kind of service, is zealous; the Russian dangerous (on account of his numerous and vigilant Cossacks); the English, heavy; the Spaniard, indolent; to which we will add, the Frenchman is often too confident.

† See *Principes de stratégie* de l'Archiduc Charles, translated by General Jomini, 1818, v. iii., p. 253, 260.

the enemy dare not attack them, and is obliged to defer the combat to the time and place when and where it will be accepted; but to attain this result, they must rely solely upon their own vigilance, and not upon the inactivity of the enemy. A single oversight committed by an outpost may lead to the destruction of the whole army; and it were better, therefore, for the army to have no outposts, and to watch over its own safety, than to have negligent and inefficient ones.

In outpost warfare, both sides act with caution, for in most cases neither party knows precisely the position of his adversary; which leads the Prussian general, Decker, to say that, in this sort of warfare, " one sword keeps the other in its scabbard."* Nevertheless, we must not push this caution to the extreme of putting all the force on foot at once, nor so far as to introduce too great regularity in surveillance; since we should thereby unnecessarily weary the men, and also expose ourselves to be surprised by the enemy, who would base his attack upon this very uniformity. It was in consequence of this regularity that, in May, 1762, Prince Henry of Prussia was able to surprise and overcome the Austrians in the environs of Freyburg.†

In accordance with their twofold mission, of both watching and impeding the approach of the enemy, the outposts are to be placed so as to overlook the

* *De la petite guerre*, traduction Unger, p. 67.
† *Vie du prince Henri de Prusse*, 1809, p. 112. This anonymous work is due to general the Marquis de Bouillé.

surrounding ground and whatever happens there, and also so as to be able to fight advantageously, notwithstanding their numerical weakness.

If the advance-guard covers the army, the chain of outposts will extend beyond the advance-guard; but if this guard camps with the army, the chain will be formed just outside the camp. In both cases the method of placing it is the same; and it is also the same whether the outposts are *transient* (as those which are established every night before an army in march), or *permanent* (as those which protect an army in winter quarters, or in a defensive position).

When the army marches, the advance or rear-guard of each column furnishes the troops for the outposts; when it occupies a position, the advance and rear-guards resume their places in the order of battle, and the outposts are supplied from the corps of the first line. In all cases, not more than one sixth of the whole army should be employed upon outpost service.

Outposts consist of:
1st. Grand guards;
2d. Small posts;
3d. Vedettes, or sentinels;
4th. Patrols;
5th. Sometimes, posts of support.

We will examine each of these in succession.

1. Grand Guards.—The network of outposts always forms at least three distinct lines: first that of the grand guards, who are nearest to the army, then that of the small posts, and lastly, that of the sentinels or vedettes. This distribution results from the necessity which every body of troops, whatever its force, is under of guarding itself against surprise, and of disclosing the ground as far as possible in advance and on all sides.

To begin with the grand guards: these are, according to the ordinance of May 3, 1832, respecting the service of the army in the field, "the advanced posts of a camp or cantonment, the approaches to which they should cover."

Their number, their force, and their position are regulated: 1st, in a detached corps, by the officer in command of that corps; 2d, in an army, by each brigade severally, for the purpose of giving to that fraction the unity which is the more necessary, since, in actual engagements, an army manœuvres and fights by brigades. Besides, when the outpost service is filled from a number of combined brigades, the general commanding the division still has it in his power to modify it, and point out to the brigades the best posts to occupy to maintain their mutual connection and protect their flanks.*

As far as possible, the infantry grand guards, which serve for support, will be combined with the cavalry grand guards, which perform the duty of advanced sentinels. If it can be done, it will be useful to attach to the infantry grand guards a certain number of horsemen, whose duty it will be to obtain prompt intelligence respecting the enemy.

The grand guard of a regiment, or even of a bat-

* Préval, *Commentaires sur le service en campagne*, p. 73.

talion, whether infantry or cavalry, is commanded by a captain. Its force depends upon its object and the means at disposal, and also upon the rule that it requires four men for one sentinel; but subsequent data may modify this force.

The grand guards are placed at the outlets whose defence is of the highest importance, else in a commanding and covered position in the centre of the region to be observed. To place them with a wood in their rear would be exposing them to destruction. Their position may be changed at the close of the day. Upon hilly ground, and especially in the midst of a hostile population, it is prudent to keep them near to the army. Even upon level ground, if they are placed at a great distance, it will be proper to establish intermediate posts.

The grand guards are seldom dispensed with, and never without orders from the general. But the ordinance authorizes those who are exposed upon a plain to attacks of cavalry, to erect barricades, dig a circular ditch, or cover themselves by an abatis. Among the ancients, all posts were required to be intrenched, or, at least, covered by embankments. This practice rendered the troops timid, by causing them to imagine that they could be secured only by a kind of rampart; besides, it was inconsistent with the rules of offensive warfare which is most congenial to the French character, and has consequently been abandoned.

The commandant of a grand guard should establish a sure communication between himself and his small posts, and also between himself and the corps from which it has been detached. For this purpose, he will open the ground and clear it of obstacles. On the side toward the enemy, he will, on the contrary, obstruct the roads, destroy the bridges, and bar defiles, to avoid surprises.

Each grand guard may receive special orders, according to the position it occupies. Its general orders will be to give notice to the neighboring posts, to the corps from which detached, and to the general, of the movements of the enemy, and of apprehended attacks; it should also examine all individuals which come into its vicinity, and arrest those who are not provided with passports signed by a known general, and all soldiers who may attempt to pass beyond the line of outposts.

The grand guard must not allow its fire to give much light, but should mask it on the side of the enemy, either by a wall, or a rise of the ground, or by kindling it in a hole dug in the ground for the purpose. In all cases, a pile of moist earth should be kept at hand, with which to extinguish the fire suddenly, if necessary, in case of surprise. The enemy may be deceived as to the position of the grand guard by means of flying-fires kept up by sentinels.

During the night, the grand guard must exercise increased vigilance, for it is then most important to be guarded against unforeseen attacks. If an infantry grand guard, one half of the men should keep watch, whilst the other half sleep: if a cavalry grand guard, the horses should be kept bridled, and the men should not sleep. The commandant of the grand guard is forbidden to rest or sleep.

In case of an attack by the enemy, the conduct of the grand guard should be as follows. As soon as it is threatened, or as soon as it is attacked, the grand guard gives notice to the general of the brigade or the colonel of its regiment; then, if it does not occupy a defile or an enclosed post, it marches toward the enemy and measures strength with it if not in too great force, or else manœuvres so as to embarrass its progress. In all cases it avoids committing itself too far, for, if once cut off, there is no longer any obstacle between the enemy and the camp; but it keeps its ground until the army is in line, or until it is relieved. When the grand guard occupies a defile, or an intrenched post, it maintains its ground so long as its supplies last, or until the greater part of the men are killed; then it endeavors to rejoin the army, still trying to inflict damage upon the enemy.

The line of grand guards is usually as much as 2,500 yards in advance of the army.

2. Small Posts.—The small posts are to the grand guards what the grand guards are to the army: that is, while the grand guard covers the army, it has need to be itself covered in turn. For this purpose it detaches advanced posts, placed between it and the line of vedettes and sentinels, the total force of which should not exceed one third of its own force. These smaller posts are placed 500 yards in advance of the grand guards.

The first care of the commandant of a grand guard is to reconnoitre all kinds of communications by which his position may be reached; and in accordance with this reconnoissance he determines the force and the position of his small posts and of the sentinels or vedettes beyond them. These positions may be modified in cases of necessity. Sometimes they are not the same by night as by day. In all cases the small posts should not change place at the same time with the grand guards.

The small posts are established at cross-roads, the débouches of villages, woods, and defiles, at the corners of marshes, or on hill tops. It is an essential condition that they should be seen by their grand guard, and that they should see their sentinels or vedettes. They should never be placed opposite to obstacles sufficiently near to cover a surprise.

A small post is, according to its importance, commanded by an officer, or non-commissioned officer. The commandant of the grand guard gives the chief of each small post detailed instructions upon the surveillance to be exercised, and the measures to be taken to defend themselves and effect a retreat.

As soon as he has taken his position, a chief of a post should reconnoitre the surrounding localities, and avail himself of the means they may offer to insure his own safety and that of his sentinels and vedettes. He will make his chief preparations to resist an attack in the rear, which is not an uncommon occurrence with isolated posts.

The small posts are forbidden to light fires, when

these fires might contribute to their being surprised. The small posts of cavalry *may* be relieved, under certain circumstances, either every four or every eight hours.

Besides the ordinary line of small posts, some of the other nations often station upon points favorable for observation, in advance of the line of sentinels or vedettes, posts of four or five men, two of whom are always on the watch. These are called *Cossack-posts*, but the French army makes no use of this kind of posts.

3. Sentinels and Vedettes.—The sentinels (or vedettes) cover the small posts, as the latter cover the grand guards. They constitute the last link of the chain of outposts, and are placed 500 yards in advance of the small posts.

The small posts of infantry detach sentinels; those of cavalry, vedettes. Whether foot soldiers or horsemen, these sentries are so placed as to command a distant view of the surrounding ground. They are to be concealed from the enemy by a wall, a hedge, a tree, a hillock, a pile of earth or of any materials, or a haystack; and they must never expose any other portion of their persons than the head. Even in level country, they can be sheltered by digging a hole in the ground about $4\frac{1}{2}$ feet deep, in which they bury themselves as far as the chest, placing around the hole, to protect their heads, some fresh branches of trees, planted in such a form as to resemble a clump of bushes.*

---

* This expedient may also be employed to cover a post, by substitut-

The sentinels and vedettes watch closely the movements of an enemy who is within range, and apprize their small posts of an attack by the discharge of a gun. If the enemy is at a distance, they listen for the slightest noise, redoubling their vigilance at the most trifling incident, and call attention by signals to everything which appears to them to be of a menacing nature. According to the character of their signals, the chief of a small post repairs in person to the point which it occupies, either alone or with a portion of his force.

The vedettes should keep the collar of their cloaks turned down, in order that they may hear the better. If they are lancers, they may take off the *flamme* of their lance in order not to be so conspicuous to the enemy. They should keep their eye upon the neighboring vedettes, to see that none of them are destroyed. In case of imminent peril, the sentinels and vedettes are doubled, so that, if there is need for it, one of them may be detached to give warning. Double vedettes are principally useful among heights; for a vedette posted upon an eminence to watch the environs, would easily be turned while his attention was engaged, if another vedette at the foot of the slope did not baffle the enemy in the attempt. During the night all the vedettes remain on the lower grounds.

Sentinels and vedettes are forbidden to talk or to

---

ing for the hole a ditch of sufficient size. To deceive the enemy, the branches of trees must be frequently renewed. We borrow this idea from the *Traité des troupes légères* (p. 589) of the general, Count de la Roche-Aymon.

smoke. They should be wholly absorbed in their important and delicate mission; for the slightest negligence on their part may involve the loss of their small post and compromise the whole army.

4. Distribution of the Outposts.—The proper distance to leave between the most advanced outpost and the camp or cantonment, may be fixed at about three quarters of a league, as an average estimate; let us say 3,500 yards.* The distance of the small posts from the grand guards, and from the line of sentinels or vedettes, will be from 400 to 500 yards each, which, if we take the higher number, gives a distance of 1,000 yards between the extreme line of sentinels or vedettes, and the line of the grand guards. The enemy will thus have at least 1,000 yards to pass over after they have been signalled, before they can reach the grand guards. Supposing the ground perfectly free from all obstacles, it will take them about three minutes to traverse this space, and this will give time enough to the grand guards to bridle and mount their horses, and to advance to the succor of their small posts. With these distances, therefore, the army will be sufficiently covered; and yet they are not so great as to prevent the parties at the different posts seeing each other distinctly, which considerations have led to their adoption.

According to these distances, the network of outposts upon level ground forms the following figure. Upon more uneven ground, the figure would

---

* Lallemand, *Traité des opérations secondaires*, t. i., p. 2.

OUTPOSTS. 229

become more irregular, and the various lines would

SYSTEM OF OUTPOSTS.

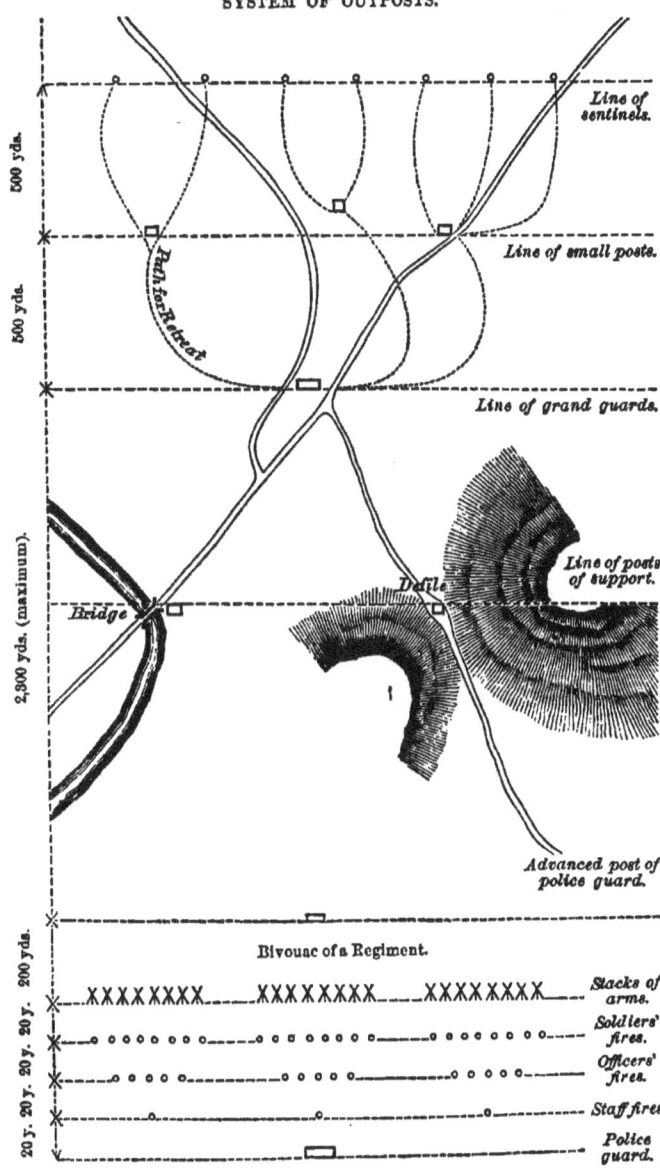

become more curved, the general proportions, however, remaining the same.

It must not be forgotten that these distances correspond to the positions assumed during the day. At night, it will often be prudent to contract the whole system of outposts, and especially to bring the line of sentinels or vedettes nearer.

5. Posts of Support.—Sometimes posts of support are established between the grand guards and the front of the camp or bivouac, for the purpose of resisting for some time an enemy who may succeed in passing the first lines of the outposts, and thus give the army time to take up arms. These posts are furnished with cannon, and composed chiefly of infantry, taken from the camp and not from the grand guards, for the latter should attend only to the ground in their front.

These posts of support, therefore, form a fourth line of outposts, nearest to the army. They are to be placed at the outlets of valleys and woods, and the approaches of bridges and defiles, which the grand guards may have to pass in their retreat.

6. Patrols, Look-outs, Rounds.—The service of outposts being one which requires to be thoroughly performed, it should be subject to an active and severe surveillance. The brigadier-general and superior officer of each regiment supervise the grand guards; the commandant of each grand guard supervises his small posts and sentinels, or vedettes, by means of patrols and rounds, the number of which, and their circuits, he fixes according to circumstances.

A *round* is the general name given to a circuit made either by a commissioned or a non-commissioned officer, attended by two or three men, for the purpose of inspecting the small posts and sentinels, and keeping them upon the alert. *Patrols* may be defined as small detachments of infantry or cavalry, taken from a post, to perambulate its vicinity and to watch over its safety. Sometimes the patrols go beyond the exterior cordon of outposts, to have a better look-out upon the doings of the enemy, and then receive the designation of *look-outs*. The latter must not be too numerous, for the sentinels, seeing them frequently coming in, would become negligent; but when there is occasion to employ them, notice is to be given to the sentinels near whom they must pass in coming in, lest they be taken for parties of the enemy. The neglect of this precaution was the occasion, near Placentia, in 1796, of a fatal mistake, whereby the French general, Laharpe, was killed by his own soldiers. We may also distinguish the patrol from the look-outs, by saying that the former is defensive and the latter offensive. The defensive patrol evidently embraces the rounds.

Arrangement of a defensive patrol.—It is composed of from three to eight men, commanded by a corporal—a small force, which can readily escape in case of need. These move not in straight lines, but in zig-zag courses, in order to embrace more ground. During the day they should preserve a distance from each other of 150 yards, which, at night, will be reduced to 20 or 30 yards.

If the patrol consists of only three men (fig. 1), they will be placed on a straight line.

If there are four men (fig. 2), they will form a lozenge, one point in advance, the corporal at the opposite point.

If there are five men (fig. 3), they will still form a lozenge, and the corporal will occupy the centre.

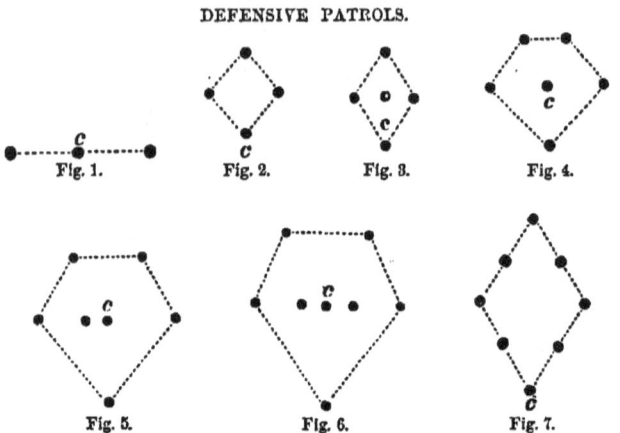

DEFENSIVE PATROLS.

Fig. 1. Fig. 2. Fig. 3. Fig. 4.

Fig. 5. Fig. 6. Fig. 7.

If there are six men (fig. 4), the corporal remains at the centre, but the lozenge will be truncated, by putting two men in advance, the figure thus becoming an irregular pentagon.

If there are seven men (fig. 5), we have the same arrangement, only the corporal will have one man by his side.

If there are eight men (figs. 6 and 7), either the same arrangement, putting two men with the corporal; or else the patrol will form a lozenge, with three men in each side.

Arrangement of an offensive patrol.—These patrols

are usually composed of cavalry, and their force varies from ten to thirty men. Like the defensive patrols, they should never remain in too compact mass, so as not to be liable to being captured at once; but they

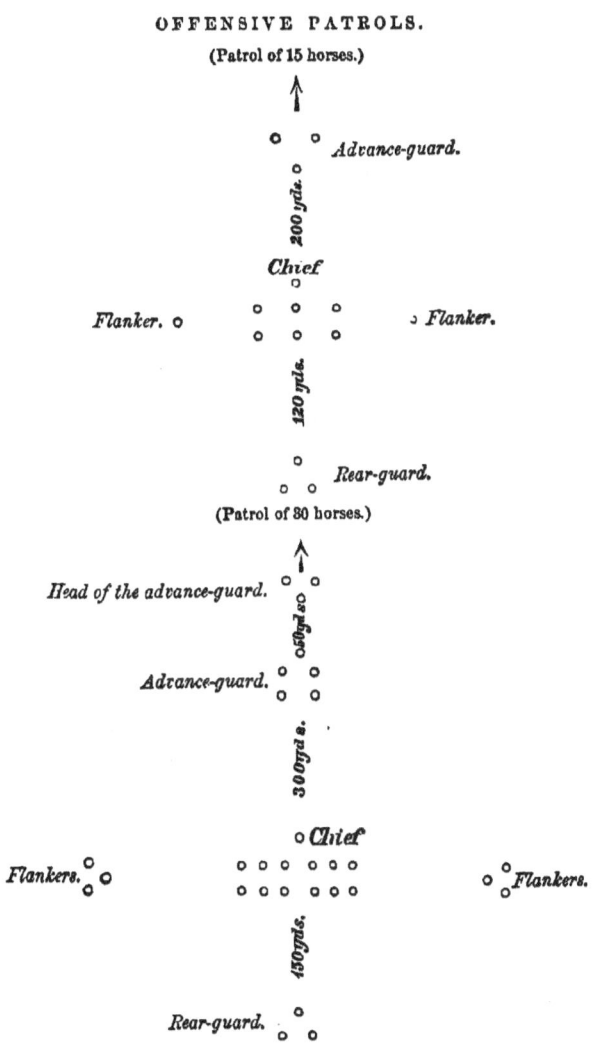

should spread out as much as their force and the localities will allow.

The foregoing diagram exhibits the mode of formation according to general La Roche-Aymon.

In each formation two men are placed at the head and rear, in order that if one has something to communicate to the chief of the patrol, the other may keep his post without taking his eyes from the object which has seemed worthy of an immediate report.

During night patrols, the chief of a patrol may need to know the hour, but he should not light a lantern, which would reveal his position to the enemy. Frederic recommended, in this case, that the officer should light a piece of tinder under his cloak, which, being passed over the watch face, would give light enough to show the hands.*

In concluding this chapter, we will recommend to our readers to refer to article VIII. of the *Ordonnance sur le service en campagne*, which contains circumstantial details, indispensable to be known, respecting outposts, the study of which will involve no difficulties after what we have above given.

---

* *Instruction secrète*, chap. iii. [In these days of friction matches, a simpler expedient will suggest itself to every reader.—*Tr.*]

CHAPTER SECOND.

DETACHMENTS.*

1. General Observations.—Outposts may be regarded as purely *defensive detachments*. The detachments which are the subject of the present chapter, may, in contradistinction to outposts, be called *offensive detachments*.

Their object is to occupy a post of observation, or to capture such a post; to protect or to attack a convoy, a foraging party, a reconnoissance, or cantonment; to levy contributions in the neighboring localities, either in kind or in money; to destroy a magazine, to make a diversion, to harass a marching column by repeated skirmishes, to lay ambuscades, to cut the communications of the enemy, to make prisoners, to take hostages, or to throw a supply of men and munitions into a besieged town.

In the composition of a detachment, we must have regard: 1st, to the object and the duration of its service; and 2d, to the nature of the country and to the

---

* Upon detachments, consult art. ix. of the *Ordonnance sur le service des armées en campagne*, of May 3, 1832.

disposition of its inhabitants. According to the nature of these various data, the detachment will be composed either of infantry alone, or of cavalry alone, or of a combination of both. Infantry and cavalry are usually to be detached only in the regularly constituted fractions of a regiment, such as the battalion, squadron, company, platoon, or section, as this method facilitates its administration, and is more conducive to discipline. The artillery and the engineers do not enter into the composition of detachments except by accident. In the following pages we will distinguish between *detachments of infantry, detachments of cavalry,* and *mixed detachments.*

By the French army regulations, the commandant of a detachment has the same authority over the troops placed under his orders as a chief of a corps. He is responsible for the safety of his force, and, *up to a certain point,*[*] for the result of the combats in which he engages. Upon his return, he makes a report to the officer who detached him, in relation to his proceedings, in conformity with his instructions and their results; and also a report to each of the chiefs of the corps which furnished soldiers for his detachment, in relation to the police, discipline, and administration of the forces.

The officer selected for the command of a detachment should be firm, prudent, and experienced; he

---

[*] This qualified language of the regulations was necessary; for a chief of a detachment may sometimes be beaten without having omitted any duty. We should also not forget the saying of Turenne: "Quand un homme n'a pas fait de fautes à la guerre, il ne l'a pas faite longtemps."

should know how to observe, and also how to relate what he observes in exact terms, without drawing upon his imagination; he should also be able to speak the language of the country, and be accustomed to estimate distances. He must supply himself with a telescope and accurate charts. He will employ good guides, and will derive from them all possible information respecting the distances and the nature of the roads over which he must pass. Before starting, he will make himself thoroughly acquainted with the precise purport of his mission, and will ask for any necessary explanations from the chief who sends him; after starting, he will execute his instructions to the letter. Some important but unforeseen circumstance may, however, compel him to depart from them in part; in this case he should conform to their spirit, and conduct himself with reference to the general interests of the service; but, to justify this, there must exist *real impossibility*. Should he extricate himself skilfully from such a position, he will prove his capacity for war, and earn a title to be selected for difficult commands.*

Before setting out, he will assemble his detachment, carefully pass it in review, and assure himself that it is provided with everything necessary, provisions, munitions, stores, etc. He will inspect the arms, equipment, and clothing. In the infantry, he will direct his attention to the shoes and the knapsacks; in the cavalry he will inspect the packing, and see that the horses' shoes are in good condition.

* Jacquinot de Presles, p. 390.

A detachment, when marching, is always in a state of feebleness, since the column is lengthened, and the order of march is not suitable for combat, especially when the distances have been lost. Hence it is indispensable that it should have time to form itself in case of a sudden attack; and on this account it is preceded by a small body, called the *advance-guard*, which explores the country and gives notice of the approach of the enemy. For similar purposes, a small body is placed in rear of the detachment, called the *rear-guard*. Thus a detachment marches between an advance-guard and rear-guard. But it is not sufficient to be guarded in front and rear; a hostile body might debouch perpendicularly to the route, and fall upon the flank or the centre of the column, and the advance and rear-guards would not be able to oppose them. This danger is guarded against by throwing out skirmishers or flankers on the right and left, upon the flanks of the detachment, whose duty it is to scour the surrounding country and to examine all the by-ways, going across the fields, if necessary, marching in various directions, watching for unusual sounds, and inspecting every suspicious object; without, however, separating too far from the main body, as they would be liable to be cut off. No fixed rules can be given for all detachments as to the force of the advance and rear-guards, and the number of flankers: it is evident, however, that their importance increases with the effective force of the detachment and the complications of the ground. Some authors consider one fourth the force of a detachment as the proper proportion for the advance-guard.*

The commandant of a detachment will usually remain at the head of its principal portion. Sometimes he will stop to see the whole force defile before him, and take that occasion of correcting the order of march. He will frequently go forward to the advance-guard to give his instructions, and to reconnoitre the country in front; or, if he has a staff officer under his orders, he may send him upon this reconnoissance, as the special qualifications of such an officer will enable him to gain speedy and exact intelligence. It is important for the chief of a detachment to know the cardinal points at night, and if he has no compass, he will regulate his course by the stars, chiefly by the *pole star*, which is very nearly at the north pole of the heavens. This recommendation is especially applicable to the war in Algeria, where, on account of the uncertainty of the Arabic roads southward, it is important that every soldier should be acquainted with this star, which will be of great use to him, in case he loses his way.

"A chief of a detachment," says Jacquinot de Presles,† "should often suppose himself on the point of being attacked, and ask himself *what course he would take if the enemy were suddenly to appear;* if

---

* The details of this paragraph have been substantially given in Part Second, chapter ii., in speaking of columns on the march; but they are so important that their repetition in connection with detachments will not be thought useless.

† *Cours d'art militaire*, p. 404.

the answer embarrasses him, if a course at once prudent and honorable does not occur to his mind, *he is not yet a good officer*, and his detachment is very much exposed; for it is probable that he will lose his presence of mind if he be attacked."

Moreover, the detachment which is commanded by a skilful chief is necessarily, at the moment of battle, more composed and better prepared for the contest, than one indifferently commanded; and the energy of its action ought to give evidence of this fact.

As a last general observation, we will add that a detachment, whether of infantry or cavalry, or of both (without artillery), should not be deterred from the fulfilment of its mission by having to cross a river.

Detachments, like partisans,* have a right to shares of booty.

2. Detachments of Infantry.—A detachment of infantry may undertake all kinds of enterprises, even the most daring. They are mostly charged with nocturnal expeditions; with coups-de-main in a hilly or wooded country; with the attack and defence of obstacles, such as houses, barricades, woods, defiles; with escorting or attacking convoys, and with ambuscades.

When a detachment is sent to maintain a position, it should at once intrench itself there, and make use of all the resources which the locality affords for the purpose. Thus, for example, for want of trees in the vicinity, it may, if necessary, demolish some huts and

---

* See, hereafter, chapter vi. of this Part.

use the wood in the construction of barricades; but the commandant must, nevertheless, remember that the regulations respecting campaign service prescribe that *all destruction of property is to be avoided which is not indispensable.*

A detachment of infantry can easily conceal and barricade itself; it can be covered by almost anything; and therefore its march, which is comparatively noiseless, is readily screened from observation; it scarcely leaves any trace of its passage, and can travel considerable distances without renewing its supply of provisions; all these are advantages which it possesses over a detachment of cavalry.

When a detachment of infantry falls in with the enemy, the best course for it to pursue, is to assume a bold front and rush to the attack. At night especially, and in favorable localities, this course will have the best chance of success. Hilly ground is the most favorable for its action; but upon a plain it will be at a disadvantage against cavalry. It should, therefore, avoid travelling a great extent of level country, at least during the day. Frequently, when it has not been able to accomplish its purpose in a single night, it will halt and conceal itself during the day behind some obstacle, and not set out again upon its march until night. In mountainous districts it may march by day, but it will yet be proper to avoid the villages and frequented roads.

In order to offer greater resistance to the enemy, a detachment of infantry should march in column by sections. It must not be obliged to put files in the rear in contracted ground, for it is a vicious formation, and an embarrassing one in case of attack; hence the sections should be formed upon a small front: ten or twelve files will be sufficient. There should be an *even number* of sections, so as to facilitate the formation of a square. Like all detachments, it will have an advance and a rear-guard; and we can here assign a more precise limit for the approximate force to be given to these two fractions of a detachment of infantry, namely *one half* (at most) of the whole force, if the latter be under 500 men; but if the force be over 500 men, the advance-guard, the rear-guard, and the flankers should not together exceed *one third* the force. For a forward march, the advance-guard will be the most considerable of the secondary portions of the detachment; for a retrograde movement, it will be the rear-guard. According to these considerations, the marching formation of a detachment of infantry is as follows:

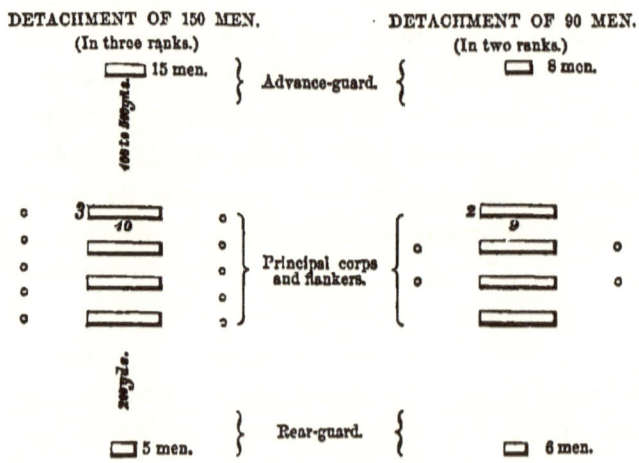

3. Detachments of Cavalry.—Detachments of cavalry are principally used in such service as requires celerity, as that of escorts, rapid reconnoissances, levying contributions, posts of observation, etc. In operations of this kind, the mounted soldier may make good use of his fire-arms.

The duty of the advance-guard of a detachment of cavalry will be to give warning of the presence of the enemy. The detachment, upon this warning, may either charge or retreat, according to circumstances; but it should not remain stationary unless it has not been itself discovered.

A detachment of cavalry has the advantage upon level ground; but irregular ground is unfavorable to it. Defiles are dangerous to it, as infantry can there easily lie in ambush; these should, therefore, be avoided by a detour; but if that is not possible, they should first be explored by scouts, or by some of the horsemen themselves (on foot, however); and afterward the defile should be passed at a gallop. When the defile is more than a league in length, the reconnoissance of it must be abandoned; and in this case it must be entered with caution, breaking up the detachment into platoons of ten or twelve horsemen each, and marching in a disconnected manner, so as to present more void than full space to the fire of an ambuscaded enemy. In this way, and aided by the rapidity of movement, the detachment will probably escape serious damage. It would be an excellent safeguard to occupy the overlooking heights before entering into the defiles, but this is often a difficult operation for cavalry.

A detachment of cavalry will usually form by platoons, which is the most suitable order for combat. The extent of the front of each platoon should be such that the detachment leaves a portion of the road free, in order that it may easily make a half turn in the event of a sudden attack, which does not permit it to deploy. It will also be prudent to keep the left side of the road; for, in a rencontre, it will then be attacked by the right flank, which is the strong side of the horseman.

4. Mixed Detachments.—Mixed detachments possess more coherence or stability than those consisting of a single arm. No others should be employed in insurgent districts. The escorts of a convoy, of a foraging party, or of a park, having to act over a great extent of country, should be mixed.

The order of march of a mixed detachment varies according to the nature of the ground it traverses. On level ground, the cavalry takes the lead, and watches over the safety of the detachment; but in a country cut up by mountains and ravines, and covered by woods, the infantry forms the advance-guard, and also flanks the column. It is the same at night, with the difference only, that the distances between the advance and rear-guards and the principal body are diminished.* In a varied region, sometimes level and

---

* Léorier, *Théorie de l'officier supérieure*, p. 138.

at other times broken, the detachment will observe the same order as in broken ground and at night; because but one order of march can be adopted, if we do not wish to disorganize the detachment by frequent interchanges of the troops of the advance-guard and of the principal body; and also because, when the infantry takes the lead, the cavalry may always, in case of necessity, come up rapidly to the head of the column.

When a mixed detachment meets the enemy, it may either retire or fight. If it fights, it will be drawn up in two lines, either in echelons, or checkerwise—the force of the echelons depending upon the total effective force of the detachment, and being, if necessary, even as small as a half squadron. The dispositions for combat, however, are of infinite variety, but are almost always determined by the nature of the ground. If the flanks of the position are covered by woods, and are thus favorable to a protracted defence, it will be well to throw out a part of the infantry upon these flanks, as skirmishers.

To complete this brief sketch, we give on the following pages the order of march of two mixed detachments, one marching on level ground, the other in broken or hilly ground. These figures (in which the symbol ◊ denotes a single horseman, and ○ a single foot soldier) explain themselves.

246 MINOR OPERATIONS.

MIXED DETACHMENT OF 300 FOOT AND 50 HORSE, MARCHING ON LEVEL GROUND.

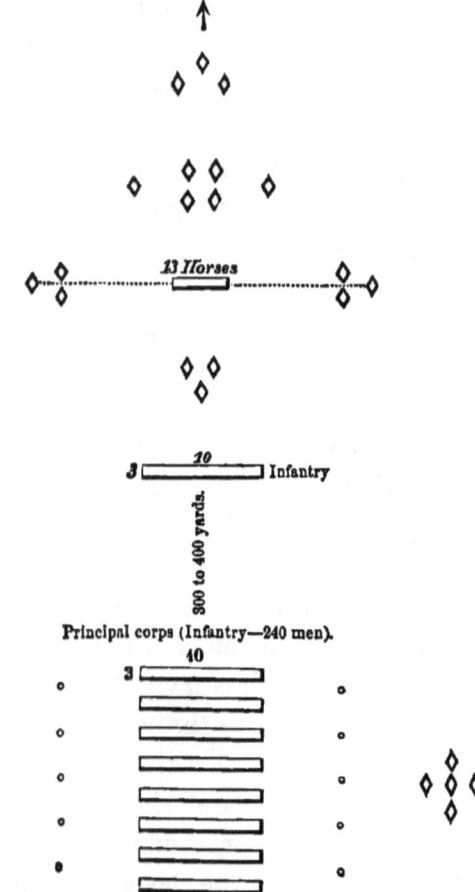

DETACHMENTS. 247

MIXED DETACHMENT OF 200 FOOT AND 50 HORSE, MARCHING IN BROKEN GROUND.

↑

◊   o o   ◊
   o   o o

   o   o o   o
             o o

    o o   5
       o 3 [====] Infry o   o
                         o

           o o
            o

Principal corps (132 men).
              11
         3 [=========]
           [=========]
           [=========]
           [=========]

Patrol of 10 foot. [ ]   [ ] Patrol of 10 foot.

         [46 horse, by fours, on left of road.]

            o
           o o
            4
     o   2[====] Infry o

          o o
          ◊ ◊

CHAPTER THIRD.

ARMED RECONNOISSANCES.

INTRODUCTION.—*Armed reconnoissance* * is the designation applied to any movement of troops, made with the object of discovering or verifying one or more particulars respecting the position, the force, the movements, or even the intentions of the enemy.

This definition shows that such a reconnoissance constitutes the basis of every military operation, and ought to precede it. Without a reconnoissance, we should be constantly liable to surprises.

Since armies generally cover their marches by flankers, and their camps and cantonments by a chain of outposts, it follows that, in order to obtain a view of their disposition, we must push beyond these flankers or this chain, by a reconnoissance, which can clear away the obstacles to such an inspection. We see, therefore, in advance, that the service of reconnoissances is attended with difficulties and complications.

We must not confound the reconnoissance by

---

* In these *Elements* we are not required to treat of *topographical* reconnoissances.

patrol, made by the grand guards for their security, with a reconnoissance proper. The patrol reconnoitres within narrower limits, confining itself to its chief purpose—that of assuring itself of the position in which the enemy is posted, without troubling itself with their tactical arrangement, or with the topographical strength of their position; while a reconnoissance examines in detail the position of the enemy, the weak points of his position, the mode of attacking it, the composition of the opposing corps in troops of the several arms, the character of the soldiers, the vigilance of the officers, the condition of their supplies, the designs of their chief, the confidence he inspires, etc.; in short, sees and collects as much information as possible.

We shall distinguish five kinds of reconnoissance:
1st. Daily reconnoissances;
2d. Special reconnoissances;
3d. Secret reconnoissances;
4th. Offensive reconnoissances;
5th. Reconnoissances in Africa.

Before entering upon these last, we shall speak of the reports which should accompany every reconnoissance, and shall cite some historical examples, calculated to show the importance of this minor operation of war.

Armed reconnoissances do not always bring back all the information needed, even when they are successful, and it becomes necessary to complete them by accessory means, which we shall also study. We shall first say a few words respecting the maps which exhibit the form and character of the country; we shall speak of the guides who conduct the columns safely through their various detours; we shall point out the questions to be put to deserters, to the inhabitants, to travellers, to prisoners, in order to make a profitable use of them; we shall treat of spies and of the proper treatment of them; and we shall conclude with details respecting the principal signs, the observation of which may develop some particulars respecting the enemy.

1. Daily Reconnoissances.*—Daily reconnoissances are made to ensure the safety either of the camps or cantonments, or of the advanced posts. They should ascertain the designs of the enemy, and whether he is preparing to march, to surprise, or to fight. Certain signs will guide them in this respect, especially what occurs at the outposts; for if they are increased, it is a sign of stagnation; if such posts are modified, it denotes a change of position.

In a level country the reconnoissances will be made by light cavalry; but in mountainous countries, they will be made by infantry, which, however, should be accompanied by some horsemen for the prompt transmission of intelligence. In a varied country the reconnoitring body will be composed of troops of both arms, and in all cases the numbers should be small.

The service of reconnoissances, like that of outposts, must be divested of regularity, for this would

---

* The reader will do well to consult, in relation to daily reconnoissances, the *Ordonnance sur le service en campagne*, art. x., chap. i.

soon give the enemy the knowledge of the usages practised, and would facilitate the destruction of the corps of reconnoissance.

It is an essential principle in reconnoissances that *to reconnoitre is not to attack*. Moreover, a reconnoitring body should march with precaution, conceal its presence, and avoid compromising itself. It should consider combat not as its end, but solely as the extreme means of obtaining information, by taking prisoners. There is also another case in which it may resort to combat; namely, when it falls in with a detachment of the enemy marching rapidly upon the camp; it will then retard their advance by assailing them, having first detached a horseman to give warning to the camp. In such a case, it should not hesitate; it should, nevertheless, take advantage of local peculiarities to the utmost extent, to compensate for its numerical inferiority.

A reconnoissance should march as a detachment, with an advance-guard, a rear-guard and flankers. The latter should take care never to be out of sight of the principal body during the day, as one or more of them carried off would suffice to guide the enemy upon the track of the reconnoissance, and would enable them to surprise it before it suspected danger.

In order to avoid ambuscades, a reconnoissance should not traverse inhabited districts before having examined them thoroughly, and taken, when necessary, hostages for the peaceful disposition of the inhabitants. It should arrest all individuals following its path or attempting to pass it, who might, otherwise, give notice of its movements to the enemy.

When a reconnoissance cannot accomplish its purpose without halting, it should do so behind some accident of ground, a wood, or a wall, which will conceal it; and should also cover itself, during the halt, by some vedettes stationed on the roads on the side from whence an attack is to be feared.

A reconnoissance may successfully reconnoitre a column of the enemy on the march. For this purpose it will follow the column, keep alongside of it without allowing itself to be perceived, see it defile before itself, count it, note the number of troops of each of the different arms, its materiel and its accessories; will observe whether it appears formidable, and how it protects itself; what are its habits in setting out, in halting, and in passing through defiles; in what part it appears most vulnerable; what its designs appear to be; whether its troops are fatigued; in a word, it will gather the most circumstantial information possible respecting the column.

2. Special Reconnoissances.—In the language of the Ordinance respecting field service, the object of special reconnoissances will be, in general, as follows:

" 1st. To determine distances, the condition of the roads and the repairs they may require, the configuration of the ground, and facilities or obstacles it presents, in order to regulate, thereby, the march of the columns and of the different arms;

" 2d. To explore, in all their parts, the positions to

be successively occupied by the columns, either for the purpose of supporting all attacks, or of sustaining themselves in case of resistance or an offensive demonstration on the part of the enemy, or of insuring their retreat.

" 3d. To reconnoitre the position and the force of the principal or intrenched posts of the enemy, the configuration of his positions, the defences he may have established there, the difficulty or the means of attacking them.

" 4th. Finally, to estimate, as nearly as possible, the forces of the enemy at every point."

Special reconnoissances belong to the province of the officers of the several staffs. Thus, for example, when the object of the reconnoissance is to prepare the way for the march of the columns, or to ascertain the force of the enemy, it is intrusted to an officer of the staff corps; if it relates to the condition of the roads, or to the intrenched posts of the enemy, or to the establishment of field works, it should be executed by an officer of engineers; when it relates to the means of reaching the enemy's position from a distance, by means of artillery favorably placed, it is put in charge of an artillery officer. Nevertheless, it is easy to imagine circumstances in the field in which such a distribution could not be rigorously observed, and in which an officer of engineers might at some point execute a reconnoissance which more properly belonged to the province of a general staff officer, while, at another point, the latter might reconnoitre the most favorable location of some field work.

The general officer who orders a special reconnoissance, gives particular instructions to the officer to whom he intrusts it: the latter communicates these instructions to the general of the brigade whose outposts he must pass. The general of brigade adds to these instructions whatever his own special knowledge of the localities and the acts of the enemy may suggest, and furnishes the reconnoitring officer with a detachment. If the latter finds it necessary to the success of his expedition to carry some posts of the enemy, he should not make the attack without the authority of the brigadier-general. The observance of this rule is indispensable, as the engagement in question might assume large proportions, compromise the brigade, and sometimes even force it to an untimely combat; and the brigadier-general is the only one in a proper position to judge of the opportuneness of a contest on his front.

3. Secret Reconnoissances.—The daily and special reconnoissances of which we have spoken, usually require but a few hours for their execution, and are usually made in broad daylight. But, besides this general case, in which reconnnoissances of this kind may be designated as *ostensible* (or *open*), there are cases where it is important to make them secretly: they are then called *secret* reconnoissances, and may occupy several days and nights, according to the greater or less distance of the enemy, his greater or less strength, and the more or less hilly character of the country.

The importance of keeping reconnoissances secret is obvious; for if it be advantageous to obtain information respecting the position and intentions of the enemy and to baffle his designs, it is still more desirable that the enemy should not know that we have obtained possession of his secrets and the key of all his operations, whereby we are enabled with certainty to paralyze his efforts. However, while it is important to conduct a reconnoissance secretly, it rarely happens that absolute secrecy is possible; the enemy frequently discovers it, and it then resolves itself into the open reconnoissance.

Let us consider these secret reconnoissances more fully.

A secret reconnoissance is a delicate and difficult operation; for it is necessary first to find the enemy without allowing one's self to be perceived, then to reconnoitre him, that is, to examine him with care, and to collect the greatest amount of information respecting him. It should be intrusted to officers of light troops, often assisted by a staff officer. The officer in charge of it should be experienced, and have under his orders none but veteran soldiers; for fresh recruits, unaccustomed to combat, might cause total failure. He will act with prudence, as his mission requires, but yet, in decisive moments, he will display boldness, or, at least, resolution, without which he would often be liable to see nothing and fail of his object; for the best conducted reconnoissance is that which brings back the greatest amount of useful information. An irresolute officer will fear to expose his detachment or his person, and at the last moment, either from negligence, or sometimes even from fear, will not approach sufficiently near; and then he will make a false report, assuredly more dangerous than the absence of all information concerning the enemy. What we have said in relation to the chief of the secret reconnoissances is applicable to the officers under him, and the non-commissioned officers to whom he intrusts some particular duty, or who accompany him in his nearest approaches to the enemy: these officers and soldiers should be mature, experienced in warfare, zealous, and faithful. To the same effect Marshal Montluc says, in his Commentaries: " *Capitaines, mes amis, il faut plus tost vous hazarder d'estre pris et sçavoir le vray, que non pas vous fonder sur le rapport des vilains. Ils ont la peur si avant dans le ventre, qu'il leur semble que tous les buissons sont des esquadrons, et l'asseurent,** *et cependant fiez-vous là; c'est comme quand ils voyent cent escus, il leur semble advis qu'il y en a mille. Envoyes tousjours quelques soldats sans peur, et que plus tost ils se hazardent; et si vous voulez faire mieux, allez-y vous mesme. Ainsi ay-je tousjours faict, et m'en suis bien trouvé.*"

A no less indispensable quality of the commandant of a secret reconnoissance is *sang-froid*, for this will often save him, and in all cases will qualify him to approach close to the enemy, and there determine with his own eyes his position and his defences. The

---

* Under the date 1545, Montluc cites the case of an officer who saw four hundred horsemen in a valley where there was not a single soldier.

career of the most illustrious of engineers furnishes in this connection a striking example. At the siege of Luxembourg (1683), Vauban, in order to reconnoitre the place, went every night to within a short distance of the outer works, accompanied by some grenadiers, who remained at the foot of the glacis, lying flat on the ground, while he ascended the glacis and approached the covered way. On one occasion he was perceived by some of the garrison, who aimed their pieces at him; but continuing to advance, and raising his hand to signify to them that they must not fire, was taken for one of their own officers, continued his inspection, then slowly retired, saved by his admirable sang-froid and his excess of temerity.

The chief of the reconnoissance should also be able to *speak* the language of the country, and if he can also *write* it, it will be still better. By employing the idiom of the country, he will not appear to be so much of a stranger to the inhabitants and prisoners whom he may question, and this will render them more communicative. This condition, which is applicable also to all kinds of reconnoissances, more especially requires to be mentioned, because we are, in France, generally too indifferent to the study of foreign languages—a study of great utility in war, as this example shows. If the non-commissioned officers of the reconnoissance can also speak the language of the country, they can supply the place of their superior officers, and can be employed upon the thousand ruses which serve to extricate a detachment from an unfortunate position. For want of a knowledge of the language of the country, that of the Latin may be of advantage to the officer, by enabling him to converse with the priests and educated persons; but for that purpose he should also have acquired the accent with which the Latin is spoken by the inhabitants.

The chief of a secret reconnoissance should supply himself with a good telescope and an accurate chart of the country he is to traverse, or, at least, with a sketch prepared at head-quarters. If he can obtain any statistical or military information from officers who have been over the surrounding localities, he will, of course, not neglect to avail himself of it.

The detachment charged with the performance of a secret reconnoissance will, in general, be composed of light cavalry. Its effective force should be sufficiently small to permit it to conceal its march, and yet strong enough to enable it to resist an enemy's patrol. From fifteen to forty horses* will satisfy these conditions. If, besides its ordinary duty of collecting information, the reconnoissance have to attempt some minor operation—such as carrying a post, firing a magazine, disorganizing a convoy—there may be some foot soldiers added to it. Unless the ground be exceedingly intricate, secret reconnoissances may almost always be performed by experienced light cavalry troops, for the horseman can go anywhere, if he is

---

* The Cossacks often make reconnoissances with a smaller number. Some five or six set out, and have been known to go as far as twenty leagues from their camp or cantonment. This results from their peculiar habits of living, for they are, in fact, mounted partisans, and, in case of need, exist upon almost nothing.

bent upon it. The reconnoissance sets out secretly, without covering itself by numerous and scattered flankers, who would attract attention. It will move with alacrity, in order to arrive near the enemy's posts before day. It should not, however, go so rapidly as to exhaust its strength before the end of the operation. "The powers of the horse," says General Brack,* " are the fortune of the horseman ; if they are all expended in one hour, what is left ? The little strength that prudence might have husbanded, would save life and obtain the cross of honor. Let the officer upon a reconnoissance especially remember this."

The reconnoissance marches with an advance-guard, which is accompanied by a guide. It will be prudent to mount the latter upon a white horse during a nocturnal march, in order that he may always be distinguished, however thick the darkness may be.

When near the enemy, the chief of the reconnoissance will point out to his men a rallying point, situated in the rear, to which every horseman, at his order, or upon a preconcerted signal, shall repair, in case it becomes necessary to disperse in order to escape from a pursuit. In anticipation of the possibility of a forced dispersment, it is prudent to send back, from time to time, to the point of departure, a note containing the information already collected. It should be written in very fine characters upon a small piece of paper, which the messenger places in his glove. In case of attack, if he sees he cannot escape, he has

* *Avant-postes de cavalerie légère*, p. 189.

orders to swallow this paper, or to put it into his pistol as a wad, so as to destroy it in firing.

After the rallying point has been pointed out, the commanding officer will form the reconnoitring body in three echelons; then, availing himself of the various obstacles of the ground as covers, he will advance with a guide and an escort of two or three horsemen to the lines of the enemy's patrols. If he is not perceived, he will observe whatever is of interest; if discovered, he will fall back to his troop, which has remained in rear. The successive appearance of the echelons will deceive the enemy as to the force of the detachment, and it is probable that some favoring obstacle may be reached while he is hesitating. If not, the troop should disperse.

The echelons formed by the reconnoissance need not be very regular. Their distance depends upon the ground, but it will be prudent not to make it more than 1,000 yards, in order that each may see the others.

When the reconnoissance has been discovered, it is often best to renew it as soon as the enemy has returned to his position, which will surprise him, and thus secure better opportunities of seeing.

Again, the officer in charge of a secret reconnoissance may accomplish his purpose sometimes, by leaving his troop at one or two leagues' distance from the enemy's outposts, going forward alone with a guide, and establishing himself by the break of day in a bush or tree, or in any position from which he can observe during the day and the following night.

Finally, when we do not succeed in gaining sufficient information by other means, we endeavor to make prisoners; but then it will be better to do so by stratagem than by open force.

We must not forget that, in secret reconnoissances, as in all others, notwithstanding the difficulty of the operation, promptness and dispatch are necessary to give reliable value to the results, for in war everything changes with such rapidity as to make any information a little old totally false.

The object being attained, the secret reconnoissance retires as quickly as possible; and, to escape the enemy's attention, makes itself as small as possible. Sometimes its return is secured by intermediate posts, which it has echeloned upon the road in its advance movement.

4. Offensive Reconnoissances.—When even the secret reconnoissances have failed, and the auxiliary resources for obtaining information prove insufficient, there is nothing left but open force. In the case where two armies, having been for some time at a distance from each other, come suddenly face to face, it is also well to obtain positive information of the situation of the enemy by a grand reconnoissance, which, like other open reconnoissances, is called an *offensive reconnoissance*. This designation is given to it, because it attacks in order to reconnoitre, whereas the other reconnoissances, already treated of, not only shun combat, but are cautious not even to put themselves in danger.

To effect an offensive reconnoissance, a detachment is expressly formed for the purpose, composed, when possible, of artillery and light cavalry, in order that it may be master of its movements. This detachment pierces the net-work of outposts, drives back whatever covers the enemy, and penetrates to some commanding point, and keeps up the skirmish until the reconnoitring officer has seen everything.

Prudence requires that a force should be in constant readiness to sustain the detachment engaged in an offensive reconnoissance, or to collect it again if it has been too quickly withdrawn. The infantry is charged with the duty of affording this support; and the whole army should be prepared to march in case some accidental and favorable circumstance should suddenly afford an opportunity of falling upon the enemy.* Care should also be taken to throw out patrols in various directions, to guard against a manœuvre to turn the flanks and rear of the reconnoissance.

It is frequently the general-in-chief himself who directs the offensive reconnoissance, and he then usually executes it with the advance-guard of the army. Frederic and Napoleon both followed this course—chiefly upon the eve of a battle—in order to reconnoitre for themselves the position of the enemy, and to settle their plans of attack. In this case the reconnoissance becomes, in a manner, an *experimental combat;* †

---

* Marmont, *Esprit des institutions militaires*, pp. 162, 165.

† The officers used to call this reconnoissance the *rehearsal of the play*.

and, if it fails, it will be better to postpone the battle until a superiority of force is secured.

As offensive reconnoissances, notwithstanding the precautions taken not to accept a serious combat, may go farther than is intended, and bring on unexpected consequences, the regulations upon field service prescribe that they shall be ordered only by the general-in-chief, and add: "They are allowed to be undertaken by other general officers only in cases where they are acting apart and out of the reach of all co-operation; or, finally, in those urgent cases in which they should not hesitate to take the responsibility."

5. **Report.**—The regulations recommend that a *report* be made of each reconnoissance, drawn up in a clear, simple, and positive manner, distinguishing information obtained from actual observation, from that obtained by hearsay, and giving the spelling of proper names with care. For special and offensive reconnoissances they prescribe, in addition, a sketch of the ground and of the defensive arrangements of the enemy.

The written report which accompanies a reconnoissance is as indispensable to the general-in-chief as the map of the country in which he operates. The clearness and precision required in its style should not prevent its embracing all the details necessary to throw light upon the *results* of the reconnoissance; and it is better that it be too explicit (provided it be correct) than too concise—for an incomplete statement always embarrasses the person who receives it. The proper preparation of a report requires an officer sufficiently accustomed to reflection not to be easily led into error, and sufficiently calm to exercise judgment and to compare with coolness that which he has observed with that which he has merely glanced at, without allowing himself to be affected either by the dangers he may have incurred, or by the rapidity with which he is compelled to conduct his operations. This rapidity, indeed, is such that, often in the space of a few hours, an officer may have assembled his detachment, executed the reconnoissance, prepared his report, and finished his sketch. For this reason, officers cannot take too much pains to qualify themselves, as soon as possible, for the preparation of such reports, by suitable studies and practice; because, if they become expert in them, they will be capable of rendering good service to armies, and while making themselves useful to their country, will earn distinction and honorable reward. In practising the preparation of such reports, the officer should aim at doing it both *quickly* and *well*—two essential conditions in many circumstances of military life, especially in war; for to do it quickly and badly is worse than doing nothing, which, at least, would not lead the general into error by an inexact account; and to do it well, but slowly, is often to work to no purpose, for in the field all things change so rapidly that exact and true information at the middle of the day becomes faulty and consequently worthless before night. It is enough to say that a mind slow to conceive is not fit for the service of reconnoissances; in the words of Allent:* "In war,

---

* *Essai sur les reconnoissances militaires.*

in those reconnoissances where the time, the general, or the enemy, does not allow more than a *coup d'œil*, all is lost if the officer stops to reflect: the moment of action passes whilst he is deliberating."

In many cases the officer charged with a reconnoissance, instead of reducing his observations to writing, should confine himself to rendering a verbal report; for example, when the operation admits of no delay. It is also very important for officers to exercise themselves in making this species of report, in order to acquire the rare faculty of describing in few words, and yet with clearness, everything of consequence that they have seen or learned.

It is evident that, to make a report, written or oral, in a suitable manner, we should have acquired the habit of putting our thoughts into shape quickly, and of giving them a form which renders them intelligible, and a dress which renders them acceptable to everybody. This habit is, indeed, almost the whole art of writing or speaking well—a more difficult art than is commonly thought, and one which is only acquired by assiduous labor, whatever may be our natural gifts.

6. Historical Examples.—The following examples will serve to demonstrate the importance of exact and circumstantial reconnoissances to the success of military operations.

I. In 1706: "If M. de la Feuillade had been better acquainted with the plain of Piedmont and the foot of the Alps, he would not have wasted two months in running after the Duke of Savoy, after the latter had left Turin with his cavalry: and when he had led that prince to the entrance of the valley of Luzerne, he would not have sent word to the king (Louis XIV.), as he so imprudently did, that he held the enemy in a country from which he could not escape; for he would have known that there are none of the valleys terminating in Piedmont, which do not possess one or more practicable routes of communication with the neighboring towns; and that, consequently, the duke could pass out of the valley of Luzerne by his left or his right, as might please him, and thus get out of the way of M. de la Feuillade, who was on his front." *

II. In the early part of the month of November, 1805, after the capture of Ulm, Marmont, charged with occupying Léoben, followed the course of the river Enns from Steyer to the village of Reifling, and after reaching the latter place was desirous of obtaining information respecting the enemy, who was endeavoring to reach the mountains: "I then sent," he states in his *Mémoires*,† "Captain Testot-Ferry, one of my aides-de-camp, an experienced and distinguished soldier, with two hundred horse of the Eighth Chasseurs, and ordered him to go up the river Salza. When within one league of the grand route, some peasants informed him that an Austrian battalion had just arrived, and had encamped a league beyond. Determining to reconnoitre it before returning, he inspected the shoes of the horses, and selected those which could best march over the ice-covered ground. The rest he left behind

---

* *Mémoires de Feuquière*, chap. liii.   † Vol. ii., 1857, pp. 331, 332.

as a reserve, and set out with 120 horses. Having arrived near the place where he had been informed the camp was situated, he went alone through a wood to observe them without being seen. He there saw the battalion wholly engaged in establishing the camp, in careless security, having placed no guard. He rejoined his detachment, left his trumpeters on the skirts of the woods, and at the instant they sounded the charge, fell upon the camp, throwing down and breaking the muskets. He collected the disarmed battalion and brought it to my head-quarters. This battalion numbered 450 men and 19 officers. This feat is certainly one of the handsomest performances of light troops on record."

III. After the battle of Austerlitz, the French army made a false movement, in consequence of a badly executed reconnoissance. Lannes and the cavalry of the reserve started in pursuit of the vanquished forces by the road to Olmutz; but only the baggage and parks of the enemy had gone by this road, and it was necessary to countermand all the orders to reach the route to Hungary by Gœding, which was the actual line of retreat.

IV. The following example exhibits the importance of boldness in secret reconnoissances. In 1809, Captain (afterward General) Curely was charged with the reconnoissance of the Austrian army, commanded by the Archduke John, in the environs of Raab. At the head of one hundred horse, he left his division behind some ten leagues, hung about the rear of the enemy, and succeeded in secreting himself in a wood about 3,000 yards from the head-quarters of the archduke. A long, dusty plain separated him from the village in which these head-quarters were established. In his ambuscade he waited for night, in the mean time questioning some Austrian marauders arrested by his soldiers, to obtain information, upon which to base his plan. A considerable drove of oxen happening to pass, he seized upon it, and penned it within the woods. At nightfall he set the drove in motion, with his horsemen in the midst of it, leading their horses by the bridle; and, covered by the thick dust raised by this pretended convoy, he approached the village without being in the least disturbed by the enemy, who imagined themselves perfectly secure on the side of the wood from which he was coming. Having thus reached the village, Curely shot down one of the Austrian sentries, and thereupon (the discharge of his pistol being the preconcerted signal), his horsemen mounted and rushed forward, dealing sabre strokes for some minutes in all directions. The surprised enemy were so completely disordered and stupefied that the detachment left the village and rejoined its division without losing a man or a horse. Upon his return, Captain Curely communicated the most precise information respecting the position of the Austrian army, and from this position was also inferred that of the French army of Italy, which was in pursuit of the Archduke John.*

V. At the battle of Busaco (1810), the position of Wellington, although very strong, " could have

* De Brack, *Avant-postes de cavalerie légère*, 1831, p. 200.

been turned by the left; and if the reconnoissances ordered by Masséna had been well executed, the army of the enemy might have been attacked in reverse and thrown upon the Mondego. But these reconnoissances were not made, or were but imperfectly made, and as the ground did not permit Masséna to embrace the whole field of battle, he had not time to change his dispositions in order to afford Ney and Reynier the coöperation which would probably have insured success."* This battle of Busaco, between Masséna and Wellington, belongs to the campaign of Portugal in 1810, and was, as is known, bloody and indecisive.

VI. Frequently an officer or non-commissioned officer may run the risk of reconnoitring alone, and should then resort to ruse. In this connection the following fact is deserving of mention: In 1814, in the vicinity of Vic-de-Bigorre, the French had posted one of their bodies of rear-guards on a hill, the end of which abutted on the high road, the slope being clothed with trees and defended by skirmishers. "Lord Wellington was desirous to know whether a small or a large force thus barred his way, but all who endeavored to ascertain the fact were stopped by the fire of the enemy. At last Captain William Light, distinguished by the variety of his attainments, an artist, musician, mechanist, seaman and soldier, made the trial. He rode forward as if he would force his way through the French skirmishers, but when in the wood dropped his reins and leaned

---

* *Mémoires de Masséna*, par le général Koch, avec un atlas dressé par le commandant Lapie, du corps d'état-major, t. i., p. lii.

back, as if badly wounded; his horse appeared to canter wildly along the front of the enemy's light troops, and they, thinking him mortally hurt, ceased their fire and took no further notice. He thus passed unobserved through the wood to the other side of the hill, where there were no skirmishers, and ascending to the open summit above, put spurs to his horse, and galloped along the French main line, counting their regiments as he passed. His sudden appearance, his blue undress, his daring confidence, and his speed, made the French doubt if he was an enemy, and a few shots only were discharged, while he, dashing down the opposite declivity, broke from the rear through the very line of skirmishers whose fire he had first essayed in front. Reaching the spot where Lord Wellington stood, he told him there were but five battalions on the hill."*

7. Reconnoissances in Africa.†—In Africa, it is almost impossible to get a view of the enemy; the Arab camp is everywhere and nowhere at the same time. It would, therefore, be dangerous to make reconnoissances in force in that region; it is better to rely exclusively upon Arab *limiers*, and to meet the enemy's cunning by cunning.

The name *limiers* (*bloodhounds*, i. e., *spies*) is applied to some native horsemen, who are under the exclusive direction of the commandant of a column, and

---

* Napier, *History of the Peninsular War*, book xxiv., chap. iv.

† This article is extracted from the pamphlet entitled *De la guerre en Afrique*, by General Yusuf.

can report directly to him at all times. They disguise themselves by putting on the bornouse worn by the inhabitants of the country. They act by day or by night, on foot or on horseback, according to circumstances; and four or five are sufficient. They take various directions, and when they have important information to give and are not able to return in person, they communicate it by preconcerted signals; for example, by fires combined in a particular manner, the light of which they conceal with their bornouses and again uncover it, alternately, so as to produce intermittent lights, the longer or shorter duration of which has a predetermined signification.

In critical moments, these spahis may feign to desert; but this desertion ought to appear to be real in the eyes of the troops, and especially in the eyes of the Arab allies, and the general alone should know that it is but feigned. By this means, in the campaign in Morocco (1844), Marshal Bugeaud knew all that occurred in the army of the enemy, and even the conversations that took place in the imperial tent.

These limiers convey their messages with certainty by scattering themselves along the road between the enemy and the body from which they have been sent. This method is especially applicable to night attacks.

If it becomes necessary to take some prisoners, they get up a mock skirmish with the rear-guard of their own column. At the sound of the firing, some veritable enemies make their appearance, and after some minutes of pretended skirmishing, in which the skirmishers of the column participate to only a small extent, the limiers seize upon several of the real combatants, from whom the desired information is afterward obtained.

These limiers are also employed to discover the secret provision pits of the Arabs, the guards of which are always invisible to Europeans. Several limiers assemble near the supposed position of the pits, and warmly discuss a project of attacking the French. Their words arousing the patriotism of the guardian of the pit, he soon comes out of his hole to join with those whom he supposes to be friends. They immediately seize upon him, and compel him to reveal the location of the pits. This ruse is not to be neglected, as an expeditionary column may subsist anywhere if it finds these pits; in fact, the corn which they contain, serves, in case of need, both for the sustenance of the men and of the horses.

8. Maps.—Maps are of indispensable utility to the officers, since, without them, they can neither make nor study war. There are two kinds, general or geographical maps, and special or topographical maps: the first serve for the ensemble of operations, the second for the details of the contest.

The great development of public works and the progress of industry at the present day, conspire to disturb the accuracy of maps; for the positions of highways and manufactories are now rapidly changed or modified. We should, therefore, even when the map is of recent date, and executed by an author of distinction, always verify it before trusting to it.

This verification presents no difficulty when we are acquainted with the country represented. We carefully examine and compare the cities, towns, villages, rivers, brooks, mountain-chains, forests, woods, roads: thus we observe whether the inhabited places are properly located on the water courses; whether the rivers are shown to rise in the mountains and to follow the valleys; whether the roads pass through certain towns or villages. If the portions compared are found exact, we may infer that the whole map is worthy of confidence.

If we are acquainted with but one portion of the country, we verify this portion, and if we find it correct, we infer the probable accuracy of the whole map.

Finally, if we know nothing whatever of the country, we survey a portion of it, and if our survey agrees with the map, the latter is considered to be reliable.

Besides this general verification of the map, we must rectify the topographical maps, especially in the environs of inhabited places, by questioning persons familiar with the recent state of the country, or else, by making a survey of some particular locality, which we first draw upon a sheet of tracing paper, and then transfer to the map itself. The importance of thus verifying the maps is illustrated by the case of the Allies who, during the campaign in the interior of France in 1814, were often led into error with respect to the roads by the maps of Cassini, which they used without testing them. The necessity of such verification is most especially felt in the case of the maps of the Algerian districts, which are, for the most part, unfinished, and are far from being satisfactory.

Of the charts which are found on sale, we should prefer those which are executed in the countries they represent, foreign maps being usually defective. We may add, however, that we may confide in the maps prepared since 1815 by the staffs of several European armies, even for foreign countries, but especially in those which emanate from the war office of the French government.

The *road maps*, that is, those on which the distances from point to point are marked, are especially useful to military men, as they save the trouble of using the dividers and scale: but unfortunately, since the introduction of railways, scarcely any road maps are made, and perhaps the only one of the kind is the station map (*carte d'étapes*). The public, therefore, no longer possesses the means of knowing the distances from point to point, except as calculated by the railroad lines and from tables of distances. Military men should not be satisfied with this, for railroads do not always follow the shortest route between two points, and, moreover, in war they may be broken up; and in no case will they suffice for operations of detail.

9. Guides.—The best topographical maps, even those which omit nothing, would not always suffice to guide the columns or detachments of an army through the labyrinth of roads and paths of an enemy's country, without the aid of men specially employed to direct them to the desired place by the most convenient route. These persons are called *guides*.

In the employment of guides, we have the additional advantage over the exclusive use of maps, of being able to gain information from them respecting the disposition of the inhabitants, the resources of the country, and the preparations of the enemy. In case of need, when we are assured of their fidelity, they may also serve as emissaries to collect on their way secret information, without exciting suspicion.

For these reasons, an army cannot dispense with men who are acquainted with the country in which it is to fight. History indeed furnishes numerous instances of detachments beaten or destroyed in consequence of not having taken guides, or of having employed bad ones, or of having neglected to watch over them.

Guides should be chosen from the class of persons best acquainted with every irregularity of the ground and its most concealed paths; such as the rural police-guards, country letter-carriers, forest-keepers and game-keepers, good huntsmen, poachers, shepherds, wood-cutters, smugglers, partisans, certain outlaws, the cicerones who in times of peace conduct travelers in their search for natural curiosities, the different categories of migratory laborers, emigrants, peddlers. All these are poor, easy to gain over, and suitable for guides. In some cases, especially when we have need of information requiring intelligence, we may take these guides from a higher class of the population, but always from among those who thoroughly understand the country, as, for example, among the employés of the excise, tax gatherers, land surveyors, constructors of bridges and roads, giving a preference to those who speak our own language.

In order to obtain guides, when they have not been procured in advance, we apply to the mayor or other prominent functionary of the locality to name them. If the individuals designated refuse from patriotic motives to act as guides, we compel them to do so by force. If we perceive that their refusal results from the fear of compromising themselves in the eyes of their fellow-citizens, we make a show of maltreating them, that they may appear to yield only to force, and afterward reward them liberally. In case the local authorities are reluctant to name suitable persons for guides, when there must always be some who are capable of acting in that capacity, we seize these functionaries themselves and compel them to march with the columns as guides. This course was often adopted by the French in the Peninsular war.

History, moreover, abounds in examples of the necessity of employing violence in order to find guides. Thus the king of Prussia, Frederic the Great, in his "Military Instruction," relates that, "in the year 1760, while crossing Lusatia to march into Silesia, we had need of guides. Some were found in the Vandal villages, but when brought in they pretended not to understand the German language, which embarrassed us greatly. We bethought ourselves of administering some blows, and they forthwith spoke German like parrots."

Before trusting a guide, we must, by questioning him, assure ourselves of his intelligence. With this object we should interrogate them separately, without formality, as if in ordinary conversation. This is an art of itself, for the peasants, especially such as usually serve as guides, are much more astute than they appear to be. We should compare their answers with each other, and with the topographical maps. If there seems to be a sufficient degree of accordance, we may conclude that they do in fact possess the knowledge to which they pretend. To facilitate this comparison, and to avoid errors, we should be careful, when speaking with the guides, to pronounce the names of towns and provinces in the same manner as the inhabitants of the country.

We should also endeavor to discover the failings or vices of a guide; for if he be a drunkard, he will lead us astray; if open to bribery, he will sell us; if a coward, he will lose his head at the first whistle of the enemy's bullets.* A knowledge of his character, moreover, enables us to draw some inferences respecting the march he is leading us; for, suppose he is naturally timid, if he appears unwontedly bold, you may be sure the road he is causing you to follow is not so fine as he represents; if he is sad and fearful, the road adopted is more favorable than he pretends.†

---

* This may happen to him though he be not altogether a coward, for he can hardly be wholly indifferent when bringing death to his own friends, and when he is liable to be struck down by a friendly ball.

† Santa-Cruz, *Reflexions militaires et politiques*, translation of Vergy, v. iii., p. 263.

The degree of confidence to be reposed in a guide also deserves some consideration. If he belongs to the nation with which you are at war, you should fear his patriotism, for he may seek to serve his country by leading you astray. If he professes a different religious faith from your own, put yourself upon your guard against his fanaticism, for he may believe he is serving God by betraying you. Therefore choose your guides as much as possible from people of your own country; or, when these cannot be found, from men who have some direct interest in your success and whose fidelity you have put to the proof.

Even when the guides are deserving of confidence, some precautions are to be observed. Take as hostages their wives and children; seize upon their property; threaten them with severe penalties if they betray you, such as the burning of their houses, or the death of their hostages and themselves: promise them abundant reward for their fidelity, and keep your promises scrupulously.

Treat them, moreover, with kindness; pay them liberally; put them on horseback if it is necessary for the rapidity of your march; though, if you distrust them, you may let them ride bareback. As you advance into the country discharge them, for they are mostly well acquainted only with the surroundings of their own villages. It will be proper, however, to detain, and even to imprison those who, from your questions, may have been able to guess your designs, which they might communicate to the enemy.

When you interrogate guides respecting the character of the roads, never rely entirely upon the representations of a single guide, not only because he may intend to deceive you, but because persons unused to military operations make no distinction between roads suitable for artillery and those suitable for cavalry or infantry. The following fact, related by Frederic, fully confirms this observation: "In 1745," he says, "after the battle of Sorr, when the Prussian army wished to retire into Silesia, I had some persons brought from Trautenau and Schazlar, to question them as to the roads over which I desired to take the columns. They told me confidently that these roads were admirable, and that they passed over them with their carriages with the greatest ease, and that many wagoners did the same. A few days after, the army made this march. I was obliged to make my arrangements for retreat in these parts. Our rear-guard was briskly attacked, but, by the precautions I took, we lost nothing. These roads, in a military point of view, were very bad; but those from whom I had obtained information respecting them understood nothing about them, and what they told me was in good faith, and with no intention of deceiving me. We should, therefore, not trust to the report of ignorant persons, but, with the map in hand, should consult them upon every configuration of the ground, and see whether we cannot sketch something additional upon the paper, which will convey a more exact notion of the road than the map itself."

In general, at least two guides are to be attached

to each column or detachment; one is to march with the advance-guard, the other to remain near the commanding officer. These two guides should not be acquainted with each other, but should be used so as to make one act as a check upon the other. It is well, besides, to have two guides, for the purpose of supplying the place of one who may be killed or severely wounded. If we have more than two, one of them is often placed with the rear-guard.

A detachment should always take a guide, even when it is pursuing a frequented road, because a sudden attack may compel it to resort to the cross roads, where, without this precaution, it might go astray.

The guide placed with the advance-guard, who, in fact, conducts the column, may be allowed to march unrestrained, if we are sure of him; nevertheless, it is always prudent to place him between two non-commissioned officers or soldiers, who are instructed to fire upon him at the least attempt at escape—a fate of which he is to be duly warned. In woody and mountainous countries, especially in night marches, even this precaution is not sufficient, for the peasants are very dexterous in slipping away and disappearing behind irregularities of the ground, and especially at the approach of danger. For this reason it is well to search them and take away their knives or any other cutting instruments, then to tie them with a rope about their middle, and even to bind their hands behind them; it will then be impossible for them to escape except by cutting the rope with their teeth— an operation which would probably be discovered in time to prevent its success. The column will thus be insured against the contingency of being left without a guide upon unknown roads.

When the guide is thus tied, an occasional pull on the rope will serve to keep him awake on his horse—for if he should fall asleep, the conducting of the column would be abandoned to the instinct of the horse. This expedient is constantly resorted to in night marches of the French columns in Algeria.

10. Deserters.—Deserters from the enemy are arrested and disarmed at the outposts. They are interrogated relative to the situation of their posts by the commandant of the grand guards, who sends them to the general of the brigade. The latter questions them, and then orders them to the head-quarters of the division, where they are subjected to a systematic examination by the chief of the staff. These are the rules laid down for them in the regulations respecting field service.

Deserters are not to be trusted: they should not be allowed to communicate with any but the proper officers, and should be promptly escorted out of the army, for they are sometimes spies in disguise.

Deserters are always very apt to give information respecting the enemy which is calculated to insure them a welcome, for this purpose exaggerating the critical situation of the army they have just left. Therefore we should not too readily put faith in the answers of these unfortunates, but should skilfully interrogate several of them separately, and compare their answers A deserter should be asked the cause of his desertion, how he effected his escape through the chain of outposts of the enemy, the number and force of his regiment, whether his regiment contains many recruits, where it is encamped, how duty is performed in it, what is the character of its superior officers, whether the camp is abundantly supplied, the proportion of sick, the various rumors that are current in it, etc. The questions are to be varied according to the character of the army to which he belongs, and according as he has left an encamped troop, or one upon a march. He is also to be questioned as to the points upon which he has seen intrenchments being erected, roads repaired, magazines established, provisions supplied, boats collected, convoys organized, arms distributed, reënforcements arriving, ambulances preparing, etc.

11. Inhabitants.—By preference we interrogate the mayor, or chief magistrate, the postmaster, the curate, the schoolmaster, the distinguished or most influential man, superintendents of work-shops or factories, the superintendent of the railway dépôt, men who have served as guides for the enemy, the directors and agents of the mails, the superiors of religious societies, tavern-keepers, messengers, etc.

The questions put to them, according to their intelligence, will be: Where is the enemy? In what direction is he marching? What is his force? What is the state of his discipline? Of what arms do the troops consist? Do the men appear fatigued, and are the horses lean? What language do the soldiers speak? Do they belong to the line, or are they of the militia? How does the enemy guard himself? Does he often make reconnoissances, and how does he conduct these operations? What route leads to the enemy? Has it any defiles, and, if so, can they be turned? How does the enemy behave toward his guides? Do the officers appear restless and dejected? What is the population of this or that village, its distance, and its resources? Is the road leading to it broad, paved, or macadamized? By what fords or bridges may the neighboring water courses be passed? etc.

The inhabitants should be separately questioned, and, as much as possible, in their own language; and this again illustrates the importance of a knowledge of foreign languages to officers of light troops, who are specially charged with making reconnoissances.

12. Travellers.—Travellers, whether on foot, on horseback, or in carriages, who come from the direction of the enemy, will probably have nothing important to communicate, as the enemy would not have allowed them to pass if he had in preparation any operation which could be jeopardized by their indiscretion. It will, therefore, be sufficient to demand, as La Roche-Aymon suggests,* their names and passports; whence they come, and their destination; whether they have met troops marching; their kind and number, or, rather, the time it required to pass the length of the column; the effective force of the

* *Des troupes légères*, p. 531.

masses of troops occupying towns through which they have passed or sojourned; the condition of these troops, the proportion of their sick and of their recruits; what villages are occupied by the enemy; whether his outposts are close together and well supported; what is the condition of the roads and bridges, and which of them is the enemy repairing; or what points is he fortifying; whether there is any scarcity of provision, of forage, or of ready money; whether the country people are suffering, and whether their cattle are preserved or have been seized by the enemy; what are the public rumors; what does the last newspaper they have read contain?

These interrogatories are to be put with the greater calmness and attention, as they often may serve to discover spies who are passing themselves off as travellers. In order to succeed in their detection, we try to bring about manifest contradictions in their answers, and then, by severity and menace, provoke confessions which usually reveal a part of the intentions of the enemy.

We should add the remark, in relation to inhabitants and travellers, that they are not military persons, and consequently do not describe the country in the way a soldier would do. This circumstance must not be lost sight of in questioning them, and their testimony must be rectified by discussing with them the positions of places and the directions of the roads laid down on the maps.

13. Prisoners.—The questions to be put to prisoners are about the same as those put to deserters.

Some authors have expressed the opinion that we should rely upon their testimony even less than upon that of deserters; but Marshal Marmont is of a different opinion: "The answers of prisoners," says he, "are almost always frank and sincere. We learn more from them than from the most faithful spies. The latter often confound the names of corps and of generals, and very imperfectly estimate the force of the troops upon which they report. . . . . It is surprising to see with what candor, simplicity, and *truth* a prisoner will reply to questions, without suspecting their bearing, without imagining that he is faithless to the cause he has zealously served, and which he is far from wishing to betray." *

There is no stronger proof of the utility of the information gained from prisoners than the pains taken to capture soldiers and stragglers of the enemy, not only in the daily reconnoissances, but even by special coups-de-main, of which the following is an example: On the 20th of February, 1814, in his defensive campaign in the south of France against the English army under Wellington, Marshal Soult, " wishing to make some prisoners in order to obtain positive information respecting the force and positions of the enemy, ordered a night attack upon the troops who were before Sauveterre (near Orthez). Two or three hours after sunset, when the enemy had abandoned themselves to repose, and the soldiers, stretched out before good fires, had become oblivious of fatigue and danger, a French detachment, commanded by an

* *Esprit des institutions militaires*, pp. 161, 277.

officer who combined prudence with audacity, crept with stealthy steps into the bivouac without being perceived. At a given signal he seized upon the allies; an outcry was raised; night increased the danger; the enemy rushed to arms, fired at random and at each other. The French handful of brave fellows, in accordance with their orders, recrossed the Gave, and returned to Sauveterre without a man wounded, bringing with them some fifty prisoners, yet half asleep, and quite ashamed at finding themselves taken in such a manner. It may be imagined that this little scene afforded no small amount of amusement to the French soldiers." *

14. Spies.—One of the most ready means of procuring detailed information consists in the employment of spies. We may define a spy as a person sent out by a military chief to examine the movements of the enemy, to discover his plans, and to report them.

There are sometimes to be found persons who, from devotion to their prince or their country, will undertake to act temporarily as spies.† "The debt which the State incurs by deeds of this kind cannot be paid by money, and the government which desires to be worthy of such subjects should proportion the reward rather to their devotion than to the service rendered.‡" These spies are rare.

---

* Pellot, *Mémoire sur la campagne des Pyrénées*, p. 104.

† Thus an officer disguised as a peasant may gain entrance to a place to discover the means of surprising it; *e. g.*, M. de Gouru (an officer of the regiment of Count Saxe), at Prague, in 1741, and Ney at Manheim, 1798.

‡ *Manuel des états-majors*, par le général Thiebault, p. 96.

As to the spies who follow this trade for money, they must be regarded as miserable beings, who, for the most part, are the slaves of passions which require gold for their gratification. These are the more numerous class. Notwithstanding their baseness, we are obliged to employ them, because they are often the only means of obtaining secret information indispensable to success. All classes furnish such spies. Even at the topmost round of the social ladder they are found, of the most devoted kind, provided they are liberally paid, according to their condition; men and women, priests and laymen, are equally open to the enticements of this shameful traffic. Here are two examples:

1st. Prince Eugene of Savoy, one of the most formidable adversaries of France during the reign of Louis XIV., for a long time had the postmaster of Versailles in his service as a spy, paying him a fat pension. This miscreant opened the dispatches addressed to the generals, and sent copies of them to the head of the imperial armies, who usually received them sooner than the chiefs of the French armies.

2d. Marshal Luxembourg had corrupted one of the secretaries of the English king, William III., who informed him of the movements of his enemies. This was discovered by the English, and the traitor was made to write to the French general that the Allies would on the next day go upon a grand foraging expedition.* Lulled into tranquillity by this announcement, which was also confirmed by numerous reports,

* *Mémoires des Marquis de La Fare*, 1734, p. 222

Luxembourg remained in his camp at Steenkirk. At break of day, the whole army of the Allies fell upon his sleeping troops; but the courage and discipline of the soldiers, the coolness and the skilful manœuvres of Luxembourg, changed this surprise into a complete victory (1692).*

The service of espionnage requires great celerity, for the information thereby obtained gets old quickly. It requires persons of adroitness and boldness, who are accustomed to find their way through any intricacies of the country, and whose faculties are stimulated by the love of gain. In every country such will be found among smugglers, peddlers, poachers, and the various traders who visit the cantonments. In the large towns, they may also be obtained among keepers of inns and restaurants, and all those who have frequent and numerous relations with the public.† Non-commissioned officers, and sometimes intelligent soldiers, are instructed to talk with these individuals, discover those who would consent to act as spies, and bring them to the chief of the staff. When the army is distributed in cantonments, these non-commissioned officers or soldiers may engage the inhabitants who lodge them to play the part of spies, which they can generally do without difficulty, as

---

* The French soldiers then wore the cravat. On the occasion of this surprise they tied their cravats in haste, and the cravat thus knotted became the fashion, under the name of *cravate à la Steinkerque*.

† From the time of his arrival in Spain (1710) and during the stay of the Austrians in Madrid, Vendôme employed as a spy in that capital, a keeper of a billiard saloon, a Frenchman who had established himself in the Peninsula, and spoke several languages.

there will almost always exist some secret means of communication between the neighboring localities of a territory occupied by the enemy. At outposts, when two armies remain for a long time face to face, the soldiers of the two sides sometimes get together to chat and drink. In these moments of familiarity, a sly overture may sometimes be made to one of the soldiers of the enemy, to try his disposition to serve as a spy, which, if favorably received, can afterward be followed up by a seductive offer.

When all these means fail in procuring spies, the usages of war authorize a last resort—cruel indeed, but justified by the necessity of obtaining intelligence of the enemy. It is to select a rich proprietor, the father of a family, to compel him to go over to the enemy under the pretext of escaping from violence, and then to require him to report all that he knows, under penalty of seeing his wife and his children imprisoned or put to death, and his property burned, should he fail to perform the part thus forced upon him. An intelligent man, acquainted with the language of the country, is often associated with him, who passes for his servant, accompanies him everywhere, and sometimes himself reports the results of the espionnage. The proprietor is answerable for this man, and is threatened with the same consequences in case he is lost, as would follow his own negligence in the performance of his mission. This plan, which should be resorted to only in the last extremity, was suggested by Frederic the Great.

When we are fighting in our own country, we

should expect almost all the inhabitants to serve as spies upon the enemy, and to hold it to be honorable to point out the way of attacking him, in defiance of the dangers to which this patriotic conduct may expose him. It is then useful to cause a soldier to assume the garb of a citizen, as he may then more completely observe whatever relates to the movements of the enemy without exciting suspicion.

If we are carrying on war in a country which is divided by two political parties, by giving our aid to one of these parties, we can know everything done by the enemy, since the party whose cause we espouse will espy the other, as occurred with the French army in the campaign of 1823 in Spain. If, on the contrary, we are fighting in the midst of an uprising people, who are undertaking a national resistance, it becomes exceedingly difficult to procure intelligence, for all espionnage fails, as the French experienced in 1812 in Russia, and in 1813 in Germany.*

We satisfy ourselves of the fidelity of spies, either by comparing the information, with respect to the same object, as furnished independently by several, or by determining whether the intelligence they bring really secures to us some great advantage over the enemy, since, in this case, it is evident that they are not betraying you to serve him; † or else by making

---

* We may then try the expedient of dressing up a detachment of our soldiers in the uniform of the enemy, selecting for this purpose those who speak the language of the country. The peasants may thus be imposed upon and led to relate what they know. But this plan is not always successful.

† *Réflexions militaires et politiques*, par Santa-Cruz, traduit par Vergy, t. ii., p. 372.

one spy act as a spy upon another. As soon as we begin to suspect a spy, we warn him that the report he has made will be verified, that he will be put under guard until this verification is completed, and that his life is staked upon his veracity.*

Notwithstanding all these precautions, spies are frequently *double*, that is, they serve both parties at the same time. If we suspect this state of things, the best course is to endeavor to gain them over by rich presents and more distinguished treatment, and then to get rid of them altogether, if their reports do not offer anything of special interest. We may also adroitly let fall some words in their presence, conveying the idea of some false movement to be executed, in order that they may lead the opposing general into error by reporting it as a real movement, which they have had the skill to discover. The celebrated Russian general Suwarrow, well known for his energy and his singularities, perceiving one day, in Poland, that there was a spy among the men of his suite, gave orders that the army should hold itself in readiness to march at the first crowing of the cock. The spy notified the enemy that they would be attacked about midnight; but at eight o'clock in the evening, Suwarrow went through his camp imitating the crowing of a cock; his troops were immediately put in motion, and the enemy, surprised by this early attack, were beaten. I cite this whimsical feat, to show the kind of ruses to which one may have recourse, in case of necessity, to deceive double spies.

* *Manuel des états-majors*, par Thiébault, p. 99.

Spies should not reside in a camp, nor communicate with the soldiers. They should not be acquainted with each other; and that they may not be compromised, they should be known under an assumed name —*nom de guerre.*

As spies adopt all sorts of disguises to obtain admission into a camp, we should watch all persons who present themselves with that object, such as beggars, traders, itinerant musicians, and even the inhabitants who are attracted by simple curiosity. Courtezans often play the part of spies; and soldiers should avoid going far to find them, for they not unfrequently pay for a moment of forgetfulness with their lives. They should never forget the case of the Duke de Guise, who, in 1647, lost Naples for a rendezvous with a woman who sold him to the Spaniards. Ecclesiastics and monks, especially in the countries of Southern Europe, also sometimes act as spies, and perform the part in a superior style, which renders them very dangerous, of which the French troops had cruel experience in Spain and in Italy. The best course in relation to them is to attach them to us as much as possible, as they may furnish useful intelligence, but yet always to mistrust them. If our army is fighting in a country where the prevailing religion is different from our own, we shall have on our side those of the inhabitants who profess our religion, and consequently a large number of spies will be at our disposal. This was Napoleon's experience in 1806 and 1807 upon the Prussian territory, where, according to La Roche-Aymon, the French army had no partisans more zealous than the Catholic priests of Rhenish Prussia.

Among other individuals attached to an army, a watch should be kept upon sutlers, who hear the conversations of the non-commissioned officers and soldiers, and also upon quartermasters' and commissaries' clerks, who must approximately know the condition and effective force of the several corps. Both often serve as spies for the enemy.

The information received from spies, as, indeed, almost every matter in war, should be kept a profound secret, and especially when in presence of the enemy; for the most trifling undertaking usually becomes impossible from the moment it is noised abroad. Therefore, do not allow it to be known that you are frequently and accurately informed of the doings of your adversary, as he will then set about discovering the sources of your information, and will adopt measures to render it useless. The king of Castile, Alphonso X., speaking one day with the Count d'Artois, heedlessly told him that he was perfectly acquainted with every secret negotiation entered upon by France. This imprudent speech put the French upon the alert, and led them to discover that the spy who gave Alphonso his information was a valet-de-chambre of the king of France.

To conclude this article, we will add that spies, as soon as they are arrested, should be thoroughly searched, and their every movement carefully watched, for they frequently endeavor to destroy the dispatches they carry. Sometimes these dispatches are concealed in some part of their clothing. Two examples will illustrate this: In 1704, a spy charged by the Elector of Bavaria with carrying a letter from Marshal Marsin to a Hungarian chief, rolled it and compressed it so completely that he succeeded in enclosing it in a button of his coat, though his dexterity did not save him from being discovered and hung.* In the campaign of 1777, during the American war of Independence, an English spy, being discovered, swallowed a silver ball. The Americans got it from him by administering an emetic. It proved to be hollow, and contained a message consisting of six lines from a general.†

15. Indications.—In addition to the various auxiliary and complementary methods of obtaining information upon a reconnoissance, which we have above considered, the observation of *indications* is of great importance. We understand by this expression the notation of any sign, mark, or signal whatever, visible or audible, which reveals in any degree the presence, the force, or the plans of the enemy.

The art of divining the intention of the enemy from slight indications is one which rarely misleads, and is one of the most precious attributes of military genius. In the familiar spirit which inspired Socrates, in the white hind which followed and counselled Sertorius, in the god Neptune from whom Scipio-Africanus the younger pretended to receive revelations, we see figured the art of using indications. To become

---

* Mauvillon, *Vie de Prince Eugène de Savoie*, 1740, t. ii., p. 189.
† Sparks' Writings of Washington.

skilful in this art, we should study the character, the customs,* and the interests of the nation, the general, and the troops with whom we are contending; we must acquire habits of observation and comparison, so as to distinguish the least sign of change in the camp† or in the movements of the enemy. This art of interpreting indications belongs to the moral part of war, and is mostly based upon a knowledge of the human heart. Marshal Villars was so well skilled in it that the Duke of Savoy remarked of him, "This Duke of Villars is a wizard; he divines everything I am about to do."

The observation of indications may be useful to non-commissioned officers as well as to their chiefs. The principal indications may be enumerated as follows:

If the enemy is distributing shoes in the cantonments, and if the soldiers are cleaning their arms, it is an indication of movement.—If numerous supplies are arriving, or if new uniforms are seen, new troops are about to be added to the old ones to make an attack. —If storehouses of provisions are established at certain points, it indicates that troops are to assemble

---

* "I have been assured that the entire success of the passage of the Po by Prince Eugene of Savoy, in 1706, depended upon a *game of cards* at which a certain general regularly played at a particular hour, and from which it was not possible to divert him." (*Essai sur les qualités d'un général*, in 4to., Milan, 1758, p. 67.)

† Before the battle of the Metaurus (B. C. 208) Hasdrubal, the brother of Hannibal, heard the command sounded *once* in the camp of the prætor and *twice* in that of the consul, and from that time had no doubt that the two Roman consuls were combined against him. (Livy, xxvii. 47.)

there.—A collection of boats brought from a distance to one point of the same bank of a river, denotes an attempt at its passage; if they are burned, an unobstructed retreat is in contemplation.—If important bridges are destroyed, the retreat will be long.—If they are collecting ladders in a bivouac, there will be an assault upon some fortified place.—When the enemy masks his movements upon the field of battle and masses his squadrons, he is preparing a formidable attack; if he deploys his troops, he is about to take a position.—If he sends his artillery, ambulances, and parks to the rear, it is an indication either of retreat or a change of front.—If the bivouac fires appear to be more numerous but smaller, or if they are, from their position, too visible, successively lighted and quickly extinguished, it denotes feebleness or retreat.—When the enemy attacks at the break of day, his movement will be general; if he attacks in the evening, his movement will be partial, and probably for no other purpose than to reconnoitre, to take position, or to gain time to cover a retreat.—Foot-prints of men and horses, tracks of wheels, observed in respect to their direction, their greater or less depth, and their number, furnish information in relation to the direction, force, and composition of a column.—The dust raised by a column gives similar indications; it forms a dense and slightly elevated cloud in the case of infantry, less dense and more elevated in that of cavalry, very dense in that of the parks and equipages; the dust of foragers is lighter and more extended than that of squadrons.—The sound of marching reveals a passing column in the vicinity.—If the glitter of the arms of a body discovered in the distance is very bright, the troops are probably facing you; if otherwise, their backs are toward you.—In an insurgent country, a timid or an insolent bearing of the population indicates that the adversary is remote and feeble, or near and strong.—By the number of bivouac fires we may calculate approximately the force of the enemy; for to each fire there are reckoned 10 Frenchmen, 4 Russians, 5 Dutchmen, 6 Englishmen, or 6 Germans. —The particular enemy that is advancing is recognized by the shape of the masses, the straightness of the lines, the form and size of the head-gear,* the color of the pantaloons and of the shoulder-straps and belts; also by the color of the coats or cloaks, which varies with the different European nations, being green in Russia, red in England, white in Austria, sky blue in Bavaria, deep blue in Prussia, Spain, Wurtemberg, and the smaller states of Germany.

In the observation of indications, we must endeavor to distinguish those which are only apparent, and which are sometimes employed by the enemy to deceive; such, for example, as running fires (*feux volants*) in bivouacs.

* Prussia and Russia have adopted a leather helmet; in other nations, the shako, the straw hat, the cap, and the chachia are found.

CHAPTER FOURTH.

PASSAGE OF RIVERS.

WATER courses are among the most frequent and most formidable obstacles to the prosecution of war; and it is therefore of the first importance to know how to overcome them. They are crossed in various ways, according to their nature and to the means at our disposal: sometimes by bridges, which always require both material and labor; sometimes in the most primitive and simple manner, that is, by passing through the water, either wading or swimming; sometimes by waiting until the cold of winter has congealed the liquid element and converted it into a firm highway.

We are here concerned chiefly with the consideration of expeditious methods of crossing rivers; in short, with *improvised* passages: but these especially require that we carefully examine the peculiarities of the water course, and for this purpose, as in all military matters, a preliminary operation is necessary.

1. Reconnoissance of a River.—The reconnoissance of a river should determine the following particulars:

1st. Its course from its source to its mouth; the windings of this course and the most decided bends; its islands, and whether these are bare or covered with plantations; the nature of its banks; the existence of any tow-path, and of roads terminating upon it; the direction of the current; dams, mills, sluices; the means of changing the channel; the nature of the bed; its periodical or sudden risings; the frequency of its freezing, and the usual strength of the ice.

2d. Its tributaries and their military importance; the distance to which the ocean tide ascends; the point at which it begins to be navigable; the kind and the number of boats existing upon its waters.

3d. Its depth and breadth; the velocity of the current; the probable time required to cross it—elements which we should determine for ourselves, and not from hearsay.

4th. The fortified places or posts which it washes; the use that may be made of it in defensive or offensive operations.

5th. All the points of crossing; either points suitable for an improvised bridge, or where fords are practicable; whether bridges are already in existence, and rest upon stone or wooden piers; swivel, draw or flying bridges (ferry or trail); giving for each its length and breadth, its degree of strength, and the mode of defending or of destroying it.

These various points are to be brought together and explained with the utmost exactness. For we must be prepared to avail ourselves of every natural or artificial advantage, if we wish to obstruct the passage of the river, and to avoid all kinds of obstacles if we wish to cross it in force.

2. Discovery, Destruction, and Repair of Fords.— A *ford* is any part of the river where the water is so low that we can cross without boats and without swimming.

The depth of a ford should not exceed three feet for infantry, nor four feet for cavalry and for vehicles whose load may be wet without injury; but for those loaded with materials that should be kept dry, the depth should not exceed two feet.

As the existence of a ford renders all other less expeditious means of crossing a river wholly unnecessary, it is important to make a careful search for them. They are to be discovered as follows:

If we see a path or road starting from each of the opposite banks, we may almost always infer the existence of a ford; but a road on one side only, often indicates merely a point to which horses are brought to water.

If, at the time of low water, the river flows rapidly between two banks of sand, there is a probability of the existence of a ford from one of these banks to the other, although this ford may not have been used, and may not be known to the inhabitants.* Fords of this kind are produced by the swollen waters at the end of winter, and are not entirely safe.

Rivers of moderate breadth are frequently ford-

---

* It is not prudent to rely upon the statements of the peasants respecting the number or nature of fords.

able below mill sites, or near their mouths or confluence with another river; for in these cases the meeting of different currents produces a loss of velocity, and hence a deposit of earthy matter, forming a bank of sufficient height to constitute a ford.

A ford is reconnoitred by an officer in a boat, rowed from bank to bank. He holds a sounding lead at the end of a rope about a yard in length (for example) from a float, and wherever the lead touches the bottom, a stake is planted; a continuous line of stakes indicating the course of the ford.

A ford may be easily traced also by a body of lancers trying the bottom with their lances; or, indeed, by a number of swimmers, wading as long as they find a foothold, and swimming over the deeper parts.

In general, a river presents fewer fordable places in the winding portions of its course, than in the straight ones, except in the case of double bends. For, as the following figure shows, the current which

FORD IN A DOUBLE BEND.

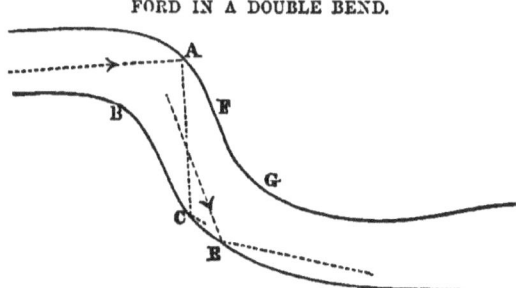

strikes at A carries off the earth from that point and throws it toward the bank BC, near which, therefore, the depth is soon diminished; in like manner the current, skirting at E, wears away the bank and increases the quantity of water on that side, at the expense of the portion near FG; thus the simultaneous elevation of the corresponding parts BC and FG may form a ford.

Sometimes rivers, which are not fordable in a direction at right angles to their banks, present a ford in an oblique direction, not suspected at first. These oblique fords possess the advantage that the current frequently aids the soldier in reaching the opposite shore.

A good ford satisfies six principal conditions:

1st. *The bank of the river from which we set out should be higher than that we wish to reach*, in order that we may manœuvre without being discovered by the enemy, and may also command his position with our batteries.

2d. *Wide fords are preferable*, because it is important to the assailant to present a strong front to the enemy.

3d. *The water should not be rapid*, for strong currents fatigue the soldier, and sometimes carry him away.

4th. *The bottom of the ford should be even and firm*, for loose soil fatigues and mires the foot soldier, while one scattered with stones wounds his feet. A rocky bottom, moreover, is too slippery. Hence a gravel bottom is the best.

5th. *The bank on the side next the enemy should have a gentle slope;* for, if it were abrupt and steep, the enemy might with great ease prevent the soldier from climbing the ascent, or from making an effective use of his weapons.

6th. *A ford which the enemy could destroy by opening sluices in his possession, would be a bad one; and the same may be said of one which could be washed away by a heavy rain or a sudden thaw.* In such cases, the enemy, or chance, might interrupt the passage at a moment when but a small number of troops, insufficient to withstand the enemy, had reached the opposite shore.

Every ford, the utility of which has been established, should be guarded and protected with as much care as a bridge; and, in case of need, by field fortifications. On the other hand, every ford which may probably be of use to the enemy should be destroyed or in some way obstructed.

From the preceding enumeration of the various conditions which a good ford must fulfil, we readily infer the mode of obstructing or destroying it.

A ford may be obstructed by throwing into it trees with all their branches, and with their tops directed toward the opposite shore, turning them obliquely to the course of the stream when the current is rapid. It would appear to be expedient, when possible, to bind these trees together, either with iron chains* or tarred ropes. We may substitute for this abatis, or combine with it, stakes of various lengths,

---

* As was done by Count de la Roche in two fords of the Montre, a small stream of Alsace. (See his *Essai sur la petite guerre*, 1770, in 12mo.)

driven with great force, which cannot be pulled up without much difficulty; also caltrops, planks filled with nails, or harrows. By distributing these different obstructions in all parts of the ford, its passage will be rendered almost impossible. We may also render a ford inaccessible by vertically cutting away the bank of which we are in possession.

To break up or destroy a ford, we may dig a broad and deep ditch, or several smaller ones, across it, following the direction of the stream; scattering the excavated earth upon the surface of the water, instead of throwing it upon the bank, where it would lead the enemy to suspect that the ford had been disturbed. These ditches being filled with water and unknown to the enemy will cause the loss of a part of their soldiers and will arrest the progress of the rest. For the same purpose we may dig wells or pits, either near the shore or in the middle of the ford, planting a heavy stake in the centre of each. The soldiers and horses plunging into these will greatly paralyze the action of a column attempting to cross. Finally, a ford may be destroyed by increasing the volume of water flowing over it, which may be done either by constructing a dam below it, or by removing dams, artificial or natural, above it.

The repair of a ford that has been broken up or destroyed, or the improvement of a defective one, is to be undertaken in the following manner:

If the volume of water has been increased by means of a dam, we endeavor to obtain possession of the dam and destroy it: if a dam has been removed above the ford, we, of course, restore it. If the enemy has dug ditches or wells in the middle of the ford, these are to be filled with stones covered with fascines. If the ford has been obstructed with caltrops, stakes, spiked planks, and harrows, all these mischievous articles are to be removed by means of rakes, the operation being protected by sharpshooters concealed behind the trees on the banks. Folard recommends for this purpose the use of iron claws or grapples, attached to long ropes, and thrown out as far as possible into the ford. As to caltrops, this author doubts " whether they can ever be entirely removed where the bottom is of gravel, and firm;"* and the best course is then to sink upon the bottom a series of hurdles loaded with stone. But sometimes this method fails, and it becomes necessary to abandon a passage that is too perilous. It is evident, moreover, that the broader the river, the more difficult will it be to clear the ford.

When the bottom of a ford is not sufficiently firm, it may be improved by sinking a bed of fascines or hurdles weighted with stones. The entrance and exit of the ford are to be rendered easy, when necessary, by constructing gentle slopes on the two banks. If only a small portion of the breadth is not fordable, the deep part may be filled with fascines loaded with stones, or with boxes filled with stone, sand, or earth.

---

* *Polybe, avec Commentaire, par le Chevalier de Folard*, 1729, t. v., p. 147. In a muddy or sandy bottom they are quickly sunk, and are formidable only to the first soldiers who cross.

A ford that is too narrow, is widened in the same manner.

It is a good precaution, especially in broad and rapid rivers, to mark out the whole ford, by planting two rows of strong stakes, upon which marks can be made which will show whether any change in the depth of the water occurs.

In reference to such changes, it is proper to observe:

1st. That, as a ford is easily broken up, we must not rely upon it as a sure means of communication between two *corps d'armée*.

2d. That it is imprudent to trust to fords in rivers and brooks in mountainous countries, where even a very moderate rain may dig them out, or swell their waters.

We will corroborate this second observation by a passage from Colonel de Carrion-Nisas.* "The river Cinca," he says, "which caused the disasters of Cæsar† and of the Duke of Orleans,‡ was no less fatal to the French in the Spanish war from 1808 to 1813. The garrison of a small town, washed by this stream, was ordered to cross it. According to the usual practice, but in this position imprudently, five companies, which were destined to form the advance-guard, were

---

* *Essai sur l'histoire générale de l'art militaire*, 1824, t. ii., p. 142.

† Read attentively chapters xl. and xlviii. of Book I. of Cæsar's Commentaries (on the Civil War). The words of the great writer suggest the improvidence of the general who neglects to obtain sufficient information, or who does not take into consideration the accidents to which he is liable from the nature of the country in which he is waging war.

‡ At the siege of Lerida (1707), which he nevertheless captured

passed over on the preceding day. During the night the river rose and cut off these five companies from their companions, who saw them slaughtered by the guerillas without being able to help them."

3. **Fording a River.**—Fords rarely answer for the passage of a whole army, but are of frequent use for detachments, and facilitate the minor operations of war.

Before allowing your troops to plunge into the water, to cross a ford, see that they are not overheated and perspiring—a hygienic precaution which prevents many serious diseases, and which should be especially observed when the waters are cold and swollen.

If the ford has not previously been staked out, let it be done by some horsemen, or take an experienced guide from the country, or stretch ropes on the right and left to confine the extreme files, so that the soldiers may not get off the track and lose their foothold.

Where a river, though fordable, is sufficiently rapid to carry away men, place in its bed, up-stream, anything which will act as an obstacle and break the force of the current, such as trees, wagons, and even horsemen. Also place below the ford a line of men on horseback, to pick up the soldiers who may be carried away. These horsemen, whether up-stream or down, must not be too close together, as they would, if in a compact body, form a sort of dam, and would have the pressure of too great a volume of water to support.

The same remark applies to foot soldiers: they should never march in close order in a somewhat rapid ford, as this would render the file on the side up stream liable to be overturned.

Infantry should enter a ford obliquely, unless the direction of the solid path of the ford prevents. They should also cross in regular platoons, with intervals between them. They take off their shoes, roll up their pantaloons, put their cartridge-boxes upon their knapsacks, and carry their arms at will, though it is best to carry them upon the shoulder which is upstream. The object of the last two precautions is to keep the ammunition and arms from getting wet. The men of the same rank grasp each other by the sword belt, so as to form a chain to assist in supporting inexperienced, feeble, or clumsy soldiers. They should not look at the water, but direct their eyes to a fixed and elevated point upon the shore.

Cavalry crosses a ford without difficulty. It is only necessary for the men to raise their feet to avoid getting wet, hold up their horses, and fix their eyes upon some tree or steeple on the opposite shore. These precautions are more particularly useful where the water course is broad.

Occasionally, each horseman may successfully carry across a foot soldier riding behind.

When the several arms cross a ford separately, the cavalry and artillery should cross after the infantry; otherwise they would break up the bottom and make the crossing for the latter difficult or impossible.

Several fords near each other facilitate the passage,

if they are not too narrow: the proceeding for each is the same as above.

Alexander the Great crossed the Granicus by a ford, *obliquely* and in *several columns*. One of the most celebrated modern instances of the passage of a river by a ford, is that of the Tagliamento, in 1797, by three French divisions conducted by Bonaparte, pushing before them the Archduke Charles in the direction of the capital—Viénna, which was the *objective* point of the campaign.

To show the importance which a ford may acquire, we will cite two facts in French history as examples: If (in August, 1346) a prisoner had not pointed out to Edward III. the ford of Blanquetaque below Abbeville, the English, being thus arrested by the river Somme and pursued by the superior forces of Philip VI. of France, would have come to the end òf their good fortune, and there would have been no Crécy to tarnish the glory of the French arms. If (in the early part of August, 1809), after the battle of Talavera, Marshal Ney had been able to find the ford of Almaraz on the Tagus, the forces of Soult would have effected a passage and menaced the rear of the English army, and ruined it, by compelling a disastrous retreat, despite the recent victory of Wellington.

4. Swimming a River.—An officer who can swim has it in his power to perform important services. We will cite two examples: At the siege of Lille, in 1708, Captain Dubois introduced himself into the place by the river Deule, often swimming below the surface. He conferred with Marshal Boufflers, betook himself again to the water with a note enveloped with waxed muslin in his mouth, and although he got entangled in the weeds, had the fortune to escape and to bring back to the Duke of Burgundy an account of the situation of the defenders.—On the 26th of May, 1800, Franceschi, an aide-de-camp of General Soult, having left the First Consul at the foot of the Great Saint-Bernard, approached the besieged and famished city of Genoa in a boat pulled by three oarsmen. He passed the English cruisers in the night, and had nearly escaped, when daylight appeared. Immediately a shower of balls poured upon his boat, killing one of his oarsmen and wounding another. In this perilous moment he did not hesitate, but resolved to swim the remaining distance to the city. Tying his dispatches about his neck, he plunged into the water, but subsequently, remembering that he had left his sword, and not being willing to allow it to fall into the hands of the English, returned to the boat, seized his weapon, and carrying it between his teeth, succeeded in reaching the shore, though almost exhausted. He bore to Massena, the general-in-chief, the promise that in three weeks Bonaparte would, by forced marches, come to the relief of the city.*

A knowledge of swimming may enable an officer to save his life. When Prince Eugene Poniatowski, while covering the French retreat after the battle of Leipsic, plunged into the Elster rather than surrender

---

* *Traité de natation*, essai sur son application à l'art de la guerre, par le vicomte de Courtivron, officier supérieur; third edition, 1836, p. 166.

(October 19th, 1813), he would not have been drowned if he had known how to swim.*

Soldiers, as well as officers, should know how to swim. In fact, a detachment of infantry composed of troops who cannot swim, will be retarded by an insignificant stream, and paralyzed in its operations.

We must confess that the French are far behindhand in the art of swimming. Notwithstanding the occasional and temporary existence of bodies of swimmers in its ranks,† their army has suffered itself to be surpassed in this respect by several foreign armies, and especially by the Prussian.‡

But notwithstanding this lamentable condition of things, we will add a few words upon the passage of rivers by swimming:

To effect such a passage, a point of the river should be chosen where the current is least rapid and the banks are of easy access. The latter condition is

---

* Poniatowski had before narrowly escaped drowning in the Sereth, at the siege of Jassy.

† For example, Soult organized a company of 150 swimmers at the passage of the Linth (September 25th, 1799). This company, commanded by the first adjutant, Dellard, threw themselves into the water, with their sabres between their teeth, and pistols tied on their heads, and, under the protecting fire of the artillery, reached the opposite shore in a few seconds and dispersed the advance-posts of the enemy. Consult the *Mémoires de Masséna*, par Roch, t. iii., p. 367. In 1853, I proposed the creation of a battalion of swimmers for the French army as a specialty, which it was desirable to establish and to perfect by study and practice. (See Duparcq's "*Commentaires sur Clausewitz*, livre vi., observation No. 22, p. 193, 197.)

‡ See Duparcq's "*Études historiques et militaires sur la Prusse*" (1854), t. i., p. 227.

desirable for infantry, but *indispensable* for cavalry; for without a point of support upon which the horse can place his hind feet, and hence spring upon the bank, he will often be drowned.

The infantry swimmers should put their effects and arms upon their heads and shoulders, their sabres between their teeth, in order to have one weapon available at the moment of landing. Sometimes they can place these effects and arms upon a small raft, or a wherry, if they can construct or procure one. They should swim obliquely to the current, and down stream, so as to be assisted by the propelling force of the water. If they are accompanied by horsemen, the latter should take to the water above the infantry, so as to break the force of the current.*

With a proper degree of boldness, cavalry may likewise cross a river by swimming. Almost all authors say the horse is a good swimmer; still, according to Warnery,† he should be exercised at it. This animal swims with his crupper under water, and hence the necessity of placing the valise of the horseman, and everything which, by being wetted, would become too heavy, either upon the rider's

---

* This method was followed by Cæsar in the passage of the Loire, and by the Prince of Orange in the passage of the Meuse (1569).—Infantry swimmers, supported by a number of skirmishers, will be of especial service in capturing boats collected by the enemy, near the opposing shore, for effecting a passage, or boats that are drifting down the stream.

† This author, in fact, informs us that in the first war of Silesia, three hundred hussars, attempting to cross the Oder, were for the most part drowned with their horses, although these horses were of the swimming species. (*Commentaires sur Montecuculli et Turpin*, t. ii., p. 183.)

shoulders, or in a boat, or upon a raft. Cavalry should also cut the water obliquely to the current, moving *in rank* and preserving some distance between the two ranks. The men should manage their horses with gentleness, and speak to them encouragingly.

Each platoon of cavalry may also be carried across a river by putting the horsemen in a boat, and letting the horses swim behind it, held by the reins in the hands of the men. This mixed mode is not entirely safe; the horses, abandoned by their riders, lose confidence, press toward the boat, and may overturn it. Sometimes a number of the horses refuse to enter the water in this manner.*

The plan of making each horseman carry a foot soldier mounted behind, has also been tried. It was in this way that Marshals Turenne and Gramont crossed the Necker in 1645.

The Tartars cross rivers on rafts constructed of trusses of straw or of reeds. They send their horses into the water in front of their frail little rafts, and while holding them by the tail with their left hands, apply stout blows with the right, drive them, swimming, to the opposite shore.

One of the most celebrated passages of a river by swimming was that of the Rhine at Tolhuys by the

---

* For want of other means, the Spanish general Sancho Davilla followed this plan in crossing the Douro with his cavalry in 1580, when going to meet the king of Portugal. According to Folard (Polybius, v. iv., p. 55), this method was successful in 1639, in the passage of the Rhine by the Duke of Longueville, and in 1708 in the passage, by a regiment of dragoons, over the arm of the sea which separates the town of Sluis from the island of Cadzand.

French army in 1672. At this place the river proved to be fordable in part, and there was only a distance of about 150 yards to be crossed by swimming. Louis XIV. directed the operation. His body-guard crossed by squadrons in regular formation, and in the words of Quincy, "it was an extraordinary spectacle to see these magnificent troops swimming in order of battle, in the midst of so broad and rapid a stream." *

5. Passage upon Ice.—Where a river is not frozen across its channel, plant two or three pointed trunks of trees, upright, in the bed of the river at a short distance down the stream, which will serve as a barrier to the floating ice, and thereby hasten the total congelation of the surface.

Ice is not to be ventured upon where it does not touch the water; for if it does not float, but forms arches, an excess of weight, and especially any sudden jar, may break it. It should be *at least* three inches thick for infantry, and four and a half inches for cavalry and light artillery. From six and a half inches upwards, it supports the largest and most heavily loaded wagons.

When the cold season continues, the thickness of

---

* *Histoire militaire de* Louis XIV., t. i., p. 322. This river passage is almost always cited as one effected by fording alone. Santa-Cruz, however, says (*Réflexions militaires et politiques*, traduction Vergy, t. ii., p. 288) that the king's guard crossed the Rhine "more swimming than fording." This is the famous crossing commemorated by Boileau, and which Feuquière characterizes as "a performance in which success was the result of temerity only, and which should never be cited as an example to be followed." (*Mémoires*, part iii., chap. lxx.)

the ice may be artificially increased, if it appears to be insufficient: for this purpose, cover it with straw, sand, and hurdles; sprinkle with water frequently, especially in the evening, and wait a night.

In crossing upon ice, the infantry should break step, and horsemen and drivers of vehicles should dismount. Sand and earth should be spread upon the ice, to save the men and horses from slipping.

As to vehicles, artillery, etc., it is important to distribute their weight over a large extent of the frozen surface, instead of allowing it to rest upon a single point: this will be accomplished by laying the road with two continuous rows of planks for the wheel tracks. But it will be still better to substitute sliding for rolling: for this purpose fasten the two wheels of each side upon a strong plank by quoins and clamps, thus converting the vehicle into a sledge, which can be readily dragged from one shore to the other.

In all passages upon ice, particularly when they are executed by an army in retreat, redouble your activity and vigilance to avoid disorder and confusion, which would inevitably prove disastrous.

We have two fine examples of river passages upon ice, in the progress of the Grand Elector of Brandenburg upon the frozen Frische-Haff (1679) with 9,000 men in sledges; and in the capture of the Netherland fleet on the ice of the Zuyder Zee, by the French cavalry, in the conquest of Holland by Pichegru, in 1795.

6. Improvised Bridges.—The construction of most improvised bridges belongs to the artillery service.

We shall briefly consider only some of the most simple kinds.

Bridge of ladders.—A foot bridge sufficient for the passage of a small detachment over a brook, may be very quickly made of two stout ladders laid horizontally from bank to bank, and firmly secured. The rounds are placed vertically, and the distance between the two ladders may be about one yard. Planks laid closely throughout the whole length and secured to the two ladders, bind the whole together, and give a solid footpath.

Bridges of undressed trees.—This is the simplest of all the bridges suitable for a river. It consists of trunks of trees in the bark, only their branches being trimmed off, thrown from one bank to the other—to the number of five or six, or more, according to the breadth desired for the bridge—and covered with any kind of planking. The possibility of constructing such bridges depends upon finding trees of sufficient length, which does not often happen except where the rivers are narrow.

Bridge of wagons.—This kind of bridge, being more ingenious than really useful, is rarely employed; but as it may serve in a case of urgency, we will describe it. One or more wagons are rolled into the water (where the stream is not more than forty yards wide, a single wagon in the middle will answer) and are secured with stakes. These serve as piers, upon which are laid beams, which are then covered with planks, to form the bridge-floor. Pieces of plank, or blocks, are inserted between the tops of the wagons and the beams, to compensate for the inequalities of the bed, and to raise the level of the floor to the requisite height.

This bridge can be employed only in a gentle current, and a depth of not more than two yards.

In the year 1543, the French army in Italy had recourse to a similar bridge; for we read in the *Commentaires* of Marshal Montluc that " the next day we passed the river Po, over which we constructed a bridge of wagons for the infantry, for the cavalry did not require it, as the water only reached the horses' bellies."

Bridge of ropes.—This bridge is used in mountainous countries, over torrents with precipitous banks, and where the construction of other kinds of bridges seems impossible.

The most simple kind* consists of half a dozen ropes, an inch and a half in diameter, stretched from one bank to the other, about twenty inches apart, and kept in position by cross-pieces of wood : upon these ropes a floor of plank is then laid. Such a bridge is only suitable for infantry. It is prudent also to provide it with guard ropes answering as hand-rails; and further, to diminish its oscillation by means of diagonal ropes fastened to the banks. Its application is confined to streams of about twenty-five yards in breadth at the maximum.

---

* In the wild parts of America, a simple cable stretched from one bank to the other answers for crossing brooks or torrents flowing at the bottom of a ravine; but as we must then make use of our hands and feet to get across, and as the passage is always long, dangerous, and uncertain, this method cannot be recommended in a military point of view.

A rope-bridge may also be constructed upon the principle employed for wire suspension-bridges. In this case, heavy pieces of timber are planted vertically on the two banks, in the place of abutments, to which two long cables are attached, which hang in the catenary form and support the floor. This floor rests upon a number of cross-pieces, which are suspended by small vertical cords from the various points of the catenary.

Small pile-bridge.—For the purpose of bringing two posts into communication, bridges are thrown over small rivers or brooks, resting upon piles, which are nothing more than heavy stakes or stout branches of trees. One or two rows of such piles, parallel to the direction of the stream, usually suffice. Strong transoms of plank are nailed upon the tops of the opposite piles, upon which beams are laid extending from bank to bank, forming the bridge-floor.

Such a bridge is easily improvised, as these small piles may be driven with a simple maul, or hand pile-driver.

CHAPTER FIFTH.

CONVOYS.

INTRODUCTION.—A *convoy* is an expedition designed to furnish an army, body of troops, place, camp, or post, either with money, arms, materiel, ammunition, provisions, live stock, or stores of any kind. The term is also applied to the conveyance of the sick, the wounded, and prisoners.

For want of convoys an army may perish,* and therefore their organization demands the greatest care. Their outfit and superintendence come under two different heads: one purely administrative, and appertaining to the military *intendance;* the other tactical, and appertaining to the command. We shall here consider only the latter, and shall regard a convoy as one of the minor operations of war

From this point of view, a convoy should never march without an escort, for it is in vain to suppose that, because it is *behind* the army, upon ground swept beforehand by the moving columns, it needs no protec-

---

* "Lines of convoys," said Bulow, "are the muscles of the military body, which would become paralytic if they were sundered." (*Esprit du système de guerre moderne*, trad. Laverne, p. 51, 52.)

tion of its own. The force and composition of this escort must be determined by the nature of the convoy and the character of the country to be crossed, by the importance attached to its success, the distance to be travelled, the situation of the enemy, the disposition of the inhabitants, and other circumstances of various kinds. The escort is always larger for a convoy of materiel, and especially of powder, which it is important to keep at a distance from the scene of combat, and out of danger from fire. It should generally be composed of infantry and a small body of cavalry, the number of the latter being diminished in proportion as the country is more woody or mountainous. This cavalry will serve to reconnoitre and watch the enemy. The principle is that the escort should be *mixed*, so as to overcome all kind of difficulties and any obstacles it may meet; consequently there should be added to it some artillery and a few sappers (or, for want of these, workmen of the country with their implements), who can be employed to level roads or to construct places of shelter.

The grade of the commandant of a convoy is proportioned to the importance of the expedition. His authority is absolute over the troops of all the arms which compose the escort. The regulations prescribe merely that in the case of convoy of ammunition, he should defer to the advice of the artillery officer in respect to the precautions to be observed *during the march* and *in halts*. The command of such a convoy is usually given to an artillery officer, an arrangement which avoids all complication.

Besides his verbal orders and explanations, the chief of a convoy receives the *most detailed written instructions* from the general who detaches him. No superior officer on the route can modify these instructions, nor can he retard the march of the convoy; but every one should rather, for the general good, endeavor to promote its object.

"The command of a convoy," says Jacquinot de Presle,* "is one of the most delicate missions with which an officer can be charged. In fact, nothing is more difficult to defend, or easier to attack, than a file of wagons, sometimes extending a long distance, which the least obstacle may impede. Whatever difficulties this operation may present, the officer to whom it is intrusted should nevertheless remember that, with intelligence and courage, obstacles are often surmounted before which an ignorant man, without energy, would succumb; for though the defence of a convoy is difficult, the attack upon it is sometimes badly conceived or imperfectly managed."

1. Organization of the Convoy.—As soon as the commanding officer has received his instructions and the necessary explanations, he collects the convoy and examines into the means placed at his disposal.

In respect to the troops, he reviews them as any chief of a detachment must, and sees that both infantry and cavalry are provided with everything necessary in the way of ammunition and equipment.

In respect to the materiel, he examines in detail

---

* *Cours d'art militaire*, 1829, p. 554.

every wagon and its harness, as well as its load, to see whether the former are in good condition and the latter suitably distributed. Should they prove otherwise, he requires them to be changed, or at least to be repaired; and should his demand not be complied with, he should represent distinctly the condition in which he is thus placed, in order to diminish, to that extent, his own responsibility in case of a reverse.

For prudence, he requires several empty wagons, and also spare pieces; for example, wheels, poles, horse-shoes, ropes, etc.

If the convoy is large, he divides it into several divisions, each of 500 wagons at the maximum,* and each division is then also subdivided into component groups of about 50 wagons each. In all cases, each isolated group should have a portion of the foot soldiers of the escort to watch over and protect it; and this will limit the subdivision and necessitate proportioning it to the number of the escort. Besides, the forces must not be so minutely parcelled off that they cannot act together; in fact, an excessive distribution would convert a military expedition into a civic procession, artistically grouped.

The more valuable wagons are placed at the head of each division, in the following order: money, the papers and documents of the staff, arms, ammunition, provisions, equipment, officers' baggage in the order of grade, sutlers' and traders' equipages. By the *head*, we here mean the portion of the convoy which is the

---

* One hundred wagons to a division is a good number.

strongest or best protected.* To speak more generally, this portion should embrace those vehicles the preservation of which is of the greatest importance, in relation to the special object in view. In a convoy of prisoners, those who are known to be the most hostile and dangerous are to be placed at the head. In a mixed convoy, composed of wagons and beasts of burden, the latter will take the head,† in order that the roads may not be cut up by the wheels before they pass, and also that they may more readily escape in case of attack.

Like every marching column, the convoy is organized with an advance-guard and a rear-guard. The latter is required, because in this operation an attack upon the rear is as probable as any other; in addition, it is well to have a reserve to act as a guard and to fight upon the most exposed flank. The advance-guard, the rear-guard, the main body, and the reserve, have each their own commander; the commandant of the convoy reserves no special command, in order to be free to go everywhere and examine everything.

In the organization of a convoy, it is necessary to bear in mind certain numerical data, the most useful of which are given in the following summary:

One caisson carries, { with horses, ...	1,650 pounds.‡
{ with oxen, ...	770 , "
One mule carries, on his back, on the average,	220 "
One horse " " "	190 "
One ox " " "	130 "

---

* The enemy frequently allows the head to pass, in order that the rest of the convoy may feel more secure.

† Thus pack horses, for example, should go *before* the wagons.

‡ Including the weight of the caisson, the load being thus only 1,320 lbs.

A caisson with four horses occupies in the file about thirteen yards, with a breadth of five feet, and requires an interval of at least one yard in the rank and one and a half yards in the file. On level ground it can move at the rate of two and a half miles per hour; in hilly country only one and three quarter miles per hour.

It will be well rather to fall below these numbers than to exceed them; and in order that the loads may not be increased beyond the amount fixed at the outset, the soldiers should be forbidden to put their knapsacks upon the wagons.

2. March of the Convoy.—Before setting out, the country through which the convoy is to pass is to be examined; this service is performed by spies or partisans, and is also to be continued during the march. The march should be performed at a uniform rate, rather too slow than too fast, in order that the slowest team may keep up with the rest; for it is important that the convoy should not increase its length, since it would become disjointed, and more exposed to attack.

The advance-guard precedes the convoy. The common rule is that it should start two hours in advance when the country is level, and only one hour when it is broken. It is better to be governed by the principle that its distance from the main body should increase with the length of the convoy, in order that it may, by reason of this very distance, give the latter time to make its defensive preparation. When this distance is considerable, it would be well to have a second advance-guard of quite small force, and very near, capable of resisting an enemy who had escaped the notice of the first.

The business of the advance-guard is to reconnoitre, to remove obstacles, and to transmit information to the commandant. For these purposes, it reëxamines places of concealment, such as woods, villages, and defiles, and keeps up a communication with the convoy through horsemen distributed along the route.

The march is generally in two files.* On the outside, two soldiers keep a watch upon the drivers of wagons which have been drawn from the country by requisition. These drivers, being also taken from the country, may be treacherous, for example, by upsetting their vehicle in some difficult spot, where there might be an ambuscade; or, not being soldiers, they may attempt to escape in time of danger. The guards have orders to fire upon any one who attempts to run away.

In each fraction of the convoy, a number of workmen are charged with the examination of the wagons during the march, and to point out, in advance, as far as possible, any one in which an accident is likely to occur. If, notwithstanding this precaution, a wagon breaks, or if for any reason it requires repair, it is

---

* If the road is too narrow, and does not admit of two files for more than a league at a time, it will be better to march in single file altogether, so as not to lose time and produce disorder by continual changes of formation.

taken off the road, and when repaired, takes its place in the rear. If the repair is impossible, the load and the horses are distributed among the nearer wagons.

The escort, in protecting the convoy, takes possession of all dangerous positions or outlets in the vicinity of the route,* and does not abandon them till all the wagons have passed. If, for example, a defile is to be passed, the escort occupies the neighboring heights, and endeavors to discover the enemy from as great a distance as possible. In this case it is proper to divide the escort into several parts—especially when the defile is not sufficient for the passage of more than one wagon—so that the defenders may be nearer to the objects which they are required to guard: they are to be reunited after the passage is effected.

When arriving at the point of destination, so far from becoming careless and negligent, the commandant redoubles his care and vigilance, to make a proper disposition of affairs in conjunction with the friendly detachment that has been sent out to meet the convoy, or else to join the outposts of the camp or the place without producing confusion.

3. Halts and Parks.—The convoy stops every hour to give the horses time to breathe, and to allow lagging wagons to come up: these are short halts of five minutes. Long halts, during which the convoy may be attacked, or at least be observed and counted by the

---

* For example, the *débouchés* of a river or of a chain of mountains, when the convoy is moving parallel to one of these almost impassable obstacles.

emissaries of the enemy, should be avoided. They should be indulged in only at strong positions, in places previously reconnoitred, and known to be favorable for defence. In all cases, the horses are not to be unharnessed, even for feeding, and the drivers should remain near them. While resting, a military guard must be maintained.

The expedition may occupy several days, and then the convoy is parked at night. Sometimes, also, it is parked by day, as well as by night, when it is obliged to stop in consequence of the occupation of the road by a considerable force of the enemy; the park then assumes a more defensive and solid form than in the first case.

In the park of a convoy, the wagons occupy the exterior, or perimeter, whilst the horses, whether harnessed or not, being more vulnerable, are upon the interior. If there are caissons loaded with inflammable materiel, they are drawn up with the horses as much in the centre and as completely sheltered from the projectiles of the enemy as possible.

The form of the park may be either closed or open. When closed, it offers more resistance, and somewhat resembles an intrenchment; it is, in fact, a barricade of wagons, sometimes circular, sometimes rectangular, employed for a regular and obstinate defence. We here give three examples of it:

The park No. 1, which we take from Joly de Maizeroy,* is protected on the outside by the grand

* *Cours de tactique*, 1785, t. ii. In this park, the wagons might also be placed at right angles to the circumference (the figure represents them

guards and several pieces of artillery, and the platoons of the infantry of the escort are placed within, behind the circle formed by the wagons. When the wagons are very numerous, this author recommends that two such parks be formed and connected tactically by cavalry placed between them in one or two lines. This cavalry takes the place of a curtain in fortification.

PARK NO. 1.

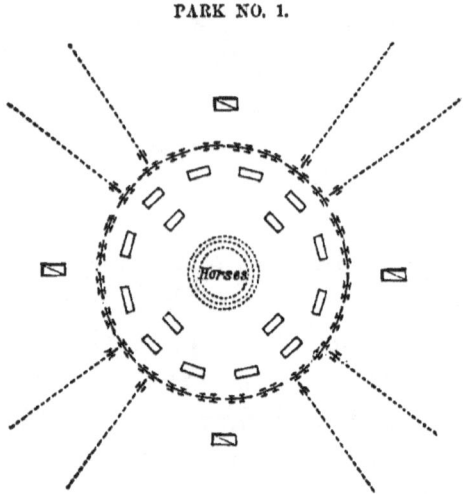

The park No. 2, taken from the "Regulations for the Prussian Cavalry," established by Frederic the Great, presents a solid arrangement with an interior space, which is very useful. With the rear resting upon a river, it is defended on the front and flanks by platoons of infantry covered by chevaux-de-frise; and upon the most advanced angles, by cannon, firing

with their length in the circumference) the hind wheels being outside and the poles toward the centre. This would require more wagons, but the barricade would be more dense and solid.

either balls or grape, according as the enemy is at a

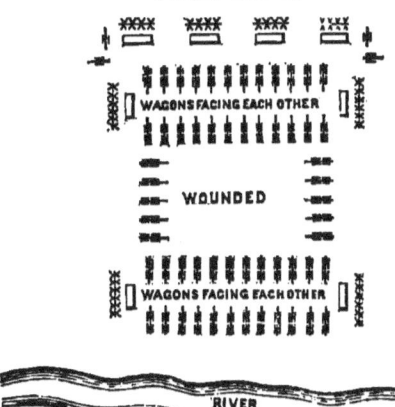

PARK NO. 2.

greater or less distance. This park is fully prepared to receive the enemy.

A close formation, with the horses in the interior, shown in park No. 3, is that to which we would naturally resort, when the convoy is marching in two files upon a wide road, and is suddenly met by an imposing force of the enemy.

The park No. 4, given by the Archduke Charles,* is suitable in cases of attacks by a small force. Being formed of partial parks by divisions, situated at the same distances as in columns, it possesses the advantage, both in forming and in breaking up, of resuming the march

PARK NO. 3.

* *Principes de la grand guerre,* p. 70, and plate ix. of Duparcq's translation.

with great facility, as all the divisions can move at the same time without incommoding each other.

PARK NO. 4.

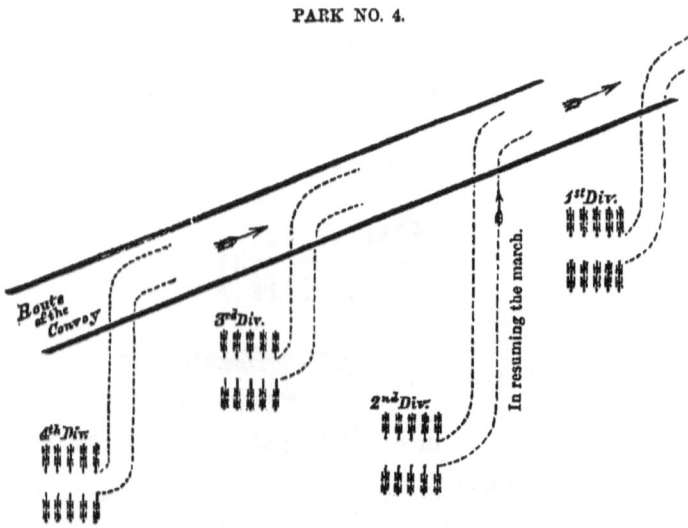

In the parks 2, 3, 4, the horses remain harnessed to the wagons, whilst in No. 1 they are stationed in the centre. In all the parks, the drivers bivouac near their horses and watch them.

In general, the parks are to be formed far from inhabited places and woods which would afford facilities to the enemy; and advantage is to be taken of any obstacles of the ground to diminish the number of points of attack.

These details respecting parks show that convoys, while supplying an army, may also become a defensive accessory: they then receive the name of *tabors* (intrenchment of baggage for defence against cavalry). Zisca, the chief of the Hussites, made great use of them in the early part of the fifteenth century; and more recently the Cossacks have employed them very successfully in resisting superior armies and extricating themselves from critical situations.

4. Defence of the Convoy.—As a convoy includes a large number of non-combatants, and may therefore be seized with a sudden panic upon the appearance of the enemy, it is prudent and useful to exercise the whole body, from time to time, in the manœuvre it would be required to execute in case of attack.

At the first intimation of the approach of the enemy, the files are closed and greater order is observed in marching. Without seeking the combat, the escort watches the positions which overlook the route, and in case of necessity disputes them; but if the enemy is in too great force, it will be necessary to halt. In this case, the best course is at once to put the horses in safety, to prevent their being hamstrung. The manœuvre is simple: the right file turns to the left, and the left file to the right, bringing the heads of the teams toward each other, as in the park No. 3: no wagons are placed across the front and rear unless the contest becomes serious, and calls for the employment of every resource.

The essential point is, in general, to keep the enemy at a distance, especially from a convoy of ammunition or of sick and wounded. This is to be done by the skirmishers, and while the fight is carried on at a distance, the convoy, covered on all sides, should file off at increased speed and endeavor to gain some woods or village, or any obstacle which may serve as a shelter. This method will be successful where the attack is only upon the flank. If the position of the enemy is not exactly known, it would be better, provided the force of the assailant is not too formidable, to halt the convoy during the action, and to resume the march after the road has been cleared.

The attack on the flank will almost always be central. As soon as this is ascertained, the reserve or the main body of the escort is to be reënforced at the expense of the advance and rear-guards. This main body is to occupy the threatened positions along the route, during the whole time the convoy is passing.

In the case of an attack on the front, the advance-guard occupies these positions, which are successively relieved, but no position is abandoned until the last wagon has passed.

An attack in the rear is repelled by the rear-guard, which makes a stubborn defence while retiring by echelons, throwing up obstructions and cutting off all communication. The rear-guard in this case keeps up a communication with the convoy, for the transmission of intelligence, by horsemen distributed along the road.

In passing a dangerous place, it is proper not only to occupy the heights and threatening positions in good season, but also to divide the convoy into small convoys completely organized, each having its own advance-guard, rear-guard, reserve, and even flankers: under this multiple protection they will be able to pass in security, one after the other.

Should the defence fail, and the enemy prove victorious, the wagons should not be suffered to fall into his hands untouched. In the first place, a certain number of them are to be sacrificed, and employed, in a dilapidated condition, to obstruct the road, while the remainder, to which the horses of the broken wagons will be added, are hurried away. If this sacrifice does not avail, everything is to be destroyed; the wagons burned, and the horses killed, or at least hamstrung; and then, sword in hand, the escort must cut its way through the surrounding force of the enemy.

The escort should be satisfied with repelling the enemy, and never attempt to pursue; for its principal duty is to remain near the wagons and protect them; besides, it would run the risk of falling into an ambuscade.

In the defence of a convoy of prisoners, it is necessary to observe the precaution of compelling the prisoners to lie down during the engagement with the enemy, and not to rise, under pain of death, until the signal is given;* otherwise, many a prisoner would be able to assist the assailant by signs, or by various attempts of a dangerous character. In this connection the regulations recommend that the convoy reach some village as soon as possible, where the prisoners can be shut up in some large building, the approach to which is to be defended. This method exposes the escort to a more destructive fire, as the enemy will no

---

* The same penalty is to be inflicted, during the march, upon any prisoner who resists orders or attempts to leave the ranks.

longer be deterred by the fear of hitting their own men when these are protected behind walls.

In the conduct and defence of a convoy, the elements of success are activity, resolution, coolness, and perpetual vigilance. In the words of Frederic, " The officer in command must preserve his temper under all provocations and difficulties, and should especially be on his guard against false reports."

5. Attack of a Convoy.—We may attack a convoy with a force inferior to the escort; for in this species of action the advantage is on the side of the assailant, who chooses his own time and place, and brings a solid force against a scattered one; and if he also resorts to stratagem and false attacks, he will stand a good chance of success in his principal attack.

The attack of a convoy is based upon previous information respecting the nature of this convoy, the management of those who conduct it, and local peculiarities. A convoy of prisoners or of animals may be carried off by cavalry alone. In other cases it is necessary to have infantry, cavalry, and a few howitzers. These last are indispensable, as, without them, we could hardly undertake an attack upon a park.

The corps of attack is divided into three masses: one destined to engage the escort, a second to fall upon the wagons, and the third to remain in reserve. The first mass commences by harassing the escort, so as to weary it and lead it into the commission of some error; then, profiting by this error, the uncovered convoy is attacked with lightning speed. In ground more or less hemmed in by elevations, attacking both extremities of the column has the advantage of throwing the centre itself into confusion and uncertainty. Upon level open ground, we should confine the attack to the centre, thereby cutting the convoy in two, and gaining a cheaper victory over the separated portions. In the midst of such an attack, a few well-timed shells spread terror among the enemy, and hasten the result.

If the convoy forms into a park to resist, the attack becomes more difficult. We must then prepare to make a breach in the park, precisely as in a wall. If we have not sufficient artillery to cut an opening through the perimeter of the park, it will be better to wait until the convoy resumes its march, and then to take it in the rear.

In attacking a convoy, it is not always intended to capture and carry off all the wagons. In general, we are satisfied with seizing those which, from certain indications, or information given by prisoners, are known to be the most valuable.

Frequently, indeed, the design of an attack is still less ambitious, the only object being to disorganize the convoy by thrusts at one or more points. For this purpose the attacking body ambuscades the convoy sometimes on one side and sometimes on the other, and rushes through it several times, each time doing as much damage as possible, by cutting the traces, hamstringing the horses, upsetting, breaking, and setting fire to the wagons. In this operation, where it is necessary to move among numerous obstacles, the chasseurs, and especially the foot chasseurs, are most suitable.

6. Convoys by Water.—We have thus far been speaking exclusively of convoys by land. Convoys by water* are also important. They transport bulky and heavy supplies with extremely simple means and at small expense: for example, we consider ourselves fortunate if we have a water conveyance for bringing a supply of siege equipage before a fortified place.

The infantry of the escort is distributed in small bodies upon the several boats; there are, in addition, an advance-guard and a rear-guard of foot, in boats specially provided for them; sometimes also flankers, on light boats, where the river is sufficiently wide to allow it. The cavalry of the escort follows upon the borders of the stream, and keeps open its communication with the convoy. It is preceded and followed by an advance-guard and rear-guard of mixed composition; these are frequently useful in bearing important intelligence to the floating convoy touching its safety. For greater security, there should be some spare boats, to convey the infantry from one side of the river to the other, when required, in order to line both banks where the progress of the convoy is retarded; as, for example, at a bridge or a dam, or in shallow water.

When the river flows between steep hills, almost all the infantry of the escort marches on land, with

---

* Upon rivers or canals. Convoys *by sea* are of much assistance in provisioning an army; but as they are in general protected by a maritime force, they do not come within the scope of this work.

advance and rear-guards, for the purpose of preventing the enemy from occupying the heights, from which they could easily annoy the convoy.

The defence of a water convoy is simple. While the attacked escort is fighting upon the bank (employing chiefly fire-arms), the convoy halts in the vicinity. If the escort gains the ascendency, the convoy proceeds under its protection; if otherwise, it makes all speed to escape; but if this becomes impossible, the boats are scuttled.

A convoy by water is easily destroyed, even with a small force.* The best plan is to ambuscade it in a bend of the river, in a wooded spot, and where the channel runs near the shore, so as to be able to attack (especially with cannon) both on the front and the flank, and even to enfilade the convoy, which is occasionally possible, as the annexed figure shows. If this multiplied attack does not bring the convoy to a halt, the cannon are aimed at the water line of each boat, to sink them by letting in water; at the same time, the conductors and defenders of the boat are picked off by musket shots. In this way, the attack being constantly renewed, the boats will be obliged to surrender.

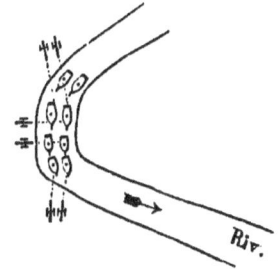

ATTACK OF A CONVOY OF BOATS.

---

* We may damage such a convoy by filling its route with obstacles in advance, such as iron chains stretched under the surface of the water, sunken boats, fireships, stockades, etc. In combination with one or more of these obstacles, the attack will be formidable.

After the convoy is captured, a difficulty presents itself: for to carry it by water is to follow a route marked out and known by the enemy, and upon which the convoy is expected; and to carry it by land requires considerable means of transportation, probably more than the country can furnish. Of these two proceedings, the latter is to be preferred, except in a case of extreme scarcity of transportation; but in order to carry it out, it may be necessary to sacrifice and destroy a considerable portion of the materiel of the convoy.

7. Historical Examples.—I. *The siege of Corbie prevented by the entrance of a convoy.*—After the taking of the towns Thionville and Arlon by the French army in 1558, the king of Spain marched with his troops in great haste to lay siege to Corbie. The French were at a loss how to get succor to the place, for, from Marches, where they then lay, to Corbie, the distance is some thirty leagues, and in that day troops marched slowly. Nevertheless, Montluc offered to undertake the expedition, promising to reach Corbie before the king of Spain. His advice was at first rejected in the council, and was attributed to his boasting disposition; but he, in his usual manner, flew into a passion and cried, "If the king will but permit, I will succor the town, or perish;" upon which he was authorized to act as he desired. Quickly enrolling in his service seven ensigns, and collecting together bread, wine, oats, hay, and a chest full of powder, drawn by three horses, this adventurous soldier, who excelled in petty warfare, was about to start, when the king sent him word that, as "colonel-general" of the infantry *ad interim*, he must remain to command the regiments in person in case of a battle, and that the command of the convoy that had been prepared was assigned to Captain Brueil. The latter acquitted himself with credit; he marched chiefly by night, with prudence and circumspection, stopping in hidden places, and avoiding the villages; and was only two nights out. At sunrise after the second night, he appeared before Corbie. At about 300 paces from the town he was assailed by the Spanish cavalry, but, putting his troop on the gallop, he reached the gate of the city, and then made a stand against the enemy upon the edge of the ditch. The convoy lost seven or eight stragglers, but succeeded in entering the place with the powder, after which the Spaniards no longer ventured to undertake the siege.

This example illustrates the value of celerity and prudence in conducting a convoy, and proves that a little timely succor thrown into a place may save it from being besieged.

II. *Partial success of a convoy introduced into Lille in* 1708.—In this year, Prince Eugene, covered by the army of Marlborough, after his conquest of Oudenarde, proceeded to lay siege to Lille. The French marshal Boufflers, with 1,600 men, immortalized himself by his defence of the city, which is regarded as one of the most brilliant defences on record. Nevertheless, Lille fell, and history proves that this was in a great measure due to the want of skill of the

French army of relief, in suffering convoys sent to the famished troops of Eugene to pass. We have, however, one instance of a brilliant coup-de-main, which makes some amends for this want of skill in other cases.

At the commencement of the siege, the Chevalier de Luxembourg, who was subsequently made Marshal of Montmorency, was sent from Douai to introduce a convoy of powder into Lille. He collected "150 grenadiers and 2,000 cavalry, each carrying a musket, a bayonet, and a bag of fifty pounds of powder. To deceive the enemy, these troops assumed the dress of the Dutch soldiers."* After several demonstrations, with a view to divert the attention of the allies, Luxembourg gave Marshal Boufflers notice of his design, and commenced his march. Upon leaving Douai, at Pont-à-Rache, several horsemen of the centre of the column carelessly spilled some powder upon the pavement, which was ignited by sparks struck from the stones by the iron shoes of the horses in the rear of the column; a number of men and horses were scorched, but the expedition was still able to proceed. It reached the camp of the besiegers upon a dark night, and represented itself as bringing ammunition to the allies, and being pursued by the French. A sentinel hailed them in Dutch, and an officer replied in the

---

* De Vault, *Mémoires relatifs à la succession d'Espagne*, t. viii., p. 107. The supply destined for Lille appears, therefore, to have consisted of 2,000 muskets and 100,000 pounds of powder. It was also designed that two regiments of infantry should be thrown into the place at the same time.

same language, "Soldiers of Marlborough." Having reached the interior barrier, a close scrutiny by the captain of the guard had to be undergone, but all his questions were satisfactorily answered, and the gate was opened. Some 1,900 had already passed, when one of the officers, impatient at the slow movement of some of the horsemen, gave the imprudent order *Serre, serre* (Close up, close up). At these words the officer of the guard at once suspected the ruse, and ordered the detachment to halt. Luxembourg paying no attention to the order, the enemy fired, and three bags of the powder were exploded, killing sixty Frenchmen with their horses. Nevertheless, nearly the whole body penetrated into the town with their ammunition, while the rear of the convoy succeeded in escaping back to Douai.

But for the untimely exclamation of the French officer, the entire convoy would have succeeded in entering the place. This illustrates the necessity of possessing sufficient presence of mind, in ruses of this kind, to carry them out successfully to the end. Better not attempt them at all, than to unmask the design too soon.

III. *Attack of a water convoy.*—In the campaign of 1710, Marshal Villars learning that a convoy was on the way, by water, to the allies, who were besieging Aire, formed a project to cut it off:

This convoy, consisting of fifty barks, came down the river Lys, escorted by 1,000 infantry and 500 cavalry. The attack was made at the village of Saint-Eloi-Vive, between Deynse and Courtrai. The convoy halted, and the escort formed its order of battle, with the cavalry on the right, without protection, the infantry in the centre and on the left, the front covered by three ditches, the left resting upon an impassable marsh connecting with the river.

The attacking corps detached by Villars was under the orders of Ravignau, and consisted of 800 grenadiers, 1,500 fusiliers, and 300 dragoons. Ravignau extended his left to outflank the enemy's right, and occupied a road by which the opposing cavalry might debouch upon his infantry. His right, composed of fusiliers, confined itself to firing across the marsh; his centre, consisting of grenadiers, crossed the three ditches and beat down the enemy at the point of the bayonet; his left, which included the dragoons, overthrew the cavalry of the allies, and, turning to the right, took their infantry by the flank. Almost all the allied detachment were taken prisoners (500 men), slain, or drowned. The horses who pulled the transports were also taken, and used by the victors to carry off their prey. As to the powder, instead of throwing it into the water, the victorious troops adopted the singular expedient of setting fire to the three transports which contained it; the consequence of which imprudence was an explosion of such magnitude that the Lys was separated into two unnavigable branches, and the village of Saint-Eloi-Vive laid in ruins.*

IV. *Attack of a land convoy.*—In the month of June, 1758, Frederic, having laid siege to Olmutz with

---

* *Histoire de Marlborough*, an anonymous work emanating from the imperial press, Paris, 1806, t. iii., p. 220 to 232.

an army of comparatively feeble force, found himself in need of large supplies of ammunition. He expected from Silesia a convoy of 3,000 wagons, which should have come by Troppau, and took, unfortunately, a road in the possession of the enemy.

The convoy started with an escort of 9,000 men, under the orders of Colonel Mosel. Its march was slow and irregular, in consequence of the bad state of the roads, which were gullied by heavy rains, and a large number of the wagons stuck fast in the mud. Mosel left one third of his wagons behind, and, thus lightened, continued his march. While passing along a deep road, he was assailed by some Croates posted in a wood, and repulsed them; but a number of the peasant drivers being panic-struck, unhitched their teams during the fight, and ran off with the horses. The convoy was thus reduced to one half. Nevertheless, being strengthened by a reënforcement sent by Frederic, it continued to advance, until it was stopped near a wooded defile by 25,000 Austrians, who, firing upon the horses to disable them, and upon the caissons of powder to explode them, spread confusion in all directions. The escort drew up by platoons upon the whole line of wagons, and covering them in this way, sustained the conflict for two hours; but being everywhere weak, they were compelled to yield to the attacking columns in spite of their brave and stubborn resistance. All the convoy was destroyed excepting only 250 wagons, including 37 loaded with money, which reached the camp of the king. The Prussians were compelled by this loss to raise the siege of Olmutz;* and this event had an important influence upon the whole campaign.

V. *Rescue of a convoy of prisoners.*—In 1806, after the battle of Jena, the Prussian lieutenant Helwig planned and executed an attack upon a convoy of prisoners. This convoy, containing 8,000 Prussian prisoners, was on its way to Mayence, and had to pass through Erfurt. He waited for it with eighty horses in ambush near Eichrodt, which is in the vicinity of Erfurt, on the route from Eisenach to Gotha, and not far from the entrance into the defiles of Thuringia. Dividing his force into three platoons, he fell upon the four companies of infantry composing the whole escort, and finally routed them, as they proved too feeble both to fight and at the same time guard so many men.† The escort retreated, and the prisoners were rescued.‡

This is one of the most striking examples of the bad consequences resulting from the employment of too small an escort, especially for a convoy of prisoners.

VI. *Re-capture of a convoy.*—In the year 1811, in the environs of Placentia, Spain, some French dragoons seized upon a convoy of seventy mules loaded with wine, which made them drunk, and in this condition attacked a body of Portuguese infantry. It

---

* Archenholtz, *Histoire de la guerre de Sept Ans,* traduction du Baron de Bock, Metz, 1789, 12mo.; t. i., p. 102 to 106.

† At the same period I find a French escort composed of eighteen companies and two pieces of artillery, for a convoy of 22,000 prisoners. This is also weak, but much less so than four companies for 8,000 prisoners.

‡ I borrow this fact from Jacquinot de Presle.

need hardly be said that they were repulsed and the convoy taken from them.*

This example shows that when a convoy has been once captured, the first care should be to put it out of reach of danger.

* Napier's History of the Peninsular War.

CHAPTER SIXTH.

PARTISANS.*

THE term *partisans* is given to isolated bodies intended to reconnoitre for the army from which they are sent, and also to protect it,† or else to harass, to retard, and to deceive the enemy; to cut off their supplies, and to weaken them, by compelling them to send off detachments; or again to punish the population by levying contributions, etc.

Partisans do not act solely at a venture, as might be supposed, nor do they trust themselves rashly to chance; but their operations are connected with the general plan of campaign, and depend upon the general-in-chief under whose orders they are undertaken. This condition shows at once the restrictions under

---

* The reader is referred to art. xi. of the *Ordonnance sur le service en campagne*. Notwithstanding the official existence of this article in respect to partisans, we would observe that in the present century the French (and also the English) have almost wholly dispensed with partisan warfare.

† Hence they are frequently also called *flankers*. The *Ordonnance* says "*corps* of *partisans*," and "*detachments* of *flankers*," whence it appears that the latter may be less numerous and have not the same need of a separate organization.

which partisans at the present day exist, being subjected (except as to the execution of their orders) to that regularity and centralization which distinguish not only modern armies, but all associations; and hence, also, we see how widely they differ from the partisans of the Thirty Years' War, and even from those of the Seven Years' War, in respect to the freedom of their movements.

The composition and force of these corps are prescribed in the French regulations, according to the object to be accomplished, the difficulties to be surmounted, the length of the route to be travelled, and the probable duration of the expedition. They may sometimes embrace troops of different arms,* but in preference should consist of light cavalry, which is able to surprise, to strike, and to retire, almost before being perceived, and certainly before being compromised. The aim should be to form them, not of many soldiers, but of very good ones—for here quality is much more important than quantity, as history fully proves. Therefore, select your volunteer partisans (I say *volunteer*, because the first condition is to secure men whose disposition leads them to this kind of service), from among men who are experienced in war and in outpost service, good marksmen, skilful with the bayonet and sabre, accustomed to gymnastic exercises, and good horsemen; men who will not object to

---

* This is stated in conformity with the regulations referred to. General Dufour (*Cours de Tactique*, second edition, p. 346), thinks there should be no mixture of the two arms (infantry and cavalry), in order that there may be less embarrassment in marching, and greater mobility.

taking hold of a spade or a pickaxe when necessary, and who are fond of the soldier's life; men of honor and self-devotion; especially let them be temperate and robust men, for they will be compelled to suffer the privations and hardships of the smuggler in addition to those of the soldier.

One half the infantry of a corps of partisans should be pioneers, with *some* artillerists.

The light cavalry will answer very well if composed of five hundred men, taken by fifties, from the regiments of chasseurs, hussars, and lancers.

The best corps of partisans will be found to be those free and irregular corps which are raised during war by officers of reputation, who are detailed both to form and command them; or better still, those who rise into notice in consequence of political events, and choose their own leaders. The latter free corps should have their existence legalized by a species of letter of marque: they may be called land privateers.*

There are certain essential qualities which should be combined in a partisan chief, even more than in a commandant of a detachment, and the proper selection of such a chief is of even greater importance than the composition of the corps. He is to be chosen from among the officers of the most willing disposition, without regard to priority of rank; further, he should be young and yet experienced, and should be able to speak the language of the country. This com-

---

* Some authors give the name of *partisans* only to these free and irregular corps; regarding those as provisional, and properly to be designated as "parties," which are composed of detachments of light troops.

bination of qualities will certainly be difficult to find; yet not impossible, if the general is possessed of sufficient penetration and decision to distinguish and at the same time disregard the jealousies which are so apt to be excited by rising talent. A partisan chief should be of an ardent temperament and glowing imagination, rather than a cool thinker or methodical calculator. He should, besides, be vigilant, firm, collected, disinterested, prompt, adroit, vigorous both in conception and in execution, of strong will, and the determined resolution to succeed.*

The operations of partisans embrace all those which belong to petty warfare; and since the corps which executes them is not strong in numbers, it must have recourse to a thousand expedients to compensate for its feebleness, relying especially upon cunning and audacity, and should make its preparations and act with secrecy. For such a corps, to obtain much with little, is a necessity; and therefore, except when upon a special mission, it may in general try its fortune and venture upon hazardous and doubtful enterprises; for if it succeeds it renders an important service, and if it perishes the loss is comparatively small.

Above all, it must cause itself to be respected. In a friendly country, there will be no difficulty in this respect, if the conduct of the corps is such as to inspire confidence and admiration. In a hostile country, it should keep the population in a state of quiet submission, and for this purpose it must not hesitate to

* Davidoff, *Essai sur la guerre de partisans*, traduction du colonel comte Héraclius de Polignac, p. 65, 66.

make examples when necessary. It must, moreover, multiply itself, so to speak, and wherever it goes must create alarm and disturbance, to conceal the feebleness of its actual numbers. Even when surprised and almost surrounded by treachery, the corps should never surrender; but, as such an event must have been provided for in advance, each soldier, at a given signal of the chief, should make his escape and steal away among the obstacles of the ground, to meet his comrades at some previously appointed place of rendezvous.

When once separated from the army, partisans should bid adieu to idleness and rest, which would lose them the chance of more than one attack. Their eyes must never close, and if they are overcome for an instant by fatigue, they must throw out a line of spies, to give them warning of the approach of danger.

They march, as much as possible, concealed from the enemy by the elevations of the ground. Information previously obtained from maps or from the inhabitants, will direct the march, which is also to be facilitated by a guide, while it is reconnoitred and protected by flankers, posts, and sometimes sentinels or vedettes. They march chiefly by night, and always with order, silence, and discipline. To ferret out everything, they make frequent and radical changes of direction. They must be hindered by nothing, for the lightness of their equipment gives them the greatest mobility.

They avoid inhabited places. When obliged to pass through them, they search them, or take hostages from among the most notable persons. When merely obliged to pass near them, they make requisitions upon them for provisions and forage for a larger number of men than their troop contains, which little ruse serves to intimidate the population, and keep them in check.

They conceal their approach to the enemy until the last moment. Having arrived at the favorable point, they attack with vigor and spirit, and so that neither their designs nor their numbers can be discovered. Their action is doubled in value by its unexpectedness and by the vigor of its blows. In this respect they have been compared to vultures darting upon their prey. Or else, they ambuscade and wait; which is a game they can easily play, especially in rainy and foggy weather.

When an engagement appears doubtful, they at once retire without hesitation.

The regulations recommend that the chief of a corps of partisans should communicate the object of his expedition to the chief who comes immediately after him. This formality should always be strictly observed; for he may perish, while the orders concerning the object and extent of the operation, as well as the point of rendezvous, are secret orders, which cannot be understood by anybody merely from an inspection and comparison of the first acts of the corps, as may be done in the case of most other detachments.

According to article 119 of the "*Service en Campagne,*" prizes taken by partisans belong to them, when it has been shown by the authentic declaration of a competent authority, that these prizes consist of things taken from the enemy.* They are sold for the benefit of the partisans, with the exception of arms and munitions of war, which are appropriated to the use of the army, an allowance nearly equivalent to their value being made for them. The division of the profits of this sale, or indemnity, among the partisans, is made according to rank:

Each superior officer receives	5 parts.
Each captain	4 "
Each lieutenant (first or second)	3 "
Each non-commissioned officer	2 "
Each corporal or soldier	1 "

The commandant of the expedition has six parts besides what his grade gives him. This arrangement applies to any isolated detachment which succeeds in bringing in a prize: "It would be unjust and impolitic," says General Préval, "to deprive detachments of this privilege."

It appears from this that the hope of gain serves also to excite the zeal and increase the courage of partisans. But another consequence is a tendency to rapacity, which is constantly fed by new gains. The general-in-chief will therefore find it expedient to force them to make an exact list of all the requisitions which they have exacted, and to produce this list upon their return, accompanied with certificates from the local authorities.

A number of partisan leaders have made themselves distinguished names. In the beginning of the

---

* Things taken from the inhabitants are returned to them.

Thirty Years' War (1618), Count Ernest de Mansfeld, a man of excessive ferocity, distinguished himself as a partisan chief. In 1700, we have in France Dumoulin, who in the midst of winter, marched with his dragoons fifteen leagues without halting, to form an ambuscade. In the wars for the succession in Austria (from 1740 to 1745), we notice among the Austrians the fierce Mentzel, Trenck, a cousin of the celebrated prisoner of Frederic II. at Magdebourg, and Nadasty, with his Pandours; and among the French, Fischer, the founder of a corps which bore his name, Grassin, and La Morlière. During the Seven Years' War, we may mention Lieutenant-colonel Emmerich, the author of a small work upon the special duties of partisans; in the campaign of 1809, the Prussian major Schill; and between 1812 and 1814, the Russians, Seslawine and Michel Orloff.

We cite a few historical examples, to illustrate the nature of the operations executed by partisans.

1st. Dangeau relates that on the 21st June, 1710, a French partisan, leaving Namur with 250 men, succeeded in entering Lille, overcame the guard which was at the gate, proceeded to the centre of the town, and took the whole guard, killing their commander. He then pillaged the houses of the minister of the emperor and the residence of a Dutch officer who commanded in Liege, and having secured a large amount of booty, left the city with 50 prisoners. In this affair, there was but one soldier killed and one wounded." *

* *Journal de Dangeau*, nouvelle éd., par MM. Soulié, Dussieux, de Chennevières, etc.

2d. In 1712, Marshal Villars detached "Pasteur, a brigadier of the troops from Spain, and a very good partisan, for the purpose of penetrating into Holland, where there were no troops. This officer acquitted himself well; he approached very close to Rotterdam, and burned the small towns of Tortolles and Sleimbourg. This expedition astonished the Dutch, who were not accustomed to see us so near to them."*

3d. "A partisan officer having remarked that two regiments of the enemy, while on a march, had encamped on the two opposite sides of a ravine, to pass the night, stole into the ravine and caused his soldiers to fire a volley to the right and left upon the two regiments. The latter fired in turn, supposing the enemy to be before them" (but, as it appears, fired upon each other), "and were very much astonished on the following day to find so many killed on each side."†

4th. "I remember," says Le Miere de Corvey,‡ "that in 1798, while in command of a company of partisans in Belgium, I was sent to Loo-Christi, some leagues from Ghent. I had no more than 25 men with me, and was surrounded by more than 400 of the enemy. I had been ordered to wait for the arrival of the rest of my company, which had dispersed, and

---

* *Vie de Villars*, publiée par Anquetil, 1784, 12mo., t. ii., p. 232.

† *Harangue latine sur l'art militaire*, traduite par l'abbé Creyssent de la Moscillo, à la suite de *l'Examin de plusieurs observations sur la littérature*, Paris, 1779, p. 379. I adduce this fact because it contains a hint of a useful ruse, but I regret not being able to give a clearer account of it.

‡ *Des partisans et des corps irréguliers*, 1823, p. 256, 257.

could not collect until the next day. This village, being open on all sides, was not tenable, and I made use of a ruse. I sent for the bailiff, and told him I was in momentary expectation of the arrival of 100 horses and 250 infantry, and ordered an immediate supply of 100 rations of forage and 350 of provisions, which the bailiff furnished in the shortest possible time. I then ordered the inhabitants to return to their homes and to keep quiet. After dark, I secretly sent out small detachments, which returned by another road with my drummer in front, beating the night march. This manœuvre I repeated several times. The ruse was successful, and I passed the night undisturbed; but the officer who relieved me the next day with 75 men was beaten two days after by the enemy, who had concentrated their forces and knew they had but 75 men to contend with."

CHAPTER SEVENTH.

SURPRISES AND AMBUSCADES.

INTRODUCTION.—Against every anticipated and open attack there exists a method of defence which is taught by the military art; and to put it in practice, even before superior forces and under unfavorable circumstances, requires only that we have sufficient time to make the proper preparations. But this time is indispensable, and if it is not given, we are *surprised*, and find ourselves in a critical situation.

A surprise, therefore, offers *à priori* an advantage to the assailant, by reason of its unforeseen character—an advantage which may enable a feeble troop to overcome and to crush a numerous one, and which compensates largely for the uncertainty incident to this kind of operations.

To succeed in them, surprises must be prepared in concealment, and hence they are most frequently employed in a hilly country. They demand prompt execution; for the data upon which they are based soon change, and delay produces uncertainty as to the position and plans of the enemy. They should also have reference to troops imperfectly guarded; and hence they will be attempted against detachments rather than against armies, for in these days the latter all make use of thoroughly organized measures for their security. These measures, remarks Clausewitz,* render surprises very rare in modern warfare; yet they are not impossible, for vigilant and experienced troops, even against an army.

Surprises may be employed either in offensive or defensive operations. The assailant effects them by an unexpected march, or the suddenness of his attack: and the defender, by the secrecy and thoroughness of his arrangements; but a true surprise is most effective in offensive warfare, and constitutes one of its most important elements.

Two methods of preparing a surprise offer themselves: 1st. To resolutely await the adversary and ambuscade him near the route he is pursuing; 2d. To advance upon the enemy by a rapid and circuitous march. Let us examine these two methods. The greater part of the precautions to be used in the one will apply also to the other.

1. Surprises by Ambuscade.—The term ambuscade comes from a word in the low Latin, copied by the Spanish and Italian languages,† and signifies *in the woods;* in fact, wooded places are favorable for this kind of operation.

* *De la guerre*, traduction Neuens, t. iii., p. 300.

† In low Latin, *emboscata*, in Spanish, *emboscada*, in Italian, *imboscata*. According to the translator of Santa-Cruz, the Spaniards in the last century said *embosques*, and *bosque* in their language signifies a wood.

The purpose of an ambuscade may be to capture a post, a cantonment, a patrol, a drove of cattle, or a convoy of military stores or merchandise; or to seize upon some of the inhabitants, especially an important personage (a prince, general, ambassador, bearer of dispatches, etc.); sometimes, also, to make a reconnoissance, or, again, to fall upon a troop, which is either on a march or already engaged in a combat.

The composition of the corps charged with an ambuscade requires the most minute attention. The officers and the soldiers should be experienced and ready, full of confidence in those who direct them, quick to strike, in darkness and in the midst of obstacles, wherever and whenever ordered. The selection of the horses is of the same importance. White ones are too easily seen at a distance; therefore take those of a dark color in preference. As the least noise might give the alarm, reject animals which snort from fear, as also those which neigh upon the slightest occasion. Hence, it will be seen that mares are to be preferred for surprises; besides, they are more quiet, support heat and thirst better, and can urinate without halting. For these reasons the Arabs prefer them in all adventurous enterprises;* but we ought to add that, in case of a pursuit, if they are wounded, they have less force and energy to carry their riders beyond the reach of danger.

Since it is evident that profound silence is here one of the first elements of success, both in the march

---

* *Les chevaux de Sahara*, par le général Daumas, third ed., 18mo., 1855, p. 76, note 2.

and in the ambuscade, no dogs should be allowed to accompany the expedition, notwithstanding their qualities as watches, for it would be difficult to prevent being betrayed by their untimely barking. The expedition should start by night to conceal its departure, and so as to reach the place of ambuscade by the break of day, which is the more favorable time for discovering. It should follow paths that are little frequented and free from stones, for the horses' feet among them would make too much noise. The horsemen should also be directed to secure their equipment in a solid manner, and to cover their scabbards with hay, in order to avoid all clanking sounds.

If the road to the place of ambuscade has been softened by rain and retains footprints, these must be obliterated by a roller or by sweeping the road with long branches of trees—an operation that may be intrusted to a small rear-guard of foot soldiers;[*] otherwise the enemy will follow your tracks and will discover you; unless, indeed, you deceive him, as has been often recommended, by going considerably beyond the place of ambuscade, and returning to it by a bend across fields and over very dry ground.

The position selected for the ambuscade should be of sufficient extent to contain the force, an "out of the way" and lonely place, but open, with a sufficiently extended front, and with at least two outlets, one suitable for retreat, the other for making a sudden attack upon the enemy. When the ambuscade is probably to be occupied more than one day, select

---

[*] Santa-Cruz, *Réflexions militaires*, t. ii., p. 242.

the position near some spring, if possible, so as to secure a supply of water: provisions you can readily carry with you.

Cavalry is in its nature more difficult to conceal and place in ambuscade than infantry;* but this inconvenience is in a measure compensated by its celerity, which enables it to attack at the instant of its discovery. This arm should lie in wait in winding valleys, in woods, in broad ravines with not very steep sides, or in isolated farm-yards; and in this last case, if but one outlet exists, care should be taken to provide a second, by removing, when necessary, any high wall or fence.

Infantry can be concealed at the bottom of a ditch, behind a bank, along a railway, under a rock, among hedges, vines, growing grain—almost anywhere, indeed, for they can, if necessary, sit down, or even lie at full length. The position of an ambuscade should also be such that the adversary can bring but a portion of his forces into action. If the purpose is to surprise an enemy on the march, the position should be not far from some steep descent, a ford, or a plateau favorable for a halt; in short, near places where the enemy will slacken their speed and preserve less order.

If, on the contrary, the enemy to be surprised is encamped or cantoned, you will place yourself so that you may emerge from the ambuscade when the men are going to their meals, or when they are leading their horses to water.

---

* Nevertheless, ambuscades are often composed of mixed troops, that is, of both infantry and cavalry.

After having decided upon the position of the ambuscade, do not, in any case, enter it until you have previously searched it. Place your troops in the most concealed manner possible. Surround them with sentinels and even vedettes, who must endeavor to fulfil the twofold and difficult condition of seeing without being seen; they must fall back, when necessary, but must never challenge any one. You can second these sentinels and increase your facilities of acquiring information by placing near the road a soldier disguised as a peasant and affecting to be engaged in tilling the ground. Let none pass, especially inhabitants, but put them under guard, and even sometimes tie them up.

As soon as the troops are in ambuscade, they should observe increased caution. Talking, smoking, moving about, or going off upon any pretext, making any kind of noise, and lighting a fire, should all be forbidden. Going to sleep should be especially prohibited. All the soldiers must remain awake,* and even in constant readiness for combat, especially in an ambuscade of cavalry. The infantry should sit or lie down, and in either case their arms should be placed on the ground; for if they remain standing with their arms in hand, or if they sit with them between their legs, a gun might be accidentally discharged (as they are all loaded), and thus betray the existence of the ambuscade.

---

* Several general officers have said that a part of the troop might sleep *during the day;* but in all cases it would be very dangerous at night, as one of the examples cited at the end of this chapter proves.

The attack upon the enemy must be sudden, and rather upon the rear than the front of his column, in order to produce more indecision and disorder in the ranks. The infantry, after discharging a full volley,* will rush upon the enemy with loud cries: the cavalry will take him in reverse by making a detour, for the purpose of blocking his way. To attack at the proper instant, neither too soon nor too late, is the most important and delicate point to be decided by the commanding officer. Soldiers in ambush cannot but feel a certain degree of emotion in beholding the enemy passing carelessly and gaily almost within arms' length, unconscious of the danger which is about to fall upon him, and against which his bravery may prove powerless; and this emotion will naturally be increased when they recall the fatigue they have undergone and the risk they have run in concealing themselves, and when they reflect that the most trifling incident may rob them of the fruit of all their labor; hence it is not surprising that, in their anxiety to put an end to this uncertainty and to grasp the coveted object, they often act with too much precipitation, and thus cause the failure of the enterprise. The success of this operation of petty warfare, therefore, depends greatly upon coolness, as well as upon the quickness of eye and the skill which are the natural attendants of coolness.

If a corps purposely fleeing before the enemy can thereby draw them in front of the ambuscade, success

---

* Some sharpshooters, properly posted, should at this time aim at the officers.

becomes almost certain. This ruse is chiefly employed in retreats, and serves to aid the vanquished party in retarding and weakening the pursuing force.

When we have discovered the existence of an ambuscade prepared by the adversary, an excellent way to meet it is to prepare a counter-ambuscade, for the enemy will infallibly be disconcerted when he finds himself surprised where he expected to surprise others.

2. **Surprises by a March.**—This kind of surprise enables us to avoid the inconvenience of a too precipitate attack, but depends upon the exactness of a calculation. The march must be calculated so as to fall upon the enemy just at the most propitious place and time, and the difficulty in this calculation is to make proper allowance for delays and for accidents.

It appears best to attack at the break of day, when the patrols of the enemy have gone in, and the fatigued outpost guards are reposing, or have relaxed their vigilance. By choosing this time we also have the advantage of daylight for the end of the operation, and are better able to extricate ourselves from any unforeseen difficulties.

In the case where we are aiming at troops that are on the march, we should follow a route either at right angles or very oblique to theirs, in order not to fall among their flankers, and to remain masters of the time when we shall choose to make our appearance.

In the present century surprises effected by means of a march are of more frequent occurrence than ambuscades. This march may remain very secret, by imitating the plan pursued by the French in the Portuguese campaign to surprise the English posts, namely, by wrapping the horses' feet in pieces of sheepskin, with the wool inside, tied above the hoof.

We cannot conclude these remarks more appropriately than by repeating, with General Kleber: "A surprise is more dishonorable than a defeat," and by quoting the following precept from his orders of the day: "The bravest man may be beaten; but whoever allows himself to be surprised no longer deserves to be an officer."

3. Historical Examples.—I. *We should emerge from an ambuscade in a solid body.*—During the war in Africa, in the 44th year before the Christian era, "Labienus, seeing that Cæsar would be obliged to cross a certain valley and a wood, placed an ambuscade there. Not knowing the existence of the snare, Cæsar had sent his cavalry in advance; and when they reached the valley, the troops of Labienus, forgetting their orders, or executing them unskilfully, or perhaps fearing to be overthrown in the valley by the cavalry, began to emerge from their ambuscade in single file and one soldier at a time, for the purpose of gaining the neighboring summit. Our horsemen (says Cæsar) forthwith went in pursuit of them, killed a large number, took many prisoners, and then, turning to the hill, obtained possession of it, having first driven off the troops that had been posted there by Labienus, who had much difficulty in saving himself, with a part of his cavalry." *

---

* Cæsar's "*Commentaries:* The War in Africa," chap. 1.

II. *In surprises, do not forget to adopt some distinguishing feature of dress, or a rallying signal.**— In 1667, Villars, then a colonel, was sent by night to reconnoitre and ascertain whether an embankment was guarded. He advanced with 300 horse, leaving the remainder of his troop in the rear, marched along the causeway, sent his drummers and trumpeters ahead to make an uproar and distract the attention of the enemy, while he fell suddenly upon him through a breach in a deserted barrier, and routed him, in spite of his force of 2,000 men. In the very height of the action, the French reserve arrived, and took the combatants in the rear. " Villars, supposing his troop surrounded, turned back. There was a short, but murderous combat of Frenchmen with Frenchmen, which ceased only with the rallying cry of '*Villars.*' This unfortunate mistake saved a part of the enemy, who, nevertheless, were dislodged." †

III. *Soldiers in ambush should not sleep.*—On this point, the Marquis of Santa-Cruz,‡ one of the best military writers of Spain, relates the following fact: " In the night ambuscade which we formed (in 1710) against our enemies near Mora de Ebro, care was not taken to prevent the soldiers from going to sleep. They were in a profound slumber when, a little before day, a horse of Don Joseph Miranda got

---

* For example, the shirt thrown over the dress, as at the taking of Pontoise in 1419. A surprise was then called a *camisade* (from *chemise*).
† *Vie de Villars*, par Anquetil, t. i., p. 18, 19. In attacking, instead of simply reconnoitring, the impetuous Villars transgressed his orders.
‡ *Réflexions militaires et politiques*, traduction Vergy, t. ii., p. 260.

loose; and hardly had he begun to run across the fields, when the soldiers, awakened by the noise, began to call to arms, some firing without knowing where, some flying, and some taking each other for enemies, so that the ambuscade was discovered before its time and came to nothing."

IV. During the siege of Mayence (1793), the besieged French failed in a surprise attempted upon the Prussian headquarters located at Marienborn, in consequence of the cry *Vive la nation*, which they gave at an untimely moment.

V. In 1796, the republicans sent a chief of a battalion with 200 grenadiers and 25 mounted chasseurs to surprise a farmhouse (la *métairie* de la Saugrenière). This small body marched in four different ways, with a column of fifty men in each, and thus debouched in silence at the four cardinal points of the plateau on which the farmhouse was situated, surrounded the house by placing four men with loaded guns at each of the corners of the ground-floor, while two patrols of four men knocked at each of the doors and summoned the Vendean chief Stofflet and the three officers who had taken refuge in this asylum, to surrender.

VI. *The vanquished party who in retreating too near to the pursuer, without some covering obstacle, may be easily surprised.*—Marshal Marmont, arriving at Champaubert on the evening of the battle of Vauchamps, February 14th, 1814, learned that the vanquished enemy had just settled themselves about two thirds of a mile off, at Etoges. He marched upon the position in the most profound silence and by night, with 800 foot soldiers, flanked on each side by 50 skirmishers, fell upon the Russian outposts, routed them at the point of the bayonet, entered the village, found the enemy scattered and engaged in establishing themselves, and took nearly the whole of them prisoners, to the number of 4,000 men, without having fired more than 500 shots.

VII. In July, 1845, in Algeria, a detachment of 300 foot and 25 horse, in command of Manselon, had marched for a night in a wooded gorge four feet wide, when they found themselves, at the first dawn of day, within ten minutes of the Douars of the Sbeahs, a tribe whose hospitality had just been shown to Bou-Maza, and which it was intended to surprise. After a moment's halt, the march continued, every one on the alert and watchful; but in making a detour around an earthwork, a foot soldier stumbled against a stone, and his fall caused his gun to go off. "*Au galop, cavaliers*," cried the commandant at once, "and try to make amends for the blundering of that fool: we will follow you upon the run." The Arabs, warned by the discharge of the gun, were already starting off, for between the untimely signal and the first charge of the mounted chasseurs, they had had three minutes to make their preparations; but notwithstanding the confusion, the coup-de-main was successful.*

* *Souvenirs de la vie militaire en Afrique*, par le comte de Castellane, in 18mo., 1852, pp. 196–198.

CHAPTER EIGHTH.

HEIGHTS.

The skilful and timely occupation of positions of this kind, and their proper defence and attack, exercise an important influence upon the final result of warlike operations. We shall therefore treat of them first in order.

1. Reconnoissance.—Before occupying a height, we must first reconnoitre it.

We first examine the *outline* of the height. In this outline there should be shown the direction of the crest or ridge which bounds the plateau, the natural line of retreat, the course of valleys bordering upon it, and the character of the slopes should be indicated. Every road, and every path, even the smallest, should also receive attention, for the light foot soldier may climb up anywhere, and we should indicate even the steep paths followed by the goats.

We must also examine the *profile* of the height, its contour, its relief from the bottom of the valley to the summit, the peculiarities of the slopes, the abrupt escarpments and projections, the intermediate plateaux, and the successive rises.

We must also indicate the places in which a combat may be engaged, either in line or skirmishing, those in which cavalry might, as an exception, have a chance of success, and finally those in which artillery may be posted with advantage.

2. **Defence.**—In a height, as upon any field of battle, there exists a line of demarcation between the ground of the defence, or *plateau*, and the ground of the attack, or *slope*. This line has been named the *military crest*, because it is, in fact, analogous in position to the exterior crest of a parapet.

Without wishing to ascribe undue importance to a military crest, we will observe that this line, which has a somewhat vague existence, and is to be found approximately by trial, has nevertheless its use in the contest. In fact, it is upon this line that the assailant is to be stopped, for if he once gains the plateau he

Defender. Assailant.

will soon master it. In order to accomplish the object in the best manner possible, the defender should be placed *in rear of the military crest, and very near to it.* By very near, we here mean from a yard and a half to nine yards, according to the inclination of the slope. Thus, while the defender, with his gun pointed, will be uncovered only to the shoulders, he will see the whole body of the assailant as he climbs the ascent, for a distance of fifty or sixty yards; whereas, if he were stationed forty yards, for example, behind the crest, he would be below the prolongation of the slope, and would, therefore, be unable to reach his

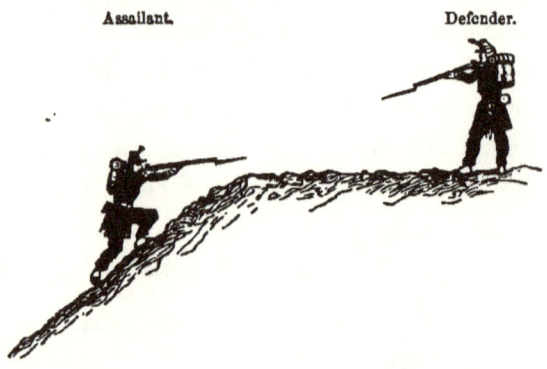

adversary while climbing; at the same time he would receive the grazing fire of his antagonist, from the moment the latter arrived within a yard and a half of the top of the crest.*

The first line of defenders will, therefore, stand on the plateau, near the military crest. I say *first* line, for it will be well to have two lines and a reserve.

* We may, however, take our position at some fifty paces behind the crest, when the assailant is ignorant of the precise position of the enemy he is attempting to find; for in this case his grazing fire will probably not take place, for he will not see the defender while ascending, whatever may be the inclination of the slope.

The first line will be in order of battle, or spread out as skirmishers if the plateau abounds in undergrowth, and will receive the assailant by a fire at a short distance, a little before he reaches the crest. If this discharge does not arrest him, they must charge upon him with the bayonet, and, having overthrown him, must retire coolly to their first position.

The second line will stand generally in order of battle, ready to second and to assist the first.

The sole business of the reserve will be to oppose any flanking movements of the enemy; for which purpose it will watch the passages by which such movements might be effected.

With such a mode of defence, repeated several times if there is a succession of plateaux, always executed with patience and coolness, and without undertaking a dangerous and useless pursuit, it is probable that the height will be preserved. We may add to our chance of success by resorting also to well-combined flanking fires. It is in the latter kind of firing that cannon may here become of real service. As to cavalry, it is evident that it should act chiefly with the reserve on the plateau.

This mode of defence, which requires solid and experienced infantry, was inaugurated and put in practice by the English against the valorous but too impulsive French soldiers in Spain; first at the battle of Talavera (July 28, 1809), and in the most memorable instance, on the heights of Pampeluna (July 28, 1813). In this last affair, the French ascended the slope in close columns by divisions, and an English line received them with a close volley, charged upon them with the bayonet and threw them back, then returned to their position upon a run, with three hurrahs. They met a second attack attempted by the resolute French columns, in precisely the same manner, and with the same success.

3. Attack.—In the first place, as an attempt upon the front would be too destructive, we should endeavor to turn the position, and until the last moment seek for a path by which this may be accomplished.

If we are finally compelled to attack in front, we should make one or too false attacks, designed, as usual, to divide the attention of the defender, and to promote the success of the principal attack.

This principal attack (the others being analogous) will be made by a large number of light troops, supported close at hand by small and mobile columns.* A single broad and deep column would be a false measure, and a failure to place skirmishers in front would be a most grave and disastrous error—the error, in fact, which was committed on the heights of Pampeluna, of which we have just spoken. For these skirmishers will break up any manœuvre by the English mode of defence, by compelling the defenders also to disperse in order to meet them, or else to waste their fire, and in any case will deprive the defenders of the *ensemble* and of the expectant situation which constitutes all their strength.†

---

* Columns of one company, for example.

† See *Quelques réflexions sur l'infanterie de nos jours*, par le général de Chambray, in the *Mélanges* of that author.

The skirmishers can go anywhere, and consequently will finally succeed in advancing up the slope. Under their protection the small columns will gain some intermediate plateau or some commanding position, from which they can fire directly upon the defenders. If this fire produces effect, they will ascend another step; a third will bring them upon the upper plateau, and if at that instant one of the false attacks makes a more violent and noisy demonstration to alarm one of the flanks, it is probable that the defenders will yield, and, fearing to be turned, will retire.

The good discipline of the assailant, his confidence, and his assurance of victory, will go far to remove the obstacles and to diminish the perils of such an attack.

4. Attack of an isolated height in Africa by a company of infantry.—A company frequently acts alone in Africa, and as a young officer may occasionally be called to command one, it may be useful to point out this mode of attack, which we derive from the verbal instructions of Marshal Bugeaud.

The company, divided into four half sections, takes

ATTACK OF A HEIGHT IN AFRICA.

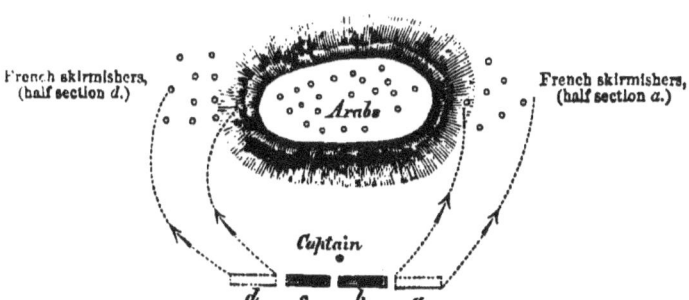

its position at 200 yards from the height. The half sections on the extreme right (*a*) and left (*d*) are detached to the right and left, scattering, so as to take the Arabs defending the height by the flanks, and even somewhat in the rear. When these skirmishers have succeeded in producing some confusion among the defenders by their firing, the two half sections of the centre (*b* and *c*) advance under the orders of the captain, with arms at a shoulder, until within about fifty yards of the foot of the height, and then fire a full volley to complete the confusion of the defenders; then they rush forward at a run with fixed bayonets and scale the height. This discharge serves as a signal to the skirmishers on the right and left, and apprises them of the instant when they must rapidly move upon the flank and almost upon the rear of the defenders, who will thus find themselves taken, so to speak, in a closed circle, unless they decide to abandon their position.

CHAPTER NINTH.

WOODS.

Woods, like heights, are positions where infantry plays the principal part, and hence their importance has grown with the increase of that arm and the multiplication of fire-arms.

1. Reconnoissance.—The greater the obstacle offered by a wood, the greater is the necessity of reconnoitring it.

The officer sent to reconnoitre a wood, leaves from a fifth to a fourth part of his detachment at the entrance as a reserve. Taking the principal road himself with four men and a guide, he sends into each of the lateral and secondary roads a patrol of from four to six men, who should keep on the same level and in communication with him. He completes the general indications contained in the map of the country, and gathers the materials for his report, from the information which these patrols furnish, from his own observation, and from the replies of the wood-cutters, gamekeepers, poachers, and other individuals whom he meets in the wood.

This report must show: 1st, *the extent of the wood,*

in order that the time necessary to pass through or to turn it may be inferred; 2d, *its exterior form*, its salient and reëntrant portions, and whether it is surrounded by a ditch; 3d, *the nature of the wood*, whether forest or coppice; forest trees furnish abatis; coppice offers little hindrance to light infantry, and, if the ground is sterile, even light cavalry may sometimes pass through it; 4th, *the openings* in the wood, and whether these openings are favorable for the operations of cavalry; 5th, the number, direction, and condition of the *principal roads*, which may be adapted to the mechanism of the defence, by permitting the employment of artillery and cavalry; 6th, the same respecting *cart roads*, and any other roads auxiliary to the principal ones; 7th, the form of the *paths*, their courses, and their points of intersection, for the paths facilitate the action of skirmishers in defence, as well as the march of patrols and guards; 8th, *the situation and sufficiency of running streams and stagnant waters*, which may be serviceable in ambuscades, and offer facilities in offensive manœuvres: in a word, those which may be a protection to the defenders and an obstacle to the assailants; 9th, finally, the neighboring villages, hamlets, country seats, abbeys, farmhouses, and isolated buildings in general, which are capable of serving as habitations or storehouses for the defender, together with their distances from the verge of the wood.

2. Defence.—The prime object of the defence is to arrest the assailant at the verge of the wood, for when once within it, the assailant will likewise profit by the nature of the obstacle (namely, by the trees and the underwood), to fight and to advance under cover.

The outlets, therefore, are to be closed, and the projecting points protected by abatis; these projecting points may also have additional protection by stationing pieces of artillery so as to give an effective fire, and yet not exposed to be readily taken. A centre of action is to be selected, either naturally or artificially connected with the skirts of the wood by convenient communications.

DEFENCE OF A FOREST.

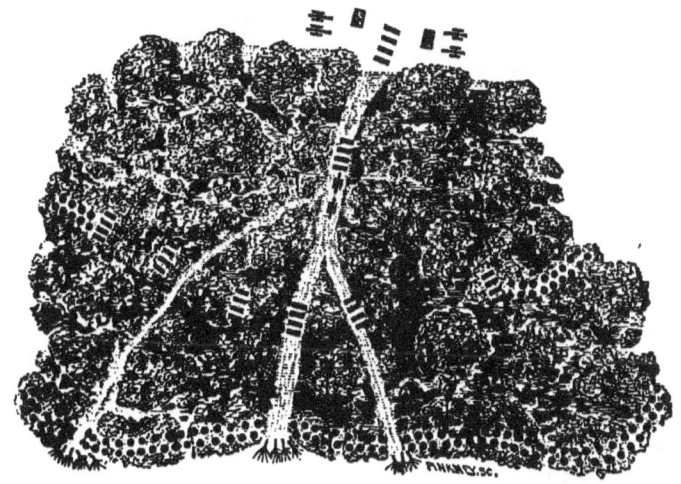

The distribution of the troops will be based upon the fact that in this case a numerous reserve would not have free scope for its action. As large a number of men as possible will therefore be put into action at once, one half the force being thrown upon the contour of the wood as skirmishers, and the remaining half divided into two parts, the first of which will be placed in a second line, while the other forms a reserve. This reserve will occupy a central position,

DEFENCE OF A COPPICE.

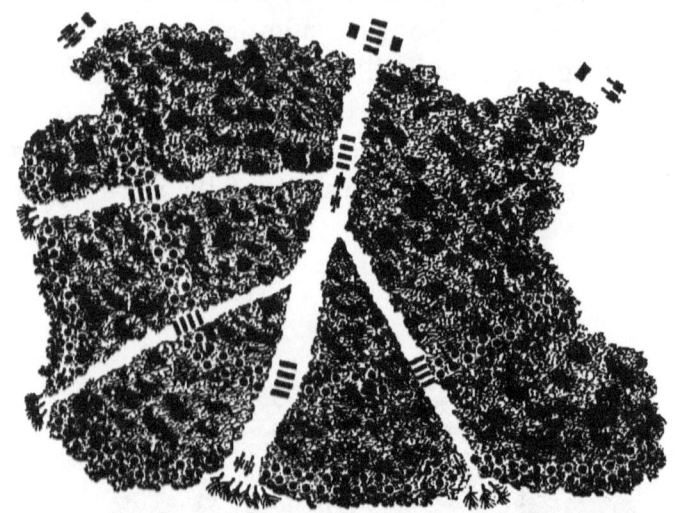

resting upon the structures prepared for the defence, if there are any, and keeping a watch upon any flank or rear movements which the enemy may attempt. In a forest, the second line will spread itself in small columns; and in a coppice, partly in small columns and partly as skirmishers; in all cases, this line should keep at about two hundred yards from the verge of the wood.

3. Attack.—The preparations for attack are made at a distance from the wood, and beyond the extreme range of the fire of the defence. When these preparations are completed, the assailant passes rapidly over the clear space which separates him from the wood, so as to be but a short time exposed to the fire of the enemy, yet not so fast as to get out of breath, for the tremor of the hand produced by running will prevent his making an effective use of his weapon.*

The point of attack is chosen so as to reach or to threaten the enemy's line of communication or of retreat. We here refer to the principal attack, which is always to be seconded by a flanking or turning movement.

The troops who attack should be vigorous and veteran soldiers; for if they fail at the verge of the wood, it will hardly be possible to renew the attack, and many lives will be uselessly sacrificed.

These troops adopt the ordinary subdivision into two lines and a reserve, the second line about one hundred yards behind the first, and the reserve about three hundred yards behind the second line.

When the wood is very dense, the two lines should remain spread as skirmishers, while the reserve follows it, in columns, along the principal roads. When the wood is sufficiently clear, the second line may form in small columns, capable of passing everywhere, the first line and the reserve acting as before. If the wood presents openings, the assailant should have a special corps, independent of the reserve, destined to fight in these openings. With this addition, the attack will be made according to the above methods.

Besides this special and exceptional corps, and be-

---

* The carbine is the best arm for forest combats.

sides the reserve, which always exists, it has been recommended to protect the rear of all the troops engaged, by placing, at some distance from the reserve, a sufficiently strong rear-guard, which should carefully watch its own flanks and preserve itself in readiness to meet any counter attack.

4. Example.—The battle of Hohenlinden (December 3, 1800), won by General Moreau over the Austrians, illustrates the advantage of a turning movement in forest combats.

The French were deployed between Hohenlinden and Harthofen; the Austrian centre, engaged in the defile of the forest extending from Mattenboett toward Hohenlinden, tried to debouch in advance of their flanks, upon the plain of Hohenlinden. This centre was twice checked and driven back by the French soldiers. In the mean time, General Richepanse, sent by Moreau, marched by the Ebersberg road upon the village of Saint-Christophe and upon Mattenboett, which he finally reached, after incredible labor. There, he obstructed the defile which Ney was defending in front, and in which the enemy was enclosed. He rushed intrepidly upon the Austrians, advanced in spite of showers of grapeshot, threw the enemy into the most complete disorder, and made a junction with Ney, who had penetrated from the Hohenlinden side. The enemy's centre, beaten on all sides and hemmed in, surrendered; and to this beautiful and persevering manœuvre of Richepanse the success of the day is almost wholly due.

We must here call especial attention to the fact that in this action the conquerors understood the art of formation better than the conquered. When they penetrated into the forest occupied by the enemy, they did so by isolated companies, marching either by sections or by the flank, and connected together by skirmishers; they could thus introduce themselves everywhere without ceasing to present sufficiently strong and formidable groups. The conquered party, on the contrary, as a contemporary writer observes, adopted and preserved "an extraordinary order of march, hardly conceivable even in time of peace. Their advance-guard remained composed of some battalions of grenadiers; then followed the whole park of artillery; then the body of the army, and then the cavalry, which was still at the entrance of the wood while Richepanse was taking his position at Mattenboett and arresting the march." *

* *Moreau et sa dernière campagne*, par un officier de son état-major à l'armée du Rhin, Munich, 1801; traduction Française, Paris et Metz, 1814, 8vo., p. 88.

CHAPTER TENTH.

FARMS, OR HOUSES.*

A FARM enclosure, or a house, rudely and hastily fortified, when occupied by some companies, within some five hundred paces of an army, or at a greater distance, according to circumstances, may, in spite of the projectiles and incendiary missiles of the assailant, disconcert all attacks, greatly promote the success of a battle, aid in the preservation of a post, and thus save an entire army, notwithstanding its own relatively small importance.

For this purpose, the farm enclosure or the house is not required to be well constructed and perfectly solid; the most wretched hovel is hard to take when its garrison possess resolution, and are determined to sell their lives or their freedom dearly.†

However, when there is a choice between two farm enclosures or two houses, we prefer the one most

---

* The French word *ferme*, used by the author (literally farm), is applied here only to the structures upon the farm; that is, the house, outbuildings and their masonry enclosure, in Europe often grouped together, and thus forming a strong defensible position.—*Tr.*

† An officer frequently gains glory by the heroic defence of the most dilapidated post.

FARMS, OR HOUSES. 383

defensible. Brick walls have an advantage over those of rubble or of dressed stone, as they are not so easily breached by cannon.

What we have to say respecting the defence and attack of a farm enclosure or of a house, will be, in the main, applicable to those of a block-house, with the difference only, that the latter is more combustible.

1. Defence.—We shall not here treat of the method of putting the farm enclosure or a house in a condition of defence, as that subject belongs rather to fortification than to the military art. We will merely observe that in all farm enclosures, as in every house which is to be separately defended, we should select a solid portion of the structure to serve as a small redoubt, that is, as a rendezvous or last place of refuge for the defenders when they have been driven out of the other parts.

In the conduct of the defence we endeavor to compel the assailant to follow a sort of regular siege.

The points which the enemy must occupy are illuminated at night by the light of burning brush or of torches, that we may be able to direct upon him the most certain and destructive fire; and in order to keep him under fire as long as possible, all the avenues and approaches, previously cleared of dangerous shelters, are to be intercepted by accessory defences.

Every enclosure, or portion of an enclosure, every court and outbuilding, should receive for its defence a portion of the garrison proportioned to its importance.

This portion of the soldiers fire from within, through loopholes pierced beforehand through the walls.

Behind the barricades of any barrier, or of a doorway, there should be eight or ten men, drawn up in a semicircle, firing with coolness and concentrically upon the point attacked, and charging with the bayonet when the obstruction is thrown down. Folard prefers to leave a door open and to obstruct it with strong abatis, protected by firing from the ground floor, and especially by firing through openings in the floor of the second story (*machicoulis*). In all cases, while the assailant is taking his position against the door and is endeavoring to break it down, we rain down upon him from the upper stories everything which can be turned into a projectile, gathered for the purpose in advance; and we take him in the rear by musketry from any neighboring outbuildings.

Any ladder placed against a wall is immediately pushed away by a pitchfork, or any other suitable implement, passed through one of the openings of the first story and worked as a lever. A similar proceeding answers against the light troops of the enemy, who may be sufficiently nimble and dexterous to have reached the roof itself.

The defenders must not be sparing of destructive sorties upon the works of the attacking party and upon their preparations for the attack, nor of counter attacks in the portions already conquered; sorties and counter attacks which require in their conception as well as in their execution a certain mixture of audacity and prudence.

He looks out for incendiary attempts, and promptly extinguishes any fire which the enemy kindles; and should the roof be set on fire, he must, without hesitation, tear it off. It is true this amounts to depriving the building of its helmet, as it were; still, even without this piece of armor, the defence may be continued.

The garrison, forced by degrees, retire from building to building till they reach the redoubt, where they make another and a final defence. When they conclude to evacuate, they leave a small troop in this redoubt, who make for a time as much noise as possible (while the main body escapes), and finally capitulate upon the best terms they can make.

2. Attack.—The method of attack is of course founded upon a preliminary reconnoissance, as in all the minor operations of war. The following is the most common:

The cavalry watches the supporting troops without, and guards the entrances through which succor can come.

In a night attack,* we commence by extinguishing the fires kindled by the defenders, while we endeavor to illuminate the exterior parts of the farm enclosure, and especially the weak portions.

If we have any cannon at our disposal, we place a battery (by preference of howitzers) about three hundred yards from the farm enclosure or the house, with which we try to breach, in its lower part or at the

---

* Ordinary attacks commonly commence a little before day.

angles, the most solid building of the first enclosure, and to burn the roofs.

Skirmishers, ambuscaded upon the flanks at two hundred yards, second this cannonade, aim at the windows and other openings, prevent the defenders from showing themselves there, and thus obstruct their firing upon the attacking troops.

As soon as the artillery and the skirmishers have produced their effect, two or three columns of assault advance upon the breaches, the doors, and other weak parts, preceded by laborers carrying scaling-ladders, tools, and sandbags,* and protected by the skirmishers, who now come nearer and shoot at everything which shows itself during the entire contest.

We burn or burst in, or tear from their hinges, the doors that have escaped destruction by the cannon. We make search for secret and concealed passages. We debouch simultaneously from several adjacent openings upon some broad front which is not too much exposed to a fire from the buildings in the rear; we convert this space into a place of arms, and, as far as possible, we enlarge the communications connecting this place of arms with the points already mastered.

If there is a second enclosure, this as well as the redoubt is to be carried, if possible, by several attacks, all supported by a common reserve.

These attacks, like those directed against the outer enclosure, should be made simultaneously, with the aid of ladders placed against those walls which are

---

* To mask the lower loopholes of the defence.

neither flanked nor commanded. If the escalade is successful, we sprinkle the roof with expert skirmishers, who, firing from behind the chimneys and dormer windows, will compel the garrison to abandon the upper stories, and especially the staircases: it is never necessary to venture in these latter until success is probable.

If the garrison make a sortie during the operation, the assailants surround them and take them prisoners, or better, pursue at their heels to enter with them, and follow them everywhere in the interior.

This method of attack, which is employed in *taking possession* of a farm enclosure or house, requires infantry troops chiefly. If we merely wish to *destroy* a house—for example, one containing large quantities of stores—cavalry is almost sufficient; for they have only to blockade the house until it is set on fire by shells from a number of howitzers, the operation being covered by a reserve of several squadrons.

CHAPTER ELEVENTH.

REDOUBTS.

WE shall be brief upon the subject of redoubts, as they belong rather to fortification.

Redoubts are employed to defend assailable points which are open to attack on all sides, but nevertheless within reach of support, such as hillocks, the entrance or exit of a defile, or the flanks of a position. They are, in certain cases, very suitable for fortifying the front of a line of battle.

1. Defence.—The troop charged with the defence of a redoubt is divided into two parts: a reserve, equal to the third of the troop, and an active part, composed of the other two thirds, for manning the parapet. To obtain a good defence, this active part should be sufficiently strong to furnish two men for each running yard of the parapet. The reserve is divided into two sections: the special duty of the first is to repulse any turning attacks upon the entrance of the redoubt; the second stands in readiness to go to any point that is threatened.

The commandant of the redoubt should explain to

the chief of each fraction of the troops under his orders, the nature of the duty he is to perform.

Up to the moment of attack, the sentinels alone are charged with guarding the redoubt.

When the enemy appears, he is to be received with cannon at four hundred yards' distance, and with musketry at only one hundred and fifty yards. It is best to execute the firing of musketry slowly and with careful aim; at the moment of beginning this firing the soldiers mount upon the banquette.

When the assailant has descended into the ditch, and is attempting to climb the scarp, the defenders mount upon the superior slope and pour a destructive fire upon him along the exterior slope. However, if during the operation of the escalade the assailant has left some men on the edge of the counterscarp to fire upon the defenders, the latter cannot mount upon the superior slope, but remain behind the parapet.

The assault being repulsed, a well-sustained fire is turned upon the enemy as he retires, and then the troops come down from the banquette. If, on the contrary, the assault succeeds, it is the part of the reserve to fall upon the first enemies who enter the redoubt, and to drive them back, forcing them into the ditch.

2. Attack.—To attack a redoubt, the attacking force is divided into three columns. Each column embraces some sappers with tools, whose principal business is to destroy the accessory defences. A supporting troop, or reserve, marches in rear of these columns.

In order to occupy the enemy, and to harass him, two of these columns make false attacks.

The principal, or veritable attack, is made at a point determined by the situation and form of the redoubt, as much as by the position and force of the attacking body.

We begin by silencing the artillery and musketry of the defence by means of a sustained cannonade. Then the columns, preceded by the sappers and protected by skirmishers, advance upon the capital, and without firing. The sappers remove the accessory defences, and, that done, the columns descend into the ditch. Meanwhile, some skirmishers posted upon the counterscarp fire without intermission to prevent the defenders from showing themselves upon the superior slope.

We scale the scarp, and after an instant of repose on the berme, we ascend the exterior slope. Having reached the top of this exterior slope, we fire upon the defenders, and when upon the superior slope we fall upon them with the bayonet. At this moment it is necessary to avoid scattering, for it is important that each attacking column which succeeds in its undertaking should present itself in mass upon a single point.

The skirmishers who had remained upon the counterscarp immediately march after the columns to support them, and the reserve endeavors to turn the redoubt by the entrance.

The columns, once in the redoubt, throw themselves upon the garrison and upon their reserve, beating them down, and advancing until they reach the entrance, from which they remove the barrier to give admission to the flanking corps.

The work being taken, the assailant establishes his reserve facing the enemy, in order to parry counter attacks, and to give his columns, which have necessarily suffered in the attack, time to form again.

Such is the systematic method of attacking a redoubt, but it supposes a considerable attacking force.

A small detachment, a half company, for example, is often all that can be spared for the attack of a redoubt. In fact, this slight force will be sufficient where but one redoubt is to be carried, as frequently occurs in battles, containing some pieces of artillery, and only twenty or thirty men. Considering the feebleness of the assailants, they should no longer think of threatening the flanks of the redoubt, nor of ambuscading sharpshooters for the purpose of firing upon the defenders with all the precision of aim attainable by the use of the new carbines. The best method of attack in this case, is a species of charge *as foragers*, that is, the attacking body, in order to escape the grape showered from the redoubt, throws itself precipitately upon it at a full run, all the soldiers spreading *at great distance*, advancing as much as possible in a *creeping posture*, and rallying together upon the berme or the parapet of the redoubt, which they endeavor to escalade on different sides at the same time. Such an attack requires much courage and skill, and especially good luck. In fact, during the wars of Napoleon, the taking of such a redoubt was found in some cases to involve the loss of two or three detachments commanded by an officer; and we may well conceive that the successful commander received a brilliant reward.

3. Example.—The most memorable example of the employment of redoubts was at the battle of Pultawa. We will permit Marshal Saxe, the great advocate of redoubts, to relate the affair in his own words.*

"In the month of July, 1709, Charles XII., having laid siege to Pultawa, Peter the Great arrived with his forces to relieve the place.

"The king of Sweden, although wounded, declared to his generals that he would attack the Russian army on the next day. The arrangements were made, the forces were drawn up, and the march commenced a little before day.

"The czar had established seven redoubts on the front of his infantry, and they were constructed with care. There were two battalions in each, and all the Russian infantry remained in the rear, with the cavalry on the flanks. It was therefore impossible to reach the Russian infantry without taking these redoubts, for the Swedish forces could neither leave them in their rear nor pass between them without being overwhelmed by their fire. The king of Sweden and his generals, who were ignorant of this arrangement, did not comprehend the state of things until they were in the very midst of them. But as the machine had been set in motion, it was impossible to stop it and to retreat.

"The Swedish cavalry of the two flanks at the outset overthrew that of the Russians, and even went

* *Mes rêveries,* liv. ii., chap. 12.

too far; but the infantry of the centre was arrested by these redoubts. The Swedes attacked them, and were met with a stout resistance. They nevertheless took three of them, but were repulsed by the others with great loss. It was impossible for the Swedish infantry not to be broken by attacking these redoubts, whilst that of the Russians, drawn up in order, were looking on at a distance of two hundred paces.

"Charles and his generals saw the danger they were in, and the inaction of the Russians gave them some hope of being able to retire; however, order could not be restored, for the whole line was broken, and to attack was to lead the troops to slaughter. To retire was the only course to be pursued: the troops who had taken some of the redoubts, as well as those who were being overwhelmed by the others, were therefore withdrawn.

"There was no way to form them under the fire which proceeded from the redoubts, and consequently they retired in confusion and disorder. At this juncture the czar called his generals and asked them what it was proper to do. One of the youngest, Allart, without giving the others time to express their opinions, addressed his royal master in these words: '*If your majesty does not attack the Swedes at this moment, it will be too late.*' The whole line was immediately set in motion, and marched in good order, with pikes erect, between the intervals of the redoubts, which were left manned, to cover a retreat, in case of necessity.

"Hardly had the Swedes halted to form, and to restore order, when they saw the Russians on their heels. Their disorder and confusion became general. Still, they did not fly at once; they even made one more valorous effort, and turned back to charge; but order, the soul of battles, being gone, they were scattered without resistance.

"The Russians, who were not accustomed to victory, did not venture to pursue them, and the Swedes retired in disorder as far as the Borysthenes, where they were all taken prisoners. Thus it is that, by skilful arrangements, we can propitiate fortune."

CHAPTER TWELFTH.

BARRICADES.

1. Construction.—Barricades are often constructed in the streets of places besieged or in revolt, for the purpose of resisting the entrance of the enemy for a longer time by obliging him to overcome successively a number of obstacles.

Barricades being nothing else than defensive works, the rules for their construction are the same as those prescribed for field intrenchments; in other words they should, as far as possible, be located, 1st, at *elevated points*, in order that they may command the portion of the street or place extending before them; 2d, at the *middle of blocks*, rather than at their extremities against the two houses forming an angle, for in the latter position they are more easily turned.

Barricades may be composed of all kinds of materials, and for those which are erected in haste anything is used that comes to hand. The best are constructed either of alternate layers of paving stones and earth, or of wood and earth, in a form resembling the sluice in dams employed in hydraulic works. In all cases, it is well to make the slope that is turned toward the enemy as steep as possible, like the face of a wall, in order to make it difficult to scale the barricade.

It need not be said that the higher the barricade, the more difficult it will be to carry by assault; and that if provided in front with a ditch and pits, it will present accessory obstacles to be surmounted in the first place.

On the inside the wall of the barricade should be provided with steps, upon which the defenders can mount for the purpose of firing on the enemy.

2. Defence.—In defending a barricade the occupants fire in succession upon the assailing columns as they present themselves. A small mine-chamber may also be prepared in advance, opening outward, some ten or twelve yards in front of the barricade, which may be sprung by a train from the inside at the instant the assailant reaches it.

When the enemy begins to scale the barricade, the crest is defended either with the bayonet and sword, or by musketry.

The defence of a barricade requires great coolness and calm and deliberate courage, not to be too readily daunted by numerous assaults upon so feeble an intrenchment; and to make these assaults fruitless, which is the important and sole object in view, we can only advise indefatigable activity and incessant vigilance.

If the defender of the barricade possesses artillery, he will throw grape-shot, but this is a rare case.

When one barricade becomes untenable, the defenders abandon it and retire to another, at the same time taking care to obstruct the way between the two barricades.

3. **Attack.**—Carrying a barricade is a dangerous operation, as we cannot here deploy an array of force, and must of necessity, on account of the narrowness of the street, fight upon a small front, which gives the chief advantage to the defenders.

In general, this obstacle should be carried by ruse, by surprise, or by a flanking movement. In fact, after a careful examination of the locality, by a reconnoissance or bird's-eye view from the top of some high building, we shall seldom fail to discover some passage or court situated near the barricade by which it is possible to gain an entrance within the barricade, or from which we may at least be able to inspect the space occupied by the defenders. We must forthwith endeavor by all means to secure the occupation of such a passage or court.

We may also occupy the upper stories of the neighboring houses, and thence dislodge the defenders by a plunging fire into the interior of the barricade.

Finally, we may resort to blowing up the barricade by running a mine beneath it, or at least to throwing it down by petards or barrels of powder placed against the outer face. But we are frequently deterred from employing these means by our unwillingness to destroy the houses in the vicinity.

On account of the small breadth of the street, it will rarely be possible to run a sap to carry a barricade: besides, we should in this operation be too much exposed to the plunging fire of the defence. The only way would be to advance against the barricade behind high movable mantlets, furnished, if required, with a banquette, such as have been proposed for this purpose.

These means failing, we must come to a direct and open attack, notwithstanding the danger it involves. It is to be conducted as follows:

If we have cannon or howitzers, we first endeavor to batter down the barricade by their heavy projectiles judiciously directed. Otherwise we dislodge the defenders by rapid and well-aimed musketry fire.

This firing is continued until the defence shows signs of hesitation; then a column of assault throws itself at full speed upon the barricade, sappers having previously filled up the ditch and pits. This column endeavors to escalade the barricade, while the sappers proceed to open it in any part that has been sufficiently damaged by the cannon.

At the same time, the sharpshooters of the assailant, posted in the neighboring houses which command the interior of the barricade, redouble their fire to paralyse the defence of the crest, and thus to promote the success of the assault.

If the street is wide, it is usual to employ two columns of assault instead of one; but in all cases the first columns should be supported by others which put themselves in motion shortly after the first.

When, after a number of assaults, we find ourselves unable to obtain possession of the barricade, we can only resort to the extreme measure of bombarding it and reducing it to ashes, together with the adjacent houses. This method unfortunately involves the destruction of a number of the inhabitants who are not among the defenders of the barricade; nevertheless, we should not hesitate to employ it rather than to suffer the destruction of large numbers of valuable soldiers, before these barriers raised by revolt or despair.

CHAPTER THIRTEENTH.

FORAGES.

1. Object.—A *forage* is the name applied to the operation in which troops who have exhausted the resources of their bivouacs or cantonments, go to more distant parts to obtain the food needed for their horses. There are two kinds of foraging—foraging upon the inhabitants, or *dry foraging,* and foraging in the fields, or *green foraging.*

Formerly, and even in the last century, forages were regarded as important operations. They were preceded by reconnoissances, and undertaken with every precaution; frequently two thirds of the army were employed in their execution. They served as *coups d'essai,* in which the young officer could test his abilities; and Folard advises officers "never to omit a single opportunity of conducting them, as they tend greatly to cultivate quickness of eye and acuteness of judgment." In the wars of the Revolution and of the Empire, forages became of secondary importance, in consequence of the extreme mobility of the armies, which, remaining but a short time in presence of each other, could subsist everywhere. From that time not a single general forage was ever made; each division and each brigade making those which their wants required.

Nevertheless, foraging is still indispensable, and especially for light cavalry. General Brack says: "I have served in eight campaigns under the Empire, and always at outposts, and in the whole time have never seen a single commissary, nor have I drawn a single ration from the stores of the army. Was there then no military administration? Never was the chief military administration in more skilful hands. Why then did this administration not have its agents at our outposts of light cavalry? Because the Emperor had judged that it was impossible, and that it was folly to subject a troop which was irregular in all its movements to the regularity of the distributions of provisions." And he explains how this system, at first practised in foraging upon the enemy, continued to exist when the French were afterward forced to the defensive, and had to draw upon their allies and their own people.*

2. **Distribution.**—As soon as the country in which we are to sojourn has been reconnoitred, its foraging resources must be distributed among the different corps of troops; that is, the fields must be apportioned for green foraging, and the houses, barns, or hay-mows, for dry foraging. This distribution is the more necessary, because it not only puts an end to vexatious rivalry between the corps and to other

* *Avant-postes de cavalérie légère*, 1831, p. 143.

causes of disorder, but prevents extravagant waste,* and thus husbands the foraging wealth of the country as long as possible, without which precaution the cavalry would soon be deprived of food for their horses.†

To effect this distribution for dry foraging, we commence by measuring the cubic contents of the granaries, stacks, or barns. This measure is converted into weight, by the rule that one cubic foot of straw weighs about eight pounds; and hence the number of rations of straw will be found by dividing the whole weight by the weight of the ration, which varies from ten to twenty pounds, and which is usually fixed by the orders of the day. The number of rations of grain will be reduced from the total number of cubic feet of grain to be disposed of, by multiplying that number by $3\frac{1}{2}$, which is about the average number of rations in a cubic foot.

For green foraging, on the other hand, we first ascertain from the inhabitants the yield of their meadows, which usually varies between 1,500 and 5,000

---

* General Brack says with reason: "In peace wanton waste is a wrong; in war it is a crime."

"The use of cut straw by the German cavalry, and the order and system of their green foraging, have often facilitated the means of their subsistence." (*Approvisionnement des armées au XIXe siècle*, par le général Roguet, p. 153.)

† In support of the distribution recommended, we will remind the reader that when Moncey was about to enter Spain in 1823 in the vicinity of Carcassone and Narbonne, he was obliged to extend his cantonments "because the first estimate of the resources of the communes had been made in an inexact manner." (Marcillac, *Hist. de la campagne de Catalogne en* 1823, Paris, 1824, p. 63.)

pounds per acre; and then, if we have time, also make an actual experiment. We mow a portion of a meadow, an acre, for example; then, having measured the area of all the meadows in our possession, we multiply the number of acres by the number of rations we have found in a single acre, to determine the whole number of rations at our disposal. We should observe that the weight of the green ration is much greater than that of the dry, its regulation weight being as much as 88 pounds,* so that a mounted forager can bring in but a small number of green rations. It will also be useful to remember that a liberal allowance should be made in the distribution of green forage, for waste—about one third†—for the forage is often mowed when short, and much of it is then lost, with all the care that may be observed in the operation.‡

When the number of rations of the locality has been determined, the assistant intendant and staff officers to whom this duty is assigned, make an exact distribution of the granaries or the meadows among the different corps, in proportion to the number of their

* For the light cavalry horse.
† Some authors allow as much as one half.
‡ The following recommendations in respect to green forage will be found useful when we have our choice of the food to be given to the horse. Green forage is more valuable than new hay; the best is mown grass that is not too young. Next comes rye, which is the most digestible of all green forage, but is not so nutritious as lucern grass and clover. These latter should be cut a day before they are given to the horses, for when fresh they contain injurious principles, particularly clover, which, if eaten in too large quantities, will kill the horses. When grasses or grain fail, give them the leaves of trees, and especially leaves of elm.

horses, and in such a manner that the limits of the grounds assigned shall present no possible confusion.

3. Dry Foraging.—Having arrived at the commune in which the forage is to be made, the detachment which has been sent for the purpose takes possession of its outlets and surrounds it by sentinels. The chief of the detachment then presents to the communal authority the requisition for forage, signed by the general-in-chief or at least by a general officer (except in case of a detached corps). If this authority complies, willingly or unwillingly, with the requisition, he is required to transport the forage to the spot where the foragers are in waiting. But the foragers are not allowed to carry away this forage on their horses until the amount of forage delivered has been verified: it will be better if we have the privilege of employing the wagons of the country for the transportation.

But if the communal authority refuses to comply with the requisition, we enter the village by force, and we assign to each company the granaries, farms, or stacks from which they are to forage. Outside the village, we take further precautions, and place additional outposts, in order not to be surprised by the enemy during the operation. Inside the village, we prevent marauding by patrols. We do not permit all the foragers to enter the houses at once, as this would be too dangerous in case of surprise; they are allowed to enter only by squads, and in succession. If we do not fear the arrival of the enemy during the operation, we may, for greater convenience, have the horses brought near to the houses; otherwise they are to be left outside the village, of course under escort. In the first case, we send off the foragers in small bodies, as fast as they are loaded; in the second, they do not start until the whole detachment is collected together.

It will be expedient to forage in but one village at a time,* so that the cavalry may not be too much dispersed in positions more or less obstructed, and always dangerous.

4. **Green Foraging.**—For green foraging, the foragers† are each furnished with two forage ropes and a bag. They retain their stoutest head-gear‡ (the helmet or shako) and their sabre, and carry sickles or scythes, according to circumstances. Each of them should make two bundles or trusses, weighing together from 200 to 300 pounds.§ He ties them with his ropes, and balances them upon his horse. The grain is put into the bag and carried on the pommel of the saddle.

In making a green forage, we first take military possession of the ground and place a reserve on the right or left. Then we surround ourselves by outposts, so as to be apprized in season of the approach of the enemy.

---

* *Instruction de Frédéric le Grand à ses généraux*, article 4.

† Often called *corvée* horsemen, in contradistinction to the horsemen of the escort.

‡ So as to be safer from sabre blows coming down upon them while they are cutting the forage.

§ As much as 550 pounds was once allowed. See the *Rêveries du maréchal de Saxe*, liv. i., chap. 3, art. 6.

In order that the horses may not be in the way during the operation, they are left outside of the foraging ground.

When all these dispositions are made, the operation is commenced and prosecuted with diligence. If the enemy appears during the operation, we first make a defence on the exterior, and the reserve goes forward to repel him; but the foragers should not quit their work until the last extremity. If we have wagons at our disposal, we load them and send them off under a small escort, while the reserve obstructs the advance of the enemy. We may thus save the forage contained in these wagons at least, by getting it to some secure place.

Green foraging, being executed wholly in the open field, is less dangerous than dry foraging, in which it is often difficult to assemble the foragers in case of alarm. We must only observe not to embrace too much ground in the operation, but should rather forage twice in succession on a smaller scale.

5. Attack of a Foraging Party.—For attacking a party engaged in green foraging, cavalry will be sufficient; but infantry will be required in an attack upon those engaged in a dry forage.

In the attack upon a forage, as in a surprise, secrecy is the great element of success.

We show ourselves toward the end of the operation, and endeavor to separate the foragers from the posts, or from their escorts, according as they are at their station, or on the march. The attack, especially, must be sudden and rapid; and several false attacks should be made, to distract the attention of the enemy.

If we succeed in compelling the enemy to abandon the forage in which he is engaged, we have completely accomplished our object, and therefore we should not pursue the foragers.*

Failing to attain so complete a result, we at least harass the foragers during the operation, both going and returning, so as to retard them, or cause them to fail in their enterprise.

Ruse, well employed, may become an excellent auxiliary in an attack upon a foraging party

---

* Carrying off the horses of the cavalry, whether on a forage or in pasture, by a special ruse, was formerly called *donner le haraux*. This ruse, described by Marshal Saxe (*Rêveries*, liv. ii., chap. 7), had almost wholly gone out of use before the middle of the eighteenth century.

CHAPTER FOURTEENTH.

DEFILES.

We apply the term defile to a certain extent of country or of ground shut in between lateral obstacles, as well as to any contraction of a road through which we can pass only in a column of small front, or by the flank.

Defiles may be divided into two classes:

1st. Those whose outlets alone can be seen and attacked by the enemy, and whose flanks may be advantageously occupied to strengthen their defence.

2d. Those which give scope to the projectiles of the enemy throughout their whole extent, as well as at their outlets, and whose flanks, therefore, can neither be strengthened nor defended.

Roads through narrow valleys, and those between mountains, ditches, woods, and passages through villages which cannot be turned, are defiles of the first class. Bridges, narrow necks of land, dikes through marshes, are examples of defiles of the second class. A defile which can be turned will often become but a fatal trap, in spite of all precautions. Nevertheless, the greater number of defiles may be easily obstructed; they afford facilities for ambuscades; they present a narrow front for the combat; and, like water courses, exert a very important influence in military operations. Those of the first class, when their flanks have been strengthened, present positions that are almost impregnable. As an example, we may cite Thermopylæ, of classic renown. Formed by Mount Œta and the sea, they close the entrance of Greece toward Thessaly, and are impregnable when the surrounding heights are also occupied. But for treachery, the Persians would have been baffled by this formidable position. Defiles of the second class are favorable for defensive operations, and are forced with difficulty, as was illustrated by the triple combat of Arcola, fought by Bonaparte in the Italian campaign of 1796, against the Austrians, commanded by Alvinzi.

The defence and attack of defiles come specially within the province of infantry and artillery. Cavalry should participate only as an exception: it is excellent for turning them, but even this requires that the roads by which it may be effected are such as they can traverse.

1. Occupation and Defence of a Defile.—The method of occupying a defile and the distribution of the troops in it, depend upon the nature and conformation of this defile, and also upon the object we propose to accomplish. This object may be, either to preserve the defile for our own use, or to prevent its passage by the enemy.

In the first case, we occupy all the points in front

and on the flanks of the defile which are suitable for an obstinate defence, and establish the reserve at the rear outlet in a position chosen so as to prevent the enemy from taking possession of it and to protect the retreat in case we are driven back. This reserve should coöperate with the supporting corps. We should especially not neglect to occupy the outlets of the various roads or transverse defiles which debouch upon the interior of the main defile. Communication must be carefully maintained between the main body and the different posts occupying these outlets on the one hand, and the favorable defensive positions situated on the front and the flanks of the defile on the other, in order that these posts may fall back or be supported in season.

In the second case, or where the object is to prevent the enemy from passing the defile, we should take a position in the rear and at the point most favorable for assailing the enemy on the front or flank at the moment he attempts to debouch. This rule is more particularly applicable to the defiles whose flanks are inaccessible, such as bridges and dikes. We may, however, in many instances, occupy some important points within the defile, especially the intersections of roads, since we may thus arrest the enemy at various points successively.

2. Passage of a Defile.—The passage of a defile, in an *advance* movement, when it is not occupied by the enemy in force, presents few difficulties. We first reconnoitre the defile, its approaches, its outlets, and the roads and paths running into it; and having assured ourselves that it contains no ambuscade nor intrenchment, we occupy it as above stated. When possession has been taken, the advance-guard passes first and clears the ground, in conjunction with some skirmishers; then the several bodies of troops pass successively, observing all the usual precautions, that is, continually throwing out scouts and never trusting to a delusive feeling of security. These troops, upon their exit from the defile, finding the front freed from the presence of any detachments of the enemy (which should have been driven off by the advance-guard and the skirmishers), can easily take position. The passage being completed, a detachment is left to occupy and defend the defile, if its possession is required for the safety of the rear of the army. We are thus saved the trouble of subsequently taking it when the necessity arises.

The passage of a defile in a *retreat* is a more delicate operation. After having taken military possession and covered its flanks, especially by detachments, the main body of the army is left in advance, facing the enemy. The cavalry and artillery accelerate their speed and are the first to pass the defile, because they require more time in passing, and are important to be preserved; then comes the infantry, which retires slowly, leaving the rear-guard before the front of the defile in the place of the main body, and rallying, as they pass, the several detachments which protect the flanks.

The first troop which debouches forms facing the defile, within musket range, in order to enfilade it with their fire, and as the other troops debouch, they successively take position on the flanks.

The rear-guard waits until the army is entirely formed before it retires. It unmasks the latter slowly, and proceeds to post itself upon the extremities of the line of battle. The retreat from the defile is a critical moment for the rear-guard; for it has to pass from a narrow field of battle, where it could resist superior forces, into open ground, where it no longer enjoys this advantage.

When there are lateral avenues falling upon the flanks of the defile, it is essential that their outlets be occupied by detachments, for the purpose of protecting the retreat of the rear-guard—a retreat which is sufficiently perilous in itself, and should not be exposed to the additional danger of a flank attack.

In irregular ground, the retreat of the rear-guard should be covered by a chain of skirmishers, but in open ground, where only the good order and discipline of the troops can give security to their march, it should be covered by some companies; and if the rear-guard should find itself pressed too sharply by the enemy, these companies must make a half turn and charge the latter with the bayonet.

A modern military writer[*] compares a column of troops in a defile to a serpent, which defends all the parts of its long body by its head, which sees best and acts best, and upon which the whole can best fold itself back. This head is the advance-guard in a for-

---

[*] *L'officier d'infanterie en campagne*, par le général Roguet, 1846, p. 111.

ward movement through a defile, and the rear-guard in a retreat. However, in both cases, this serpent column should have eyes not only in the head, but also in the tail, and often on both sides, in order to prevent a surprise; hence, besides its advanced guard, it should throw out skirmishers on the flanks.

3. **Attack of a Defile.**—In this attack we are, *à priori*, at a disadvantage, on account of the small front upon which we are compelled to fight.

In respect to the method of attacking, two kinds of defiles are to be distinguished; those whose flanks are difficult of access or well defended by field fortification, and those whose flanks are not covered by detachments of troops.

It is difficult to attack those of the first kind, nor should we attempt to take them unless their possession is of essential importance to the success of the campaign. The available means of attack are, first, to drive away the troops who guard the entrance of the defile, and then to protect the operation of passing. To accomplish this, we should commence by staggering the enemy with an overwhelming fire, and as soon as we perceive hesitation in his ranks, the infantry should fall upon him with the bayonet in close column. The artillery of the enemy being by this time dismounted, at least in part, the close column should advance without firing, protected on the front by an advance-guard and on the flanks by skirmishers, who generally succeed in insinuating themselves everywhere. As fast as the infantry debouch from the defile they should deploy, taking care to rest their flanks upon the obstacle formed by the defile. The reserve should remain massed at the entrance of the defile, to guard against a counter attack and reinforce the centre and flanks when necessary. As soon as we have mastered the defile and the obstacles which support it, a part of the reserve and the whole of the cavalry will pass through it and go forward. The main body of the artillery, which had also remained in the rear, will take position on the flanks of the defile, as soon as the infantry has completed its passage and gained ground in front, and will then fire briskly upon the retiring enemy as long as he is within range.

When the ground does not permit a direct attack of this kind, we must have recourse to ruse. We should harass the enemy by false demonstrations, especially by making a pretence of forcing a passage in some other quarter; and we should search for some road or path comparatively little known, which the enemy has neglected to guard, and by which we may be able to turn the defile. The important point is to succeed by these means in pushing some companies quite to the extremity of the defile, as these companies, thus advantageously posted, assist the march of the column, support its flanks, and thereby facilitate the capture of the defile.

As to the attack of defiles whose flanks are covered by detachments, the following is the usual method of proceeding:

We begin by attacking these detachments briskly, with the select detachments which flank the march of the column intended to force the defile. These select detachments are followed by reserves, who support them when necessary, and enable them to rally and make head against the enemy.

If these attacks are repulsed, they are nevertheless renewed again and again, until the detachments which cover the flanks of the defile are completely driven from all the points which they have occupied.

Meanwhile the main body, stationed in front of the entrance of the defile, keeps the enemy in check by making demonstrations of attack, and throwing forward skirmishers, in order to prevent the enemy from reinforcing the posts which cover their flanks.

When these posts have been driven out, we endeavor, by still pushing forward, to take the enemy in the rear, availing ourselves of the paths, cuts, and valleys which present the shortest and most favorable route. If we succeed, in this way, in reaching the openings leading into the defile and in rear of the posts of the enemy, he is necessarily forced to retire without delay, or to take the alternative of laying down his arms.

4. Historical Examples.—I. *Omit no precaution when near a defile.*—In the campaign in Silesia, about the middle of December, 1745, when the Prince of Anhalt arrived before the city of Meissen, his cavalry suffered a slight check, because, being fatigued, they neglected to reconnoitre the approaches of the places which they had to traverse. They had to defile, man by man, through a deep cut in the road before entering that city. This occupied quite a long time, during which two Prussian regiments of dragoons dismounted to wait their turn to warm themselves. But a Saxon detachment, perceiving their situation, stole into a neighboring wood, and falling unexpectedly upon these two regiments, killed 180 of their men before being repulsed. This instance aptly illustrates the importance of always reconnoitring, especially when a defile is to be passed. "The smallest mistakes in war are punished," says Frederic in relation to this subject, "for the enemy never pardons." *

II. *Cavalry may, as an exception, force a defile.*— The attack of the defile of Somo-Sierra, in Spain (Nov. 1808), is often cited as proving *that no obstacle can resist the impetuosity of good cavalry.*

This attack was made by the third squadron of the regiment of Polish light cavalry of the Guard, which regiment was commanded by Count, afterward General Krasinski.

The position seemed to be unassailable, for the contracted road, situated between rocks whose sides and summits were covered with infantry, formed four bends or angles, at each of which four cannon were stationed, defending the passage and sweeping everything which appeared on the road.

Across the road the Spaniards had made a ditch, fortunately, however, not very broad. The fire of their infantry and artillery not only prevented the French infantry from carrying the position, but even from

---

* Example taken from my *Histoire militaire de la Prusse avant* 1756, p. 338.

filling this ditch with fascines. It was proposed to carry the defile by cavalry, which, from its rapidity, would be less exposed to the effect of the fire. The third squadron of the Polish light cavalry, under the command of Kozietulski, rushed forward in column *by fours*, kept on in spite of their heavy losses, fell upon the cannoniers, sabred them before they could reload their pieces, and were so impetuous in their attack, that the Spanish infantry abandoned their positions in terror and fled, thus in a moment leaving an insurmountable obstacle without defence, and opening the route to Madrid to Napoleon and his whole army.

If the squadron had stopped during the charge, it would probably have been lost, for the Spanish cannoniers would have had time to reload, and having decimated it by the first discharge, would doubtless have annihilated it by the second. The charge was executed *with the rapidity of lightning*, without regard to killed and wounded, and the squadron scarcely perceived that its chief (Kozietulski), having had his horse killed under him at the commencement of the charge, and being unable to follow on foot, had retired.*

III. *Employment of flanking attacks.*—Marshal Moncey (July 24, 1808), forced the supposed impregnable defile of *las Cabreras* by two turning attacks on the flanks, executed by General Harispe,† the intrepid

---

* Extracted from the pamphlet *Les Polonais à Somo-Sierra en* 1808 (being a refutation of a passage in the ninth volume of Thiers' History of the Consulate and the Empire), by Colonel Niégolewski, a lieutenant of the squadron which forced the defile ; Paris, 1854.

† Since a marshal of France.

chief of the Basque chasseurs, at the head of a body of good marksmen *without knapsacks*, who conquered the position rock by rock, and thus descended upon the rear of the defenders.

In Algeria, at the beginning of its conquest, to pass the defile of Mouzaia (November 21, 1830), an attack by the front was combined with a flanking attack upon the ridges on the left.

IV. *Passage of a defile.*—Before the battle of Castiglione (August 5, 1796), Marmont, wishing to deploy for the action with five companies of artillery (nineteen pieces), found himself compelled to pass through a rather wide defile, swept by the enemy's fire. He threw forward his column (with a front of two pieces), *at a gallop*, placing at its head the company upon which he counted least. This head was crushed, but the rest passed, deployed, and quickly dismounted half the pieces of heavy calibre posted on Mount Medola.*

This example, which again illustrates the importance of passing defiles as rapidly as possible, justifies the saying of the Archduke Charles,† that " every passage of a defile is subject to difficulties in proportion to the space to be passed over and the *delay* to be suffered."

V. *An army may sometimes be drawn up in order of battle in front of a defile.*—This has been much disputed, but seems at the present day to be more favorably considered. The Emperor (Napoleon III.),

---

* *Mémoires de Marmont*, 1857, t. i., p. 209, 210.

† *Campagne de* 1799, traduction française, t. ii., p. 123.

in his great work,* remarks, in reference to a position of this kind, which was assumed (so to speak) by Gustavus Adolphus at Leipsic and at Lutzen, that " its sole advantage lies in compelling the soldiers to conquer or to die." General Jomini goes farther; he says: " It is still a question to be resolved, whether defiles behind a beaten army do not rather favor the retreat than render it difficult." †

5. Defence and Attack of a Bridge.—It frequently happens in war that we wish to preserve a bridge in order to make use of it subsequently; at other times we wish to destroy it, but our troops have not the necessary tools or powder for the purpose, especially if it is of stone. In both cases we must seek to defend it.

Suppose then, for example, an officer to be sent upon such a mission at the head of a detachment of fifty men. He will station about thirty men as skirmishers on the right and left of the bridge, along the bank of the stream, in the places which have been shown to be favorable by a previous reconnoissance, and will so dispose them that their fire will cross in front of the bridge and thus keep the enemy from approaching it. He will knock down its parapets to facilitate the fire of the defence.‡ He will obstruct the bridge at both

---

* *Études sur le passé et l'avenir de l'artillerie*, 1846, t. i., in 4to., p. 341.

† *Traité des grandes opérations*, fourth edition, 1851, t. i., p. 130. On this point of tactics, the reader may consult the *Histoire de Wellington*, par M. Brialmont, 1857, t. ii., p. 412, 413.

‡ There is a historical fact in support of this recommendation. At the attack of the bridge of Goito (April 8, 1848) by the Piedmontese, the

extremities. The first obstacle cannot be directly defended; it will consist of a low barrier, or an abatis, or, better still, of a simple cut, with the object of retarding the march of the enemy, and bringing him to a stand at the entrance of the bridge. The second obstacle will be defended with the greatest energy by the remainder of the detachment. If the number of defenders were greater, a reserve would assist in this second defence. Finally, one or two posts may be established to oppose any flanking manœuvres. Artillery would here be an excellent auxiliary.

A chief of a detachment, charged with the attack of a bridge, will first make a minute reconnoissance of the bridge, to ascertain the defensive arrangements of the enemy. He will then distribute his skirmishers and his artillery along the bank; the latter for the purpose of silencing the fire of the enemy, or of distracting their attention, while he throws himself upon the bridge at the head of his best soldiers, climbs over the obstacles in his way, and strives to drive off the defenders.

We should, however, always endeavor to turn a bridge by fording or swimming, at a point above or below it, in order to avoid an attack by the front upon a position in which the enemy has fortified himself and is prepared to make a firm stand.

---

explosion of a mine rendered the bridge impassable; but the parapet of the bridge remained almost uninjured, and the sharpshooters (*bersaglieri*), using it as a foot bridge, crossed the Mincio and pursued the Austrians, who retired by the road to Mantua.—As an analogous instance, it may be remembered that, in 1796, the French crossed the Lavis upon the beams of a bridge from which the planking had been removed.

As an example, we will cite the attack of the bridge of Lodi (May 11, 1796). The Austrians had not had time to cut away the bridge, and Beaulieu, instead of defending it solely in the rear, had committed the error of leaving some battalions in front of it. The French reached Lodi at five o'clock in the evening, after a march of ten leagues, and immediately made their preparations. The columns of grenadiers charged with the attack were sheltered behind the ancient ramparts of the city from the grapeshot of thirty pieces of artillery (drawn up concentrically upon the opposite bank), until the signal for the attack was given. This attack, seconded by the fire of the French artillery, was made with such impetuosity that its success was instantaneous (notwithstanding the 175 yards' length of the bridge), and remained a long time engraved in the memory of the Austrians. The retreat of the latter was precipitated by the appearance on their right flank of 2,000 French horsemen, who had crossed the Adda above Lodi by the ford of Montanaso.

6. Defence and Attack of a Dike.—As combats in marshes can seldom take place except on dikes, it will be useful to say a word upon their defence and attack.

The dikes best adapted for defence, are those which can be defended both in front and on the flanks, especially when the troops intrusted with the defence of the flank can occupy an inaccessible post. But in general a dike can only be defended in front.

In this case, when its length does not exceed musket range, our force is to be placed in rear of the dike, and is to be divided into three troops of about equal numbers, one posted (with the artillery, if we have it) at the terminus of the dike, to receive the first attack of the enemy, the second about thirty yards in rear, to fall upon the enemy when he debouches from the dike, and the third as a reserve, still farther in the rear. But if the length of the dike is greater than musket range, our force is usually to be placed at first in advance of the dike, to defend it; then, having defended it as long as possible in this position, retire rapidly over the dike and make a second defence from a position in the rear. There is, however, danger in thus placing ourselves in advance of the dike, as in this position the enemy, if in superior force, may easily surround us, and, as it were, corner us. Besides, he will often avail himself of our retreat to pass the dike at the same time with ourselves.

The attack of a dike by the front, when it can neither be turned nor attacked by the flank, consists in first driving back the defenders to the rear of the dike by an overwhelming and well sustained fire, and especially by the galling fire of a large number of skilful sharpshooters; and then, at the moment the defenders show signs of hesitation, rushing upon the dike at a run and forcing the passage. In such an attack we must exhibit great vigor, for the longer we remain on the dike exposed to the fire of the defenders, the more men we shall lose, and the greater will be the probability of our being obliged to retreat—

especially if the defenders possess any pieces of artillery loaded with grape, which enfilade the whole length of the dike. In this case, the assailant will be obliged to employ artillery to silence these pieces; otherwise he will fail to pass, or will succeed only by losing many men.

CHAPTER FIFTEENTH.

VILLAGES.

1. Occupation.—Villages should be occupied only when the locality is favorable for defence (for if it is unfavorable, their occupation by the enemy will produce but little inconvenience), and when, also, this defence is connected with the execution of the general plan of operations. This rule will save us from unnecessarily drawing away troops from the main object in view. Villages of a rounded form, in which the houses are pretty close together and have streets of a certain degree of regularity, are always more favorable for defence, other things being equal, than those of an elongated form, or those composed of habitations scattered here and there without connection or plan: for regular and short streets possess the advantage of being good strategic routes, in which the troops and the artillery produce most effect.

The villages the occupation of which may be of importance to an army, are: 1st, those which form a defile, that is, those which are the key of a defile, or protect a defile; 2d, those which form the salient angle of a position; 3d, those which cover the front or flanks of a line of battle, and would consequently become dangerous if the enemy were to take possession of them; 4th, those which may enable us to stop a pursuit and insure a retreat; that is, in many cases, those which are in defiles; 5th, those which come into a chain of posts, as it is necessary that everything which occurs in that chain should be known; 6th, and finally, those which are within a short distance of the army, and contain magazines, convoys, and manufactures, which we cannot dispense with, and are, therefore, to be protected, as places of supply, with as much care as our lines of communication.

A glance by the general-in-chief at the general and particular position of a village may have given sufficient ground for ordering its occupation; but to effect this occupation in a suitable manner, we must first obtain information respecting a number of particulars which may be classed in seven categories: 1st, as to the environs, their advantages and disadvantages as a battle-field, and the kind of troops that can be employed there; 2d, whether they are commanding positions or otherwise, and their relative advantages in this respect; 3d, the distribution and construction of the houses, which may be of wood, clay (*torchis*), brick, or stone; 4th, as to the church, the chateau, the court-house, the large factories and other considerable edifices, which may serve as redoubts; 5th, as to the time and means necessary to prepare these and the whole village for defence; 6th, as to the number and kind of troops to be placed there; 7th, as to the resources of all kinds which the place may offer in provisions, forage, materials for accessory defences, and for making powder and balls.

An isolated village, which would not be protected by escarpments or by a water course, or by a disposition of troops in the rear and on the flanks of the village, in a word, one which the enemy could approach on all sides, could not be efficiently defended, and should not be occupied. Nor should any one be occupied which the enemy may without inconvenience neglect and pass by, for our object in occupying a village is to arrest the enemy and obstruct his progress.

2. Defence.—The first thing is to organize the defence. If time permits, we close all the avenues by ditches, abatis, épaulements, and barricades of sufficient solidity to compel the enemy to breach them; we make loopholes in the walls and banquettes behind the hedges, in order to obtain a fire from the whole perimeter; we give especial care to the organization of the defence of the church, of the chateau, and of every position the fire from which may arrest the assailant, and most especially of those houses which have a commanding view of the entrances of the streets; in short, we make use of all the resources of field fortification. The redoubt is to be selected in a strong and central spot, situated in the part where the final defence is made. Although the artillery should be at first placed at the most vulnerable points, and where it may produce the greatest effect (as, for example, points from which it can sweep the open spaces and enfilade the streets), we should nevertheless be able to move it at all times, and carry it to the points most threatened, and have épaulements and platforms prepared in various places, to receive it. Firing is the principal agent of the defence, but especially flank and oblique firing, at short ranges.

A small body of cavalry may remain in the interior of the village, but the greater part of this arm should be echeloned in rear of the two flanks, to prevent our being turned. It may frequently be employed also for repelling the enemy in front.

The infantry is divided into three portions. The first covers the village, and defends the approaches, because we must, if possible, repulse the enemy on the exterior. Behind hedges, loopholed walls, and palisades, a single rank of soldiers will be sufficient; but the streets and other wide passages, although they may have been closed, when there was time, by abatis, barricades, épaulements, or ditches, should be occupied by companies in mass. Detached men occupy those houses from which they may protect the exterior line of defence. The second portion, divided into small posts communicating with each other and easily rallied, is placed behind the most exposed points, and in the cross-roads near the boundaries of the village, these posts being destined to support and relieve the advanced troops. The third portion remains concentrated in the centre of the village, in as open a place as possible, equally distant from all the points of attack. The purpose of this reserve is to repulse the enemy at any point at which he presents himself, and to receive the advanced troops and cover their retreat in case we are obliged to evacuate the village. In this formation in three masses we find reproduced the two lines and the reserve of the usual order of battle. As to the numerical force of each of these portions, it must depend upon the configuration of the village; the reserve should amount to about one fourth. The principal point being to keep up a prompt and easy communication between the centre and circumference, we make as many openings in the walls and hedges as may be necessary for that purpose. The sorties, if a favorable occasion offers, should be conducted briskly, but still with caution; strengthening the side of the village by which the troops must return, and enjoining upon these troops to confine themselves to repulsing the enemy, and not to abandon themselves to an imprudent pursuit. The resistance should be displayed at first in the defence of the exterior, and afterward in that of the village itself, and there the ground must be defended inch by inch. If the enemy gets in, the reserve charges upon his flank, while he is arrested by the barricades and the firing from the houses. If we are forced to evacuate certain portions of the village where we find ourselves too seriously threatened, we assume a new line of defense marked out within the village, we attempt counter attacks, and fight to the last extremity, always taking care, however, while maintaining ourselves in the redoubt, to keep open a line of retreat.

3. **Attack.**—" Attacks upon villages cost too many men," is the confession of Frederic (*Instruction*, art.

23), and, in fact, villages form obstacles which it is proper to attack only when other means are not available for accomplishing the end in view. The mere fact that the localities are against the assailant, makes it necessary that he should possess a superiority of force. He should, especially, have a great number of howitzers, in order to set on fire and destroy the obstacles which are thrown in his way.

It is considered that, in general, our efforts against villages should be reduced to three points: a genuine attack and two false attacks. We therefore divide our force into six parts: three to act at once; two to protect the flanks of the attacks, supporting and reinforcing them, and manœuvring at small distances in the rear; and the sixth, of greater force than the others, to act as a reserve. If the enemy occupies some positions outside, he must first be driven from them and thrown back into the village. In this, cavalry will be useful. The batteries, directed upon the village at the outset, form the most advantageous positions possible, and having produced sufficient effect, the first three parts advance in columns, accompanied by a detachment of sappers, and preceded by numerous skirmishers, who expel the defenders from the circumference, and silence their fire. The other three parts follow the movement at variable distances. We take care to avail ourselves of every local peculiarity, however trifling, to conceal our march, to put the enemy on the wrong scent, and to keep ourselves under cover. We must be neither imprudent nor rash: courage alone is required. The time of starting of the three columns, and the velocity of their march, must be so regulated that they may come upon the village in succession to renew the alarm of the defenders, and to commence the false attacks, whilst they are engaged in repelling the true one. These columns will generally be formed by sections, and will consist of a half battalion at most. Having arrived within range of the first obstacles, the sappers advance with their implements to open passages. The heads of the columns, which up to this time have not fired, will now unite their fire with that of the skirmishers, in order to protect the work of the sappers, upon which the success of the attack mainly depends.

The columns penetrate by the openings, attack and beat down the masses opposed to them, pushing them with vigor both in the streets and in the open places. The skirmishers, whose circular chain has naturally closed in while advancing, leap the hedges, scale the walls, and take possession of some house or eminence from which they can fire with effect. Being free in their movements, they are frequently the first to penetrate. If the attack is repulsed, we renew it with fresh troops. When the outer precincts have been mastered, the sappers open the secret communications of the defenders or make new ones, tear down whatever interferes with combining the attacks, or which favors counter attacks, and thereby diminish the difficulties which the permanent obstacles (namely, the houses) present to the assailant. Then, as soon as we have gained a footing in the interior of the village, the reserves come up quickly, either to aid in overthrowing the reserve of the enemy, or to secure the occupation of the village or of the conquered parties. In fact, we should be well assured of the possession of one portion before passing to the conquest of another.

The cavalry of the assailant repulses that of the defenders, clears the field, and endeavors to flank the village.

4. Sudden Attack.—In battles, we depart more or less from the regular attack which we have just considered: we give quicker blows, we act by surprise, we carry positions by assault, and we make but one or two attacks. These are then two flanking attacks, which are executed while a strong reserve remains on the front. This mode is especially employed in Algeria, where the villages are often carried by the infantry at a run, without artillery, to put which in battery would alone leave the soldiers too long exposed to the skilful fire of the Arabs. It compels the enemy to abandon his position without giving time for any real engagement.

5. Historical Examples.—It is easy to cite battles in which villages have played a part.

On the day of Nerwinden (July 29, 1693), the allies had their army drawn up from the Gehte to the brook of Landen, between the villages of Nerwinden and Romdorf, their front covered by intrenchments. Luxembourg commenced by attacking the two villages, and carried the first, from which, however, he was soon driven. A second attack was followed by the same result, because when they had got into Nerwinden, the French officers neglected to tear down the hedges and low walls with which the streets were filled, so that our columns were unable to communicate with each other, and their action was disjointed. Luxembourg did not allow himself to be discouraged: he took fresh troops, returned a third time to the attack of Nerwinden, and this time remained in possession of it. The enemy had stripped his left to defend Nerwinden, in consequence of which the attack of our right, being throughout well conducted, was successful, and we were able in that quarter to carry the intrenchments of the allies. Upon this, Luxembourg passed beyond Nerwinden, outflanked the enemy's line, threw it into confusion, and drove a large part back upon the Gehte.

In the battle of Fontenoy (May 11, 1745), the village of Fontenoy was three times attacked by the English, and the village of Antoin twice by the Dutch.

At Essling (1809), the villages of Essling and Aspern were each taken and retaken several times.

At Leipsic (1813), the village of Schœnfeld was retaken eight times.

APPENDIX.

NOTES UPON HYGIENE IN THE FIELD.

It is difficult for one who is not a physician to write upon hygiene. We will confine ourselves to a few simple notes.

Hygiene is the science, the object of which is the preservation of health and the prolongation of the average duration of human life.

Now that the foot soldier wears a cotton shirt, a flannel waistband, easy-fitting garments, light headgear, the cravat instead of the stock, trowsers inserted in the gaiters, and cloth trowsers only, a cloak* over his whole dress for cold weather, and often an overcoat with a folding-down collar, he is no longer dressed in obedience to the caprices of fashion, but more in accordance with the rules of hygiene. It may be, however, that in endeavoring to give him a greater degree of lightness and to fit him for service in all climates, we have had too much reference to warm, and not enough to temperate and cold ones. But we shall not enter into details respecting the hygienic preparations

---

* The Zouaves and foot *chasseurs* have a dread-nought with a hood.

for a campaign, either for the foot or mounted soldier; our present purpose being merely to point out the precautions necessary for the troops *after* going into the field, in the observance of which every officer, in a certain measure, should coöperate.

1. Marches.—We must limit marches to the human strength, make them at the most suitable hours,* and avoid passing through unhealthy districts.

We must especially be careful to husband the strength of the soldier when he is obliged to climb steep ascents, for this purpose diminishing the weight of his baggage,† moderating his gait,‡ and stopping from time to time to allow him to breathe.

In every kind of march, we must carefully guard against sudden transitions, which are always pernicious.§ Thus, during halts, the men should not lay off their coats, especially if perspiring, and they should not drink until after a moment of rest. In preference to water alone, their drink should consist of water mixed with a little brandy or coffee, which they may carry with them. We should add, however, what M. Michel Lévy says, that " soldiers on a march who

---

* In summer, we should avoid the heat of the day.

† In all circumstances the men, when fatigued, may be permitted to put their knapsacks on the wagons, and invalid soldiers should ride in them.

‡ The step should in general be such that the left will not be obliged to run.

§ These transitions are as objectionable in military life generally as in a simple march. We send our southern soldiers in preference to the colonies. The English detail for the Indies those regiments which have already been acclimated at Gibraltar, Malta, or Corfu.

drink cold water and *immediately continue* their journey, do not suffer." *

In a warm climate a march is fatiguing, and should be abridged, if possible. We should not give the soldier much to carry, and should allow him to march with the route step. He may, for example, be allowed to unbutton his coat and loosen his cravat, with the proviso that he shall observe a stricter bearing if the breeze springs up. It is also a good precaution to cover the back of the neck with a white handkerchief fastened to the cap. A ration of wine or coffee should be added to the ordinary fare.

If the march is in a cold climate, we should try to accustom the soldier to it by degrees. He should be well clothed and abundantly fed. He should warm himself rather by active motion than by a fire.† He should avoid alcoholic drinks.

In the summer, at the end of a march, it is salutary to wash the face and eyes; and at all seasons the feet should be washed at each stopping-place at least. A strict attention to cleanliness conduces greatly to the soldier's power of endurance.

When the halting-place is reached, the sick are to be visited, and those threatened with any serious affection sent to the hospital.

2. Camps.—The French regulations recommend that the site of a camp be chosen near wood and water. Water, indeed, is necessary for the preservation

---

* *Traité d'hygiène*, third edition, 1857, t. ii., p. 31.

† In extreme cold, if a fatigued person lies down, he goes to sleep; and sleep, in this case, in the open air, is death.

of the health of the men; a running stream is preferable, and the camp may be pitched near its banks. Woods in the vicinity are desirable for furnishing fuel for cooking, but as the soil of forests is moist, we should avoid pitching the camp within them, if we would avoid miasmatic influences.

The position of the camp should, moreover, be sufficiently high to be well ventilated, and gently sloping, that the rain may flow off;* under these conditions, a dry and sandy plain will be suitable.†

In camp, the troop is lodged in huts or in tents. If the rapidity of our operations does not prevent their construction, the former are preferable to tents, which are too close in summer and too cold in winter. The straw used for beds should be renewed every two weeks, and that which is removed should be *burned*, as a precaution against infection. With the same object, the dung should be carried off and burned every day, and offal of all kinds buried in the ground.

The soldiers should be prohibited from going out at night in their shirts and with bare feet, as this practice is highly injurious, and produces dysentery.

We should keep a camp as free as possible from all incumbrances; a crowded camp is always fatal where there is a large collection of men.

Inactivity is also attended with danger to the health of the troops, and we should therefore multiply

---

* Otherwise the camp will be liable to be inundated. Ditches or drains should be made, to assist in carrying off the water.

† An eastern (western, on this side of the Atlantic) exposure will be preferable.

detachments as much as possible, and employ large numbers of the men in extra work.

3. Bivouacs.—" A bivouac," says Jacquinot de Presle, " although unhealthy in a rainy time, is not generally so much so as is commonly supposed. The soldier sleeps with his feet to the fire, which at the same time dries the ground. This is impossible in a tent, where the cold is felt severely, and the men collected in so small a space soon vitiate the air they breathe." *

Although this remark is, on the whole, correct, yet the bivouac is always attended by more discomfort than the camp; and therefore bivouacking is frequently prescribed only to the troops who are charged with the duty of watching over the safety of the army, and a double ration of brandy is allowed them.†

The location of a bivouac should fulfil the same conditions as that of a camp.

If fires cannot be lighted, on account of the proximity of the enemy, the condition of the men in the bivouac becomes more critical, as they may be overcome by the cold. In this case, we must give a general order making it the duty of every one who sees another falling asleep, to shake him until he is thoroughly aroused.

The portable tent (*tente-abri*) is especially suited

* *Cours d'art et d'histoire militaire*, 1829, p. 321.
† In general, the drawbacks of the bivouac are compensated in a great degree by good food, but it is prudent also to combine attention to cleanliness as in marches, and activity as in the camp.

to the bivouac.* The officers should see that it is properly set up.

4. Field Hospitals.—These temporary establishments are divided into field hospitals of the regiment, of the division, and of head-quarters. They are designed to afford the first relief to the wounded and sick, and to serve as places in which surgical operations may be performed before sending the men either to the temporary or permanent hospitals. The field hospitals of the head-quarters, however, are usually of such dimensions that the soldier may be taken care of in them for a longer time.

Field hospitals are established in houses, under a tent, or even in the open air; but in all cases in rear of the army, sheltered from the fire of the enemy, and where water can be readily obtained. The army surgeons attend to those placed in them. Each corps is provided with litters and stretchers.

Every wounded man, deprived of consciousness or loss of blood, or with a deep wound in the breast or abdomen, will be sent at once to a field hospital, and, if possible, to the special field hospital which the case requires. Others may be temporarily aided on the spot, by stopping the wound from which the blood flows with a plug of lint, bound tightly with a linen bandage.

* Captain Zaccone published, in 1850, a small pamphlet on the *tente-abri*, to which the reader will do well to refer.

CONTENTS.

	PAGE
PREFACE OF THE TRANSLATOR,	3
PREFACE OF THE EDITOR,	5

PRELIMINARY DEFINITIONS.

War, offensive and defensive, ... 7	Ployed and deployed formations.......... 8
Art of War................................ 7	Manœuvres............................... 8
Army.................................... 7	Column................................. 8
Arm..................................... 7	Echelons............................... 8
Infantry arm............................. 7	Head or foot of column.................. 8
Cavalry arm.............................. 7	Distance and interval of troops.......... 8
Artillery arm............................ 7	Checker-form........................... 9
Engineer arm............................. 7	Order, or combined disposition of troops.. 9
Light and line infantry................... 8	Tactics................................. 9
Light, line, and reserve cavalry........... 8	Strategy................................ 9
Field, siege, coast, and mountain artillery.. 8	Logistics............................... 9
Sappers and miners....................... 8	Base of operations...................... 10
Unit of force, or tactical unit............ 8	Line of defence......................... 10
Formation, or order...................... 8	Objectives, or objective points........... 10
Front, rear, and flanks of formation...... 8	Line of operations...................... 10
Rank, file, and depth of troops........... 8	Line of retreat......................... 10

PART FIRST.
HISTORY AND TACTICS OF THE SEPARATE ARMS.

CHAPTER I.
HISTORY OF INFANTRY.

INTRODUCTION............................. 11	Sarissa, or long pike................... 16
1. Ancients.	Psiletes, or light troops............... 16
	Proportion of hoplites to psiletes........ 16
Cavalry and war chariots most used...... 13	Subdivisions of psiletes................ 16
Infantry more solid than mobile.......... 13	Mobile formation of phalanx............. 16
Egyptian infantry........................ 13	Peltastes............................... 17
Jewish infantry.......................... 13	Greek education chiefly military......... 17
Persian infantry......................... 14	Heroism of Spartan mothers.............. 17
Phalanx, or deep formation.............. 14	Excellence of Greek infantry............. 17
2. Greek Phalanx.	Immobility of phalanx formation......... 17
Character and formation................. 14	Alexander, Xenophon, &c., victorious with
Subdivisions............................ 15	phalanx............................... 18
Complete phalanx........................ 15	**3. Roman Legion.**
Mode of action.......................... 15	Characteristics......................... 18
Hoplites and their arms................. 15	Organization more mobile than phalanx.. 18

CONTENTS.

Maniple formation.................. 18
Hastati, principes, triarii, and velctes..... 18
Strength and subdivisions of legion....... 19
Turma of cavalry added to legion........ 19
Arms of legionaries................... 20
Veletes the skirmishers of the legion..... 20
Mode of action of the classes of legionaries, 20
Military character of legionary.......... 21
Heavy loads and long marches of legionary, 21
Intrenching customary with legions...... 21
Mobility of legion................... 22
Adaptation to universal conquest........ 22
Roman government suited to war.,...... 22
Objections to formation by maniples..... 22
Marius' formation by cohorts........... 22
Cohorts comprise but one class of troops.. 23
Cohorts armed with pilum............. 23
Legion divided into ten cohorts.......... 23
Cæsar's cohort formation.............. 23
Cohort compared with maniple formation, 23
Deterioration of legion under the Empire, 24
Degeneration of soldiers in decline of Rome, 25

4. Barbarous Nations.

Barbarians mostly foot soldiers........... 25
German infantry..................... 25
Frank foot soldiers described............ 25
Combat of Frank soldiers............... 26
Deep formation of Frank infantry....... 27
Massing infantry disappeared with Charles Martel................................ 28

5. Feudal Infantry.

Charlemagne's army half cavalry......... 28
Nobles monopolized profession of arms... 28
Knights wore armor and rode mailed chargers............................. 28
Infantry powerless against gensdarmes.... 28
Infantry composed of servants and peasants, 28
Menial condition of feudal infantry....... 28
Arms of feudal infantry................ 29
Used as rampart at battle of Bouvines.... 29
Slaughtered at battle of Crécy.......... 29
Condottieri substituted................. 30

6. Communal Infantry.

Infantry regenerated in 12th century..... 30
Origin of communal militia............. 31
Communal force chiefly infantry........ 31
Arms of communal infantry............ 31
Marched under parochial banner........ 31
Served within or not far from commune.. 31
Maintained by king on distant service.... 32
Position in battle..................... 32
Superior to feudal infantry............. 32
Nobles not relieved from military service. 32
Infantry more ready to pillage than fight. 32
Grand Master of the Bowmen instituted.. 32

7. Soldiers of Fortune.

Names of vagabond bands in 12th century, 33
Depredations committed by bands....... 33

Du Guesclin drives them from France.... 33
Formation in battle of French infantry... 33

8. English Archers.

Archers best infantry of 14th century..... 34
Arms and mode of fighting.............. 34
Hussite infantry under Ziscа........... 34
Tabor, or barricade of wagons........... 34

9. Swiss Infantry.

Swiss resuscitate infantry in 14th century, 34
Compact formation of Swiss infantry.. .. 34
Arms of Swiss infantry................. 34
Culverins used by Swiss in 1386......... 35
Swiss squares at Granson and Morat..... 35
Echelon formation of Swiss............. 35
Discipline and courage of Swiss......... 35
Swiss infantry extensively used in Europe, 36

10. Spanish Infantry.

Character of Spanish infantry........... 36
Arms of Spanish infantry............... 36
Desperate mode of fighting............. 36
Arquebus substituted for culverin........ 36
Monsquet, or improved arquebus........ 37
Spanish infantry terror of Europe....... 37
Education and esprit of Spanish soldier... 37
Tercios of Charles V................... 37

11. Frank Archers.

Charles VII. established a standing army, 38
Free companies of cavalry.............. 38
Frank archers the infantry of Charles VII., 38
Recruiting and exercises of archers...... 38
Mode of compensation of archers........ 38
Arms and dress of archers.............. 39
Force and command under Louis XI..... 39
France divided into military departments, 39
Causes of decline of Frank archers...... 39
Substitution of Swiss and other troops.... 40
Lansquenets adopted Swiss pike......... 40
Pikemen in most European armies 40
Foreign, substituted for French infantry.. 40
Louis XII. dismounted the gentry....... 41
Improved infantry victorious in Italy..... 41

12. Legions of Francis I.

French superior to Swiss at Marignan.... 41
Machiavelli's estimate of infantry........ 41
Francis I. created a national infantry.... 41
Organization of legions of Francis I...... 42
Command and force of legion........... 42
Proportion and duties of arquebusiers.... 43
Privileges of legionaries................ 43
Isolated bands substituted for legions.... 43

13. French Bands.

French band corresponded nearly to battalion................................ 43
Officers of band....................... 43
Anspessades, or first class infantry....... 44
Arms of heavy and light troops of bands.. 44

CONTENTS.

Formation and mode of fighting of bands.. 44
Formation in battailles.................. 45
Fire-arms increased during religious wars, 45
Loss of pikes felt till invention of bayonet, 45
Bands of Piedmont and Picardy.......... 46
Bands of Champagne and Navarre........ 46
Isolated bands suited to French character, 46
Necessity of combining bands........... 46
Regimental organization of old bands..... 47
Character and name of bands............ 47
Order of battle of regiments.............. 47
Arms of French regiments................ 47
Mounted infantry served as cavalry....... 47
Arquebus superseded by musket.......... 48
Henry IV. diminished depth of infantry, 48
French battalion about 1610.............. 48

14. Swedish Infantry.

Gus. Adolphus gave mobility to infantry, 49
Formation of infantry under Gustavus.... 49
Depth diminished and fire-arms increased, 50
Improvement in arms by Gustavus....... 50
Advantages of Gustavus' innovations..... 50
Mixed formation of horse and foot........ 51

15. Infantry of Louis XIV. and XV.

Flint-lock musket introduced in 1652..... 51
Turenne adopted six-rank formation..... 51
Lighter arms and formation advantageous, 51
Formation of battalion under Louis XIV. 52
Company square in 1673................. 53
Musket and bayonet universally adopted.. 53
French battalion in 1703................ 54
Grenadiers originated under Louis XIV.. 54

Light Infantry introduced by Fischer..... 54
Chasseurs introduced by Fischer in 1743.. 55
French infantry formed in four ranks..... 55
Cadenced and lock-step introduced by Saxe, 55
Formation of grenadier company (1757)... 55

16. Prussian Infantry.

Excellence of Prussian infantry........... 55
Superiority of Prussian gun.............. 55
Firing, the mode of battle of Frederic II.. 56
Tactics greatly improved by Frederic II.. 56
Formation of Prussian battalion (1752).... 56
Formation of Prussian company.......... 57
Firing while marching to the charge...... 57
Mobility and solidity of Prussian soldiers, 58

17. Modern Infantry.

Three-rank formation adopted in France.. 58
Prussian drill introduced in French army, 58
Chasseur and élite company of regiment.. 58
Voltigeurs substituted for élite in 1804.... 58
Voltigeur and grenadier company to each battalion........................... 58
Army corps of select troops for a reserve, 59
Infantry organization nearly fixed........ 59
Success due to legs as much as to arms... 59
Two-rank formation of some armies...... 59
Approval of two-rank formation.......... 60
Percussion substituted for flint-lock...... 60
Rifled arms and elongated balls adopted.. 60

18. Remarks.

Depth of infantry constantly diminished.. 60
One-rank formation probable............. 61
Success chiefly due to good infantry...... 61

CHAPTER SECOND.

INFANTRY FORMATION AND TACTICS.

1. General Principles.

Advantages of infantry over other arms... 63
Infantry the basis of an army............ 63
Qualifications for infantry soldier......... 63
Clothing suitable to infantry............. 64
Arms requisite for infantry.............. 64
Physical and moral force, how increased.. 64
Load and march of infantry.............. 65
Infantry outmarches cavalry............. 65
Instruction, from individual to the mass... 65
Step and different marching paces........ 66
Space occupied in rank and file.......... 66
Two and three-rank formation compared. 66
Infantry and cavalry necessary to each other, 67

2. Modes of Action of Infantry.

By firing, or with sabre and bayonet..... 68
Sabre a poor arm for infantry............ 68
Bayonet an inferior weapon............. 68
Bayonet the "weapon of the French".... 68
Bayonet only good for a demonstration... 68

Bayonet collision of rare occurrence...... 68
Bayonet charge produces moral effect.... 69
Bayonet mêlée at siege of Genoa......... 69
Marching prepares, firing secures victory, 69
Firing—simultaneous and at will........ 69
Firing in three ranks difficult............ 69
Firing by battalions, divisions, and ranks, 70
Firing by command impracticable in battle, 70
Fire by file best for combat............. 71
Direct and oblique firing................ 71
Firing improper while marching.......... 71
Bugeaud's maxims on firing............. 71
Saxe condemned excessive firing......... 72

3. The Battalion.

Tactical unit of infantry................. 72
Composition of, in France............... 72
Conditions necessary in its constitution... 72
Subdivisions same for drill and discipline........................... 73
Subdivisions symmetrical and equal...... 73

CONTENTS.

4. Manœuvres.
	PAGE
Tactics consist of manœuvres	73
Requisites for their success in war	73
Drills indispensable to train troops	73
Manœuvres should be prompt and covered	74
Fixed by regulations	74

5. Order of Battle.
Positions of infantry in order of battle	74
First line deployed, second ployed	75
Evolution of lines generally separate	75

6. Marching Formations.
Infantry has four marching formations	75
Marching in line	75
Marching by the flank	76
Marching by column	76
Marching in square	77
Historical examples of marching in square	77

7. Formations of Attack.
Infantry has five formations of attack	78
Attack in line	78
Advantages and defects of attack in line	78
Attack in column	79
Double-central column best for attack	79
Columns of attack by platoons and sections	80
Depth of column limited	80
Column should steadily move to attack	80
Advantages of attack in column	80
French successful in attack by columns	81
Infantry mode of attacking intrenchments	82
Exposure of columns to artillery fire	82
Mixed formation for attack	82
Historical examples of attack in column	82
Attack as skirmishers	83
Skirmishers *en grande bande*	83
Skill and valor required in skirmishers	83
Bayonet useful against horsemen	84
Attack in echelons	84
Echelons should mutually flank each other	84
Direct and oblique echelons	84
Echelon cannot exceed six battalions	85
Attack in squares	85
Attack in squares in Egypt	85
Square by battalion best for offensive	85
Rectangular formation of battalion	85

8. Formations of Defence.
Infantry has five formations for defence	86
Defence in line	86
Action of deployed line in defence	86

	PAGE
Formation defending intrenchments	86
Genoa's defence aided by outside reserves	87
Defence in column	87
Column good only against cavalry	87
Defence in square	87
Regulation square	87
Russian and English manœuvre against cavalry	87
Schramm's square	88
Square half full formed from column	88
Square by regiment best for defensive	88
Square by battalion best for offensive	88
Bugeaud's square of a battalion	89
Weak points of square	89
Bayonet better than fire against cavalry	89
Squares echeloned to flank each other	89
Artillery formidable against square	89
Cavalry may break square	89
Square termed formation of resistance	90
Square has defects of a redoubt	90
Desaix' square	90
Wurtemberg square	90
Defence in echelons	90
Echelons good defence in retreat	90
Defence in checker-form	91
Advantages and disadvantages of checker-formation	91

9. Light Infantry.
Light troops now all regularly organized	91
Light troops have special tactics	91
Chasseurs à pied of France	92
Drill, arms, duty, and organization of chasseurs	92
Deployed and rallied group by fours	92
Signals by whistle as well as bugle	93
Selection and instruction of chasseurs	93
Important functions of light infantry	94

10. Skirmishers.
Fight dispersed, leaving reserve of a third	94
Qualifications for skirmishers	94
Should keep moving, or lie down to load	94
Chasseurs furnish best skirmishers	94
Line infantry sometimes used as skirmishers	94
Skirmishers of march	95
Skirmishers of battle	95
Skirmishers *en grande bande*	96
Service of each kind of skirmishers	96
Historical examples of use of skirmishers	96

CHAPTER THIRD.
HISTORY OF CAVALRY.

1. Antiquity.
Mounted combatants first prevailed	97
War chariots much used by ancients	97

Chariots armed with scythes	97
Chariots carrying military machines	97
Chariots little used by Greeks and Romans	98

CONTENTS. 443

	PAGE
Rows of stakes defence against chariots..	98
Cavalry existed in China 2,000 years B. C.,	98
Cyrus introduced cavalry in Persia......	98
Greeks early used cavalry...............	98
Epaminondas appreciated value of cavalry,	98
Cavalry increased after Epaminondas....	98
Thessalian and Etolian cavalry..........	99
Proportion of cavalry in Grecian armies,	99
Roman cavalry mediocre................	99
Vicious method of Roman use of cavalry,	99
Causes of inferiority of Roman cavalry...	99
Cavalry of Hannibal superior to Roman..	100
Cavalry of Roman citizens or knights....	100
Auxiliary cavalry of allies of Rome......	100
Proportion of cavalry to Roman legion..	100
Arms of cavalry of Greece and Rome....	100
Ancient cavalry moved slow............	101
Deep formation of Greek cavalry........	101
Thessalian lozenge.....................	101
Cavalry of legion divided into ten *turmæ*,	101
Roman turma, or squadron..............	102
Position of cavalry of legion............	102
Depth of auxiliary cavalry less than Greek,	102
Superiority of cavalry of Numidians, &c.,	102
Increase of cavalry in decline of Rome...	102
Barbarians had little cavalry............	102
Cavalry much increased in feudal ages...	102
Saddle invented in reign of Constantine,	103
Stirrups invented by Franks............	103
Advantages of stirrups..................	103

2. Middle Ages.

Chivalry contributed to good police.....	103
Tactics and chivalry antagonistic........	104
Service of knights and their retinue.....	104
Qualification and installation of knights.	104
Knighthood conferred before battle......	104
Banneret and bachelor knights...........	105
Lance and coutillier....................	105
Names of pieces of a knight's armor.....	106
Offensive arms of knights...............	107

	PAGE
Villains prohibited use of lance..........	107
Knights, except in battle, rode a courtaud,	107
French cavalry charged in single line....	107
Pages, or varlets, in second line.........	107
Cavalry ignored tactics and discipline....	107
Cavalry fought battles and laid sieges....	107
Cavalry often fought dismounted........	108
Mode of fighting of knights as infantry...	108
Causes of decline of chivalry............	108

3. Modern Times.

Feudal, supplanted by standing armies...	109
Charles VII. institutes permanent troops,	109
Compagnies d'ordonnance...............	109
Horses for gensdarmes and archers......	109
Gendarme tax..........................	109
Nobles prefer being captains to cavaliers,	110
Companies of Charles VII. best.........	110
Formation too thin against German horse,	110
Causes of German deep formation.......	110
Fire-arms adopted by cavalry...........	110
Chevaux-légers and stradiots............	110
Cranequiniers and malandrins...........	111
Argoulets and carabins.................	111
Reitres, or pistoliers...................	111
Origin of dragoons.....................	111
Change to deep formation...............	111
Mobility of cavalry lessened.............	112
Reduction to five rank formation........	112
Light cavalry formed into regiments.....	112
Improvements of Gustavus Adolphus...	112
Mixture of infantry with cavalry bad....	113
Company in order of battle in 1750......	113
Changes in arms and armor.............	113
Improvements made by Marshal Saxe...	113
Improvements made by Frederic II.....	114
Excellence lies in the charge, not firing...	114
Frederic's formation mostly two ranks..	114
Improvements made by Seydlitz........	114
Two-rank formation generally adopted..	115
Uniform loose, and load of horse distributed...........................	115

CHAPTER FOURTH.
CAVALRY FORMATION AND TACTICS.

1. Use of Cavalry.

Strength of cavalry mostly in speed.....	116
Pursuit after rout main use of cavalry...	116
Offensive, the mode of combat of cavalry,	116
Heavy, light, and mixed cavalry.........	117
Carabiniers and cuirassiers..............	117
Heavy cavalry for decisive charges......	117
Dragoons include all mixed cavalry.	118
Dragoons rarely fight on foot............	118
Service of dragoons....................	118
Chasseurs, hussars, and lancers..........	119
Duties of light cavalry..................	119
Irregular cavalry seldom used...........	119
Cossacks charge boldly only on fugitives,	119

2. Armament.

Uniform and arms of cavalry............	120
Fire-arms useful only for skirmishers, &c.,	120

3. Numerical Data.

Cavalry one-tenth to fifth of infantry....	120
Weight carried by cavalry horses........	120
Rate of travel of a horse................	121
Rate of march of cavalry column........	121

4. Tactical Unit.

Squadron, tactical unit of cavalry........	121
Composition of French squadron........	121
Squadron in order of battle.............	122

CONTENTS.

	PAGE		PAGE
Length of front and depth of squadron	122	Object of two lines in charges	129
Oldest troops in front and on right	122	Formation for the charge	129
Effective force of squadron	123	Successful charge completed by pursuit	129
Two-rank formation best for cavalry	123	Pursuit, how conducted	129
		Position of officers in the charge	129

5. Manœuvres.

Charge as foragers against artillery … 130
Charge as foragers against Arabs … 130

Movement by fours … 124
Oblique marches by fours discontinued … 124
Movement by platoons … 124
Trot ordinary gait in manœuvres … 125

8. Formations.

Order in line, column, echelons, and square, 130
Cavalry attacks cavalry in line … 130

6. Mode of Action.

Attacks infantry in echelons or column … 130
Advantages of attack in echelons … 131

Danger to horseman less than to footman, 125
Instruction to man and horse essential … 125
Compactness and velocity in charge … 126

Attack in column against square … 131
Cavalry forms square for defence … 131
Column by platoon for marching … 132
Cavalry should march on left of road … 132
Checker-formation little used … 132

7. Charge.

9. Eclaireurs.

Charge made at beginning or end of battle, 126
Charge made on flanks of infantry … 126
Mode of charging … 126
Charge to be persevered in to the last … 127
Cavalry should not fire in charging … 127
Few killed or wounded in charge … 128
Charge often fails from small cause … 128

Skirmishers of the cavalry … 132
Duties, and how selected … 132
Advantages of combination with infantry, 132
One-fourth of troop from which detailed, 132

CHAPTER FIFTH.

HISTORY OF ARTILLERY.

Balista, onager, and catapulta	133	Artillery increased and systematized	140
Weight of projectiles, and how far thrown,	133	Examples of success of artillery in battle,	140
Moved with armies like field pieces	134	Grand master and captain-general	140
Increased use among ancients	134	Sully held it as an office of the crown	140
Destroyed by fire, or by cutting cords	134	First inspector-general of artillery	140
Causes of decline of ballistic art	134	First cannon made of bars and hoops	140
Projectile machines during Crusades	135	Cast iron, copper, and bronze adopted	141
Porrière and mangonneau	135	Materials of projectiles	141
Invention of gunpowder	135	Swiss and German infantry, guard of pieces,	141
Cannon introduced in 14th century	136	Artillery of Henry II. and IV	141
Genoese used funnels or vases in 1319	136	Artillery of Germany in 16th century	141
Field artillery first on stationary frames,	137	Gus. Adolphus' improvements in artillery,	141
Bombards	137	Introduction of 12 and 24-pounders	142
Huge dimensions of bombards	137	Bombs introduced in France	142
Bombards superior to ancient machines,	137	Light pieces only carried to field	142
Bombards supplanted in 1376	137	Vauban invented ricochet firing (1688)	142
Artillery derived from artillier	137	Breaches made by cannon	142
Duties of masters of artillery	138	Carcasses invented and used in 1672	142
Cannoniers instituted about 1411	138	Fusiliers, the guard of artillery	142
Master-general of artillery of Charles VII.,	138	Name of fusilier from fusil	143
Distribution of artillery in armies	138	French artillery corps instituted	143
Cannon effective by noise chiefly	138	Artillery under Louis XIV	143
Importance for defence	138	Position of artillery in battle	143
Unsuitable for open country	138	Vallière's system of artillery	144
Duties of chief of artillery divided	138	Horse artillery introduced by Frederic II.,	144
Louis XI. maintained much artillery	138	Howitzers used in field by Frederic II	144
Twelve peers of France	139	Artillery tactics improved by Frederic II.,	144
Single chief of artillery reëstablished	139	Amount of artillery large under Frederic,	144
Charles VIII's use of artillery in campaign,	139	Gribeauval's system introduced (1765)	144
Lighter artillery adopted by Louis XII.	139	Great improvements by Gribeauval	145
Two chiefs of artillery under Louis XII.	139	Battery established as unit of artillery	145

CONTENTS. 445

	PAGE
Battalions of the train adopted (1801)	145
Napoleon used large masses of artillery	145
Valée's system, adopted from English	146
Four guns and two howitzers to battery	146
Simplicity of Valée's system	146
Cannoniers ride on ammunition-chests	147
Mobility of artillery of new system	147
Modifications in Valée's system (1854)	147
Napoleon-gun introduced	147
Light, line, and reserve artillery	147
Advantages of these three divisions	147
Train-corps form park-batteries	147

CHAPTER SIXTH.
ARTILLERY FORMATION AND TACTICS.

1. Purpose of Artillery.

Destruction of troops and obstacles	148
Facilitating attack of infantry or cavalry	148
Artillery should act in large masses	148
Object of field and siege artillery	148
Mountain artillery carried on mules	149
Artillery movable in march and battle	149
Division and reserve batteries	149
Duties of French artillery corps	149
Artillery requires support of other arms	149

2. Numerical Data.

Proportion of artillery to infantry	150
Proportion of artillery to cavalry	151
Weight considered in fixing amount	151
Supply of ammunition carried	151
Space occupied by artillery carriages	151

3. Tactical Unit.

Battery the tactical unit	151
Composition of field-battery	151
Napoleon-guns adopted in France	152
Subdivisions and commands of battery	152
Composition of mountain battery	152

4. Formations.

Field artillery no defensive formation	152
Formation in column	153
Formation in line	154
Formation in battery	155
Advancing and retiring by half-battery	156

5. Manœuvres.

Necessity of manœuvres	156
Artillery should manœuvre promptly	156
Manœuvres more as cavalry than infantry	156
Manœuvres mostly at a trot	157
Oblique movements and wheeling	157
Right or left oblique	157
Artillery disregards inversions	158
Formation of column of attack	158
Formation from column to line	158
Change of front from line	158
Evolutions of batteries on same principles	159
Guides not used in manœuvres	159
Wheeling made on moving pivot	159
Countermarches and abouts	159

6. Positions.

Battery also applied to artillery in position	159
Choice of positions important for batteries	159
Commanding open ground eligible site	160
Soil should be solid, but not stony	160
Commodious and safe exits necessary	160
Concealed, to see without being seen	160
Fixed to produce greatest damage	160
Direct, oblique, and reverse batteries	160
Enfilading and cross batteries	161
Division batteries fire throughout battle	161
Reserve batteries act temporarily	161
Former in front and on flanks of lines	161
Latter for menaced points and attacks	161
Caissons placed in strong and safe places	161

CHAPTER SEVENTH.
HISTORY OF ENGINEERS.

Engineer arm not of ancient origin	162
Italian engineers employed in all Europe	162
French fortifications repaired by Sully	162
Ingénieurs ordinaires du roi (1602)	162
Engineers part of staff till 1690	162
Military corps serving with armies in the field and on fortifications	163
Louis XIV. largely increased engineers	163
Eminent services of engineers under Vauban in siege and battle	163
French fortifications, methods of attack, and usages, imitated everywhere	163
Vauban made marshal for his services	163
Vauban much advanced art of engineers	163
Immense lines of field-works constructed	163
Extent made them weak everywhere	163
Engineers united with artillery in 1755	163
Separated after but three years' trial	163
Uniform of French engineers	163
Engineers fixed at 400 in 1762	163
Styled, in 1776, *Corps Royal du Génie*	164
Duties of *gardes du génie*	164
Revolution caused emigration of engineers	164
Numbers during French Revolution	164
Employed more as staff officers till 1800	164
Engineers too few in 1813 to defend France	164
Employed in sieges in Peninsular War	164
French consulting committee of engineers	164

CONTENTS.

	PAGE		PAGE
Cost and extent of fortifications of Paris,	164	Convention established engineer troops..	165
Engineers fixed at 400 by Napoleon III.,	165	Number and organization of engineer troops under Napoleon	165
Sappers created in 1671, and miners in 1673,	165		
Vauban, &c., commanded sappers and miners	165	Meagre force of engineer officers and troops in United States army	166

CHAPTER EIGHTH.
FUNCTIONS OF THE ENGINEERS.

	PAGE		PAGE
Engineers one of the arms of service	167	Arms and tools carried by sappers	169
Duties of engineers	167	Proportion of tools to a company	169
Construction and repair of permanent fortifications	167	Miners carry special mining tools	169
		Miners accompany engineer train	169
Construction, &c. of military buildings	167	Articles carried by engineer train	169
Construction of all field works and ovens,	167	Sappers and miners drilled as infantry	169
Making and destroying military roads	168	Devotion to duty of sappers and miners,	170
Construction and destruction of bridges with fixed supports	168	Floating bridges, transported with armies, built by artillery in France	170
Works for attack and defence of places..	168	Pontonniers belong to engineers in most armies	170
Military reconnoissance	168		
Works executed by contract in peace	168	Pontonniers a distinct corps in Austria and Russia	170
Executed by military workmen in war..	168		
Engineer troops recruited from mechanics,	168	Pontonniers should belong to engineers in France	170
Company of sappers to a division, in war,	169		
Company the unit of engineer force	169	Arms and equipment of French engineer troops	170
Wagon to each company	169		

PART SECOND.
COMBINATION OF THE ARMS.

CHAPTER FIRST.
ORGANIZATION OF ACTIVE ARMIES.

1. Principles of Organization.

	PAGE		PAGE
Brigades, how organized and commanded,	171	Napoleon used an army-corps for reserve,	177
Divisions, how organized	172	Imperial guard and grenadiers in reserve,	177
Division, fundamental element of an army,	172	Withdrawal of select troops objectionable,	177
Advantages of division formation	172	Withdrawal should be only temporary..	177
Army composed of several divisions	172	Solid reserves indispensable in field	177
Relation of commanders in armies	172	Composition of brigades	178
Permanent and temporary fractions	173	Mixed brigades for advanced-guards, &c.,	178
Organization by divisions best for armies,	173	Appendages of an army-parks, trains, &c.,	178
Organization by army-corps in some cases,	173	Special reserve of heavy cavalry	178
Cases where army-corps preferred	173	Dépôts of an army, and where established,	178
Fractions in order of importance	174	**2. Commands.**	
Army-corps must be self-sustaining	174	Command of army or corps, how regulated,	178
Army-corps usually composed of all arms,	174	Command of wings, centre, and reserve,	179
Army-corps of cavalry under Napoleon..	174	Command of divisions and brigades	179
Limits of cavalry army-corps	174	General assigns temporary commanders..	179
Composition and strength of army-corps,	174	General-in-chief assisted by staff officers,	180
Order of battle of an army-corps	175	Chief of staff and sub-chiefs	180
Order of battle of a division	175	Duties of the état-major (staff-corps)	180
Divisions had better be of equal force	176	Administrative services for an army	181
Purpose and proportion of reserves	176	Duties of intendant and his assistants	181
Reserves for defence as well as for offense,	177	Duties of chief and staff of engineers	181
Reserve composed of veteran troops	177	Duties of chief and staff of artillery	181
Embrace heavy cavalry and artillery	177	Command and staff of divisions, &c	182

CONTENTS.

Aides-de-camp and orderly officers...... 182
Duties of commandant of headquarters.. 182
Duties of provost marshal-general....... 183
Duties of wagon-master of headquarters, 183
Command, &c., of division headquarters, 184

3. Standing Armies.

Organized in France and Austria for war, 184
Organized in Prussia for peace and war.. 184
Advantages of both systems............. 184

CHAPTER SECOND.

MARCHES.

1. Marches of Concentration.

Performed at a distance from enemy.... 186
Mode of conducting and details.......... 186
Made by day if practicable.............. 186
Rate of travel and halts................. 187
Uniformity of gait essential for cavalry.. 187

2. Marches of Manœuvre.

Performed in presence of the enemy..... 187
Made cautiously, and prepared for attack, 187
Made in strong, short columns.......... 187
Position of different arms in march...... 188
Number and distance apart of columns.. 188
Column must be covered by light troops, 188
Duties of advance-guard of a column..... 189
Duties, &c., of commander of advance-guard............................... 189

Strength of advance-guard, and position.. 190
Duties of rear-guard of a column........ 190
Qualifications of chief of rear-guard...... 190
Duties of flankers of a column.......... 191
General advance and rear-guard of columns, 191
Ruse to deceive the enemy as to march.. 191
Conveyance of messages................ 191
March of manœuvre by front, flank, or rear, 192
March by flank in single long column.... 192
Precautions to be taken in march by flank, 193
Examples of flank marches.............. 193
Marches of manœuvre must be rapid.... 193
Massena's celebrated march at Rivoli.... 193
Defeat of Austrians in 1809 from inactivity, 194
Rapidity of march indispensable in pursuit, 194
Retreat, a series of retrograde marches... 194
Precautions to be taken in retreat....... 194

CHAPTER THIRD.

BATTLES.

1. Primitive Order of Battle.

Three lines in battle.................... 196
First line brings on the action.......... 196
Second line supports first............... 196
First line is deployed in order of battle.. 197
Second line in columns, by battalions.... 197
Second line deployed if exposed to artillery, 197
Reserve in column, by brigades......... 197
Second line should be 300 yards from first, 198
Reserve 1,000 to 1,200 yards in its rear... 198
Cavalry should be on, and support flanks, 199
Exception when cavalry may be at centre, 199
Artillery in front, opposite intervals..... 199
Second line in rear of flanks and intervals, 199
Artillery of reserve close to main reserve, 199
Parks, &c., in safe place in rear of reserve, 199
Entire division usually in same line..... 200
Primitive order of battle delineated..... 200
Circumstances modify this review order, 201

2. Orders of Battle.

Parallel order of battle.................. 201
Parallel, the ancient order of battle..... 202
Modifications of parallel order.......... 202
Oblique order of battle.................. 202
Examples of oblique order of battle...... 203
Perpendicular, a case of oblique order.... 203

Concave order of battle................. 203
Examples of concave order............. 204
Convex order of battle.................. 204
Convex, a bad order, except in few cases, 204
Turks' transformation of convex to concave............................... 204
Practically, orders are mere approximations............................. 205
Continuous lines preferable............. 205

3. Conduct of the Battle.

Object and necessity of battles.......... 205
Superiority of force not indispensable.... 206
Victors try to cut enemy's line.......... 206
Vanquished try to preserve its line...... 206
General conforms his order to circumstances............................ 206
Point of attack determined by strategy,&c., 207
Avoid obstacles, and strike at weak points, 207
Genius and experience decide battles.... 208
Long circuits to be avoided in flanking.. 208
Attacks on many points objectionable... 208
Examples of attacks.................... 208
Attacks should be sudden and concealed, 209
Provision to be made for reverses.. 209
Orders completed by verbal instructions, 210
Discretionary powers to subordinates... 210

448 CONTENTS.

	PAGE		PAGE
Mode of conducting an offensive battle...	210	Squares to be used in defensive battles..	214
Conduct of pursuit after victory........	212	Reëstablishing an uncovered flank.......	214
Requisites of position for defensive battle,	212	Assuming offensive from defensive......	214
Precautions for vigorous defence........	213	Mode of conducting a retreat............	215
Mode of conducting a defensive battle...	213	History of battles to be studied.........	216

PART THIRD.

MINOR OPERATIONS.

CHAPTER FIRST.

OUTPOSTS.

Introduction.

Portion of army must guard the whole... 217
Functions of outposts................... 217
Outposts take place of scouts of ancients, 218
Outposts the eyes of an army............ 218
Composed to watch most active enemy.. 218
Covering, not fighting, corps of army.... 218
Safety in vigilance...................... 219
Surveillance active, not too regular..... 219
Posted to watch and impede enemy..... 219
Outposts extend beyond advance-guard.. 220
Transient or permanent, posted alike..... 220
Number for outposts, and how supplied.. 220
Constituent parts of outposts........... 220

1. Grand Guards.

Advanced posts of camp or cantonment.. 221
Number, force, position, how regulated.. 221
Infantry and cavalry guard combined.... 221
Force and command of regimental guard, 221
Positions to be occupied by grand guards, 222
Seldom dispensed with.................. 222
Posts protected by temporary defences.. 222
Intrenching, like ancients, disapproved.. 222
Communications to be secured.......... 222
Obstructions made toward enemy....... 223
Duties of grand guards................. 223
Precautions to be taken by grand guards, 223
Conduct of grand guard when attacked.. 224
Posted 2,500 yards in advance of army... 224

2. Small Posts.

Covering force of grand guard........... 224
Positions, force, and communications.... 225
Instructions and duties of commanders.. 225
Precautions at small posts.............. 225
Cossack-posts.......................... 226

3. Sentinels and Vedettes.

Covering force of small posts........... 226
Posted 500 yards in front of small posts.. 226
Infantry sentinels and cavalry vedettes.. 226
Duties of sentinels and vedettes......... 227
Precautions by sentinels and vedettes... 227

4. Distribution of the Outposts.

Distances and system of outposts........ 228
Modified by nature of ground............ 228
Distances diminished at night........... 230

5. Posts of Support.

Location, object, and armament......... 230
Form fourth line of outpost defence..... 230

6. Patrols, Lookouts, Rounds.

Outposts must be under surveillance.... 230
Duties and object of round, patrols, &c... 231
Arrangement of a defensive patrol...... 231
Arrangement of an offensive patrol..... 232
Patrols should not remain in mass....... 233
Precautions to be observed by patrols... 234

CHAPTER SECOND.

DETACHMENTS.

1. General Observations.

Object and duties of offensive detachments, 235
Made up of fixed fractions of regiments.. 236
Artillery and engineers not included..... 236
Qualifications and duties of the chiefs.... 236
Feeble on the march.................... 238
Advance and rear-guard and flankers. .. 238
Force of guards and flankers............ 238
Precautions to be taken by chief........ 239
Should always be ready for defence..... 239

Should not be stopped by a river........ 240
Have a right to shares of booty......... 240

2. Detachments of Infantry.

Duties and precautions to be taken...... 240
Marching formation and force........... 241

3. Detachments of Cavalry.

Used where celerity is required......... 243
Duty of their advance-guards........... 243

CONTENTS. 449

PAGE	PAGE
Dangers of defiles to be avoided......... 243	Duties for which most suitable.......... 244
Formation and march.................. 244	Order of march in different cases........ 244
	Dispositions for combat................. 245
4. Mixed Detachments.	Marching formation on level ground..... 246
Possess more stability than of a single arm, 244	Marching formation on broken ground... 247

CHAPTER THIRD.

ARMED RECONNOISSANCES.

Introduction.

Armed reconnoissance defined......... 248
Basis of every military movement...... 248
Difficult and complicated.............. 248
Designed to see and collect all information, 249
Five kinds of reconnoissances........... 249
Proposed manner of treating the subject, 249

1. Daily Reconnoissances.

Object, and indications for guidance..... 250
Kind of troops varied by nature of country, 250
Must be divested of regularity........... 250
Aim, information and not combat....... 251
Cases where combat is proper........... 251
Has advance, rear-guard and flankers.... 251
Flankers not far from main body........ 251
Precautions to avoid ambuscades........ 251
Precautions when halting............... 252
Manner of observing columns on march, 252

2. Special Reconnoissances.

Facilitating march of columns........... 252
Exploring positions to be occupied...... 252
Ascertaining enemy's posts and defences, 253
Estimating enemy's forces at all points.. 253
Made by officers according to speciality.. 253
Instructions to whom and how given.... 254
Posts not to be attacked without authority, 254

3. Secret Reconnoissances.

Occupy sometimes several days and nights, 254
Secret if possible, and open if necessary, 255
Intrusted only to veteran light troops,... 255
Requisites in the chief and subordinates, 255
Striking example of Vauban's sang-froid, 257
Chief should know language of country.. 257
Chief should have telescope, maps, &c... 258
Detachment composed of light cavalry.. 258
Composed of fifteen to forty horsemen... 258
Moves secretly and rapidly.............. 259
Accompanied by advance-guard and guide, 259
Rallying point to be designated......... 259
Messages to be destroyed to avoid capture, 259
Formed in three unequal echelons....... 260
Mode of conducting reconnoissance..... 260
When discovered to be renewed......... 260
Chief sometimes advances with guide only, 260
Prisoners to be made if other means fail.. 261
Promptness and despatch indispensable.. 261
Retires after object is accomplished..... 261

4. Offensive Reconnoissances.

Made openly by force of arms........... 261
Composed of artillery and light cavalry.. 262
Penetrates to point where all can be seen, 262
Supported in force if necessary.......... 262
Made by general himself on eve of battle, 262
Ordered usually by general-in-chief..... 263

5. Report.

Drawn up in clear and positive manner.. 263
Accompanied by sketch of ground, &c... 263
Better to be too explicit than too concise, 263
Indispensable to be made quickly and well, 264
Made verbally often to avoid delay..... 265
Written or oral, must be clear and concise, 265

6. Historical Examples.

Pursuit of Duke of Savoy from Turin... 265
Capture of Austrian battalion in 1805.... 266
Lannes' false march after Austerlitz..... 267
Ruse of Capt. Curely near Raab in 1809, 267
Defeat of Masséna at Busaco in 1810..... 268
Capt. Light's exploit near Vic-de-Bigorre, 269

7. Reconnoissances in Africa.

Difficulty and danger................... 270
Arab limiers' various ruses............. 270

8. Maps.

Indispensable in conducting war........ 272
Verification of correctness necessary..... 272
Mode of verifying maps................ 273
Cassini's maps deceived Allies in 1814... 273
Foreign maps usually defective......... 274
Governmental maps to be trusted....... 274
Road and station maps.................. 274

9. Guides.

Give information not on maps.......... 275
Indispensable to success of armies....... 275
Class of persons from whom selected.... 276
How procured and treated.............. 276
Mode of ascertaining their intelligence... 277
Must obtain knowledge of their character, 277
Selected from those in your interest..... 278
Punishment and rewards................ 278
Interrogate several, and not rely upon one, 279
Two necessary to every detachment.... 279
Precautions to prevent their escape..... 280
Must be prevented falling asleep........ 281

29

10. Deserters.

Disarmed and interrogated.............. 281
Not to be trusted, often spies in disguise, 281
Exaggerate information to be welcomed, 281
Manner of interrogation and questions... 282

11. Inhabitants.

Officials and other persons interrogated.. 282
Questions to be asked.................. 282
Questioned separately in their language.. 283

12. Travellers.

Questions asked of comers from enemy.. 283
Interrogated to ascertain whether spies.. 284
Testimony to be rectified.............. 284

13. Prisoners.

Questions to be put same as to deserters, 284
Information from them quite reliable.... 285
Capture of prisoners to obtain information, 285

14. Spies.

Definition of a spy.................... 286
Spies from devotion to prince or country, 286
Spies procured from all conditions of life, 287
Examples of noted spies................ 287
Qualifications for spies, and where found, 288
Inhabitants and soldiers of enemy spies.. 288
Cruel last resort to obtain spies........ 289
Soldiers, disguised as inhabitants, used.. 289
Spies easily got among a divided people, 290
Difficult to obtain among uprising people, 290
Verification of spies' information...... 291
Double spies, how treated and made use of, 291
Whimsical ruse of Suwarrow in Poland, 291
Spies must not reside in camp.......... 292
Spies kept apart with assumed names.., 292
Precautions against disguises of spies.... 292
Sutlers and clerks must be watched..... 293
Spies' reports should be kept secret..... 293
Imprudent speech of Alphonso X....... 293
Arrested spies searched and watched.... 293
Examples of concealed despatches....... 294

15. Indications.

Divining enemy's intentions gift of genius, 294
Mythological illustration of indications . 294
Historical illustrations of indications.... 294
Skill by observation and comparison..... 295
Interpreting, a moral part of war......... 295
Principal indications enumerated....... 295
True from false, how distinguished....... 297

CHAPTER FOURTH.

PASSAGE OF RIVERS.

Introduction.

Water-courses formidable obstacles in war, 298
Various modes of crossing streams....... 298
Improvised passages chiefly considered.. 298

1. Reconnoissance of a River.

Particulars to be ascertained enumerated, 299
Various points to be exactly explained.. 299

2. Discovery, Destruction, and Repair of Fords.

Maximum depth of fords for different arms, 300
Careful search should be made for fords.. 300
Existence of fords, how indicated........ 300
Below mills and near mouths of streams, 301
Mode of reconnoitring a ford........... 301
Mode of tracing a ford................. 301
Ford usually found in double bends..... 301
Oblique fords.......................... 302
Essential requisites of a good ford....... 302
Fords useful to us must be protected.... 303
Enemy's fords destroyed or obstructed... 303
Modes of obstructing fords............. 303
Modes of breaking up or destroying fords, 304
Modes of repairing and improving fords, 304
Fords should be staked out............. 306
Fords not to be relied upon for passage.. 306
Fords of mountain torrents not reliable.. 306
Disasters by changes of the ford of Cinca, 306

3. Fording a River.

Fords suffice for detachments, not armies, 307
Troops when heated must not pass a ford, 307
Stakes or guard-ropes required for fords, 307
Precautions taken in fording rapid streams, 307
Mode of fording by the several arms..... 308
Precedence of arms in fording.......... 308
Fording of Granicus and Tagliamento... 309
Historical examples of importance of fords............................... 309
English won Crécy by discovering a ford, 309
Soult's failure to ford Tagus saved Wellington............................ 309

4. Swimming a River.

Examples of swimming with despatches, 809
Lille saved, in 1708.................... 310
Defence of Genoa prolonged, in 1800.... 310
Poniatowski, not a swimmer, drowned.. 310
Importance of swimming to soldiers..... 311
French soldiers not good swimmers..... 311
Passage of Linth, in 1799............... 311
Choice of place for swimming a stream.. 811
Precautions essential for infantry........ 312
Passage of Loire by Cæsar............... 312
Passage of Meuse by Prince of Orange.. 812
Precautions to be observed by cavalry... 312
Horses drowned in crossing Oder........ 312
Swimming horses behind boats.....'.... 313

CONTENTS 451

	PAGE
Horseman carrying a foot soldier behind,	313
Passage of Douro, in 1580	313
Passage of Rhine, in 1089	313
Arm of sea crossed, in 1708	313
Mode of Tartar cavalry swimming rivers,	313
Celebrated swimming of Rhine by Louis XIV	313

5. Passage upon Ice.

Hastening congelation of channel of river,	314
Ice not trusted if it does not lay on water,	314
Thickness of ice for passage of all arms..	314
Artificially increasing thickness of ice	314

	PAGE
Precautions to be taken in crossing ice..	315
Disorder and confusion to be prevented..	815
Crossing the frozen Frische-Haff, in 1679,	315
Dutch fleet captured by cavalry, in 1795,	315

6. Improvised Bridges.

Construction belong mostly to artillery..	815
Foot-bridge of ladders	316
Bridges of undressed trees	816
Bridge of wagons for shallow streams...	816
Rope bridges on narrow mountain torrents,	817
Suspension bridges of ropes	818
Small pile-bridges	318

CHAPTER FIFTH.
CONVOYS.

Introduction.

Definition and object of a convoy	319
Convoys, muscles of army	319
Organization of convoys demand great care,	319
Outfit, &c., both administrative and tactical,	319
Convoys never march without escort	319
Force, &c., determined by circumstances,	320
Composed of infantry and a little cavalry,	320
Ready to overcome difficulties	320
Some artillery and sappers attached	320
Grade of commandant of convoy	320
Artillery officer usually convoys ammunition	320
Chief has detailed written instructions..	321
Not to be modified by any one on the route,	321
Command of convoy a delicate mission..	321

1. Organization of the Convoy.

Chief collects and examines convoy	321
Everything necessary must be provided..	321
Materiel must be examined in detail	321
Spare wagons and parts carried along	322
Large convoys divided and subdivided...	322
Portion of escort guards each subdivision,	322
Wagons of most value at heads of divisions,	322
Hostile prisoners at heads of convoys	323
Beasts of burden precede convoy-wagons,	323
Convoy has advance and rear-guard	323
Chief reserves no special command	323
Weight carried by wagons and animals..	323
Space occupied and rate of travel of wagons,	324
Forbidden to put knapsacks on wagons..	324

2. March of the Convoy.

Examination of route of march to be made,	324
March made slow at uniform rate	324
Advance-guard precedes convoy sometime,	324
Duties of advance-guard	325
March in two files, and drivers watched,	825
Wagons kept repaired, or thrown out	825
Escort holds all dangerous positions	826
Vigilance never relaxed	826

3. Halts and Parks.

Long halts made only in strong positions,	326
Horses kept harnessed and wagons guarded,	327
Convoy parked at night and on halts...	827
Wagons occupy exterior, and horses and valuables interior of park	827
Park resembles barricade or intrenchment,	327
Circular park, with horses in interior....	827
Rectangular park used in Prussia	828
Park formed from marching column	829
Archduke Charles, parks, by divisions....	329
Parks far from towns, woods, &c	830
Defensive accessories, called tabors	330

4. Defence of the Convoy.

Convoys should be drilled to resist attack,	331
Measures taken on approach of enemy...	331
Skirmishers keep enemy at distance	331
Convoy gains shelter and halts	331
Enemy dispersed, and march resumed..	332
Escort reënforced to resist central attack,	332
Threatened positions to be occupied	332
Attack in rear repelled by rear-guard	332
Convoy subdivided in dangerous places,	332
Defence failing wagons to be destroyed,	333
Escort does not pursue enemy	333
Prisoners must lie down during attack...	333
Prisoners confined in defensible houses..	333
Requisites for the defence of a convoy..	334

5. Attack of a Convoy.

Advantage in attacks with assailant	334
Attack based on previous information...	334
Corps of attack divided into three masses,	834
First engages the escort	334
Second falls upon the wagons	334
Third remains in reserve	334
Attack made on centre in level ground..	835
Parks attacked in rear or breached	335
Attacks generally for seizing valuables..	335
Often limited to disorganizing convoys..	335

6. Convoys by Water.

	PAGE
Transport bulky and heavy supplies	336
Distribution of escort on boats and shore	336
High banks to be occupied	337
Convoy halts during attack	337
Convoy proceeds if escort is victorious	337
Boats sunk if escort is beaten	337
Attack of convoy of boats in bend of river	337
Captured convoy best be removed by land	338

7. Historical Examples.

	PAGE
Corbie relieved by entrance of convoy	338
Success of convoy introduced into Lille	339
Attack of water convoy for relief of Aire	341
Attack of land convoy for relief of Olmutz	342
Rescue of a convoy of Prussian prisoners	344
Recapture of convoy in Spain, in 1811	344

CHAPTER SIXTH.
PARTISANS.

Definition and duties of partisans	346
Act not at a venture, nor trust to chance	346
Operations of, part of plan of campaign	346
Disponsed with by French and English	346
Sometimes termed flankers in France	346
Modern restriction in movements	347
Composition &c., vary with circumstances	347
Quality more than quantity necessary	347
Qualifications needed for partisans	347
Free corps, specially raised, good material	348
Corps, rising through political events, best	348
Essential qualifications of partisan chief	348
Partisans rely mainly on expedients	349
Inspire respect at home and terror abroad	349
Must bid adieu to idleness and rest	350
March concealed and discipline maintained	350
Discover everything and be stopped by nothing	350
Avoid towns, take hostages, resort to ruses	350
Dart on their prey like vultures	351
Success being doubtful, should retreat	351
Chief's orders given to next in command	351
Apportionment of prize money	351
Statement of requisitions to be made	352
Mansfeld, and other celebrated partisans	353
Historical examples of partisan operations	353

CHAPTER SEVENTH.
SURPRISES AND AMBUSCADES.

Introduction.

Surprises aid the weak against the strong	356
Essential conditions and preparations	356
Used in offensive or defensive operations	357

1. Surprises by Ambuscade.

Derivation of the term ambuscade	357
Purpose of an ambuscade	358
Requisites in composition of force	358
Precautions on march to designated place	359
Selection of position for an ambuscade	359
Locations for concealing troops	360
Surprise of camp or cantonment	360
Position of ambuscade to be first searched	361
Precautions in guarding ambuscade	361
Noise, fire, lights, sleep, &c., forbidden	361
Conduct of an attack from an ambuscade	362
Ruse employed in retreats	362
Counter-ambuscade against ambuscade	363

2. Surprise by a March.

Calculated for the proper time and place, 363

Break of day best time for surprise	363
March at right angles to enemy's march	363
More frequent than surprise by ambuscade	363
Wrapping horses' hoofs in sheepskin	364
Surprise more dishonorable than defeat	364
Kleber's precept respecting surprises	364

3. Historical Examples.

Should emerge from ambuscade in a body	364
Example of Labienus in 44 B. C.	364
Badge or rallying signal necessary	365
Example of Villars' reconnoissance in 1667	365
Soldiers in ambush should not sleep	865
Example of night ambuscade in Spain	865
Failed at Mayence through imprudent cry	866
Capture of the Vendean chief, Stofflet	866
Covering obstacle against surprise	366
Marmont's surprise of Russian outposts	366
Surprise in Algeria nearly frustrated	367

CHAPTER EIGHTH.
HEIGHTS.

1. Reconnoissance.

Heights first to be reconnoitred	368
Essential information to be obtained	368
Places for combat to be indicated	369

2. Defence.

Military crest between slope and plateau	369
Position of defender to repel attack	869
First line near military crest	870

CONTENTS. 453

	PAGE
Assailant fired upon before reaching crest,	871
Second line placed to support first	871
Reserve to watch flanking movements	871
Plateaux to be successively defended	871
Flanking fires particularly useful	871
Cavalry acts chiefly with reserve	871
Sold and experienced infantry necessary,	871
Examples of Talavera and Pampeluna	871

3. Attack.

Should seek to turn position	872

	PAGE
Attack in front accompanied by false ones,	872
Main attack chiefly by light troops	872
Supported by small and mobile columns,	872
Attack must be covered by skirmishers,	872
Columns, so covered, advance step by step,	873

4. Attack of Height by Company of Infantry.

Bugeaud's instructions for attack	873
Company divided into four half-sections,	873
Conduct of the attack described	874

CHAPTER NINTH.
WOODS.

1. Reconnoissance.

Necessity of reconnoitring woods	875
Mode of conducting reconnoissance	875
Objects to be noted and fully reported	875

2. Defence.

Assailant to be arrested at verge of wood,	876
Close outlets and protect projecting points,	877
Centre of action to be selected	877
Distribution of troops for defence of forest,	877
Distributing troops for defence of coppice,	878

3. Attack.

Preparations for attack made at a distance,	878
Force moves rapidly to attack woods	879
Principal attack to cut line of retreat	879
Vigorous and veteran troops required	879
Distance between lines and reserve	879
Mode of attack of different kinds of woods,	879
Rear-guard to cover reserve	880

4. Example.

Richepanse's success at Hohenlinden (1800),	880

CHAPTER TENTH.
FARMS, OR HOUSES.

Introduction.

Importance of farm or house for defence,	882
Hovel oven hard to take if well defended,	882
Brick walls best, not being easily breached,	883
Attack or defence of block-house	883

1. Defence.

Engineers prepare defence	883
Strongest structure converted into citadel,	883
Assailant should be compelled to lay siege,	883
Points of attack must be lit up	883
Enclosures or buildings are garrisoned	883
Loopholes must be pierced through walls,	884
Barricades of openings to be well defended,	884
Flank and machicoulis fires upon openings,	884
Ladders must be overthrown immediately	884
Climbers must be dislodged from roof	884
Vigorous sorties and counter-attacks made,	884
Fires kindled by enemy to be extinguished,	885

Garrison makes final defence in redoubt,	885
Main body escapes while few hold redoubt,	885

2. Attack.

Reconnoissance preliminary to attack	885
Cavalry watches supports and entrances	885
Defenders' night-fires extinguished	885
Exterior and weak points lit up	885
Breaches to be made and roofs burned	885
Ambuscaded skirmishers fire on openings,	886
Columns assault breaches and openings	886
Scaling-ladders, sand-bags, &c., provided,	886
Skirmishers cover assaulting columns	886
Doors to be forced and passages explored,	886
Sheltered area seized for place of arms	886
Communications made to place of arms	886
Second enclosure carried like first	886
Skirmishers secure roof and staircases	887
Sorties captured, or followed into house	887
Infantry troops chiefly employed in attack,	887
Houses fired under protection of cavalry,	887

CHAPTER ELEVENTH.
REDOUBTS.

Introduction.

Redoubts properly belong to fortification,	888
Defend points assailable on all sides	888
Protect hillocks, debouches of defiles, &c.,	888
Used for fortifying front of line of battle	889

1. Defence.

Garrison, a reserve and active part	888
Active part, of two-thirds, man parapets,	888
Two men to every yard of parapet	888
Reserve (first section) to protect entrance,	888

CONTENTS.

Reserve (second section) for assailed points, 388
Commandant explains duties to troops... 388
Sentinels guard redoubt till attacked..... 380
Artillery fire opens at 400 yards......... 389
Musketry opens at 150 yards............. 380
Mode of repelling assault................ 389
Repulsed enemy fired upon in retreat... 389
Successful enemy to be attacked by reserve.............................. 389

2. Attack.

Force divided into three columns....... 389

Sappers destroy accessory defences...... 389
Supports march in rear of columns...... 389
Two columns make false attacks........ 390
Principal point of attack, how selected.. 390
Systematic mode of attack of redoubt.... 390
Duties of assailants when within redoubt, 390
Precautions taken after gaining redoubt, 391
Attack of small force made as foragers... 391

3. Example.

Attack on redoubts at Pultawa.......... 392
Retreat of Swedes to Borysthenes....... 394

CHAPTER TWELFTH.

BARRICADES.

1. Construction.

Barricades often constructed in streets... 395
Rules for construction same as field works, 395
Placed at elevations and middle of blocks, 395
Constructed of all kinds of materials..... 395
Best of paving stones and earth.......... 395
High and steep, with ditch and banquette, 396

2. Defence.

Defenders fire in succession on assailants, 396
Prepared mine outside fired from within, 396
Defence, if necessary, hand to hand..... 396
Activity, vigilance, and courage required, 396

Artillery, if any, will fire grapeshot..... 397
Retreat how made, and way obstructed.. 397

3. Attack.

Dangerous when made on small front.... 397
Carried by ruse, surprise, or turned...... 397
Reconnoissance made for rear approach...397
Defenders dislodged by fire from houses, 397
Destroyed sometimes by mine or petard, 397
Streets too narrow for attack by sap..... 398
Moving martlets have been suggested.... 398
Open attack the last resort.............. 399
Mode of assault by open force........... 398
Assault failing, bombardment made..... 399

CHAPTER THIRTEENTH.

FORAGES.

1. Object.

Forage, the obtaining food for horses.... 400
Dry foraging, and green foraging........ 400
Forages formerly important operations.. 400
Forages unimportant at present time.... 400
Forages indispensable for light cavalry.. 401
Brack's experience in eight campaigns... 401

2. Distribution.

Foraging distributed among troops...... 401
Necessity of, and mode of distribution... 402
Number of rations of forage, how settled, 402
Unit of measure determined by trial..... 403
Distribution, by whom made............ 403

3. Dry Foraging.

Place of foraging surrounded and guarded, 404
Supplied on requisition, or taken by force, 404

Surprise or marauding, how prevented... 404
Forages made in but one village at a time, 405

4. Green Foraging.

Preparations for making a green forage.. 405
Occupation and guarding place of foraging, 405
Horses left outside of foraging ground.... 406
Defence and escort of foraging party..... 406
Green foraging less dangerous than dry.. 406
Must not embrace too much ground..... 406

5. Attack of a Foraging Party.

Cavalry attacks green, and infantry dry.. 406
Secrecy great element of success in attack, 406
Foragers cut off from posts and escorts.. 406
Attack sudden and rapid, with false ones, 407
Foragers to be driven off, but not pursued, 407
Forage, if not broken up, to be harrassed, 407
Ruse excellent auxiliary in attack....... 407

CHAPTER FOURTEENTH.

DEFILES.

Introduction.

Defiles defined and divided into two classes, 408
Roads in gorges, ditches, &c.—first class, 408

Bridges, necks, dikes, &c.—second class.. 408
Easily obstructed, good for ambuscades, &c. 409
Exert important influence in war........ 409

CONTENTS. 455

	PAGE
First class almost impregnable	409
Example of defile of Thermopylæ	409
Second class forced with difficulty	409
Example of dike of Arcola	409
Arms used in attack and defence	409

1. Occupation and Defence of a Defile.

Depends upon character, &c., of defile	409
Preserved, or use by enemy prevented	409
Positions to be occupied for defence	409

2. Passage of a Defile.

In advance not difficult, if unoccupied	410
Mode of advancing through defile	410
Passage of a defile in retreat more difficult	411
Mode of passage of defile in retreat	411
Precautions to be observed by rear-guard	412
Troops in a defile assimilated to a serpent	412

3. Attack of a Defile.

Difficulty of attack with narrow front	413
Difficult to attack with flanks protected	413
Not attacked unless essential to success	413
Mode of conducting the attack of a defile	413
Ruse tried if direct attack impracticable	414

	PAGE
Capturing defile by false demonstrations	414
Attacking defiles with occupied flanks	414

4. Historical Examples.

Omit no precautions when near a defile	415
Passage of defile near Meissen, in 1745	415
Cavalry may, as an exception, force a defile	416
Passage of defile of Somo-Sierra, in 1808	416
Employment of flanking attacks	417
Harispe's forcing defile of Cabreras, in 1808	417
Passage of defile in Algeria, in 1830	418
Passage of a defile rapidly	418
Passage of defile on Mount Medola, in 1796	418
Army in order of battle before a defile	418
Gus. Adolphus at Leipsic and Leutzen	419

5. Defence and Attack of a Bridge.

Mode of defending a bridge	419
Mode of attacking a bridge	420
Bridge should be turned by fording, &c.	420
Passage of bridge of Lodi, in 1796	421

6. Defence and Attack of a Dike.

Dikes, generally, only defended in front	421
Mode of defence of a dike in front	422
Mode of attack of a dike in front	422

CHAPTER FIFTEENTH.

VILLAGES.

1. Occupation.

Villages occupied when defensible	424
Select those compactly and regularly built	424
Occupied if important to the army	424
Information to be obtained before occupation	425
Without some natural defence not to be occupied	425

2. Defence.

Preparing a village to make a good defence	426
Redoubt to be in central position	426
Artillery posted at vulnerable points	426
Artillery sweep streets and open places	426
Flank and oblique firing most effective	427
Cavalry, how posted for the best defence	427
Infantry, how divided and posted	427
Reserve should amount to about one fourth	428
Communications to be opened	428
Sorties conducted briskly and with caution	428
Enemy to be repulsed, but not pursued	428

Exterior and interior defence	428
Reserve charges, while enemy is checked	428
Counter-attacks made and retreat secured	428

3. Attack.

Attacks on villages cost too many men	428
Superior forces and howitzers required	429
One real and two false attacks to be made	429
Division of force, and mode of attack	429
Duties of cavalry in assault of a village	431

4. Sudden Attack.

Made by surprise or vigorous assault	431
Adopted in Algeria in attack of villages	431
Villages carried by infantry on the run	431

5. Historical Examples.

Attack of Nerwinden, in 1693	431
Attack of Fontenoy, in 1745	432
Attack of Essling and Aspern, in 1809	432
Attack of Schœnfeld, in 1813	432

APPENDIX.

NOTES UPON HYGIENE IN THE FIELD.

Introduction.

Difficult for soldier to write on hygiene	433
Science of hygiene defined	433
Comfortable clothing contributes to health	433
Attention paid most to warm climates	433

1. Marches.

Limited to strength, hours, and districts	434
Care observed in climbing steep ascents	434
Sudden transitions to be guarded against	434
Indulgences allowed in warm climate	435

	PAGE
Men well clothed and fed in cold climate,	435
Warmed by exercise, not alcoholic drinks,	435
Strict attention to be paid to cleanliness,	435
Sick seriously threatened sent to hospital,	435

2. Camps.

Must be located near wood and water....	435
Pitched near banks of running streams..	436
Wood required for cooking and fuel.....	436
Forests moist and miasmatic............	436
High, ventilated, sloping, and drained...	436
Huts preferable to tents except on march,	436
Straw bedding renewed and old burned..	436
Offal burned, buried, or carried off......	436
Night exposure, in shirts or bare feet, bad,	436
Incumbrances to be removed from camps,	436
Crowded camps fatal to troops..........	436
Troops should be kept active and at work,	436

3. Bivouacs.

	PAGE
Generally more healthy than tents......	437
More uncomfortable than camps.........	437
Outposts and guards generally bivouac...	437
Should fulfil same conditions as camps...	437
Troops must not sleep in cold without fires,	437
Shelter tents especially suited to bivouacs,	437

4. Field Hospitals.

Regimental, division, and of headquarters,	438
For immediate relief of sick and wounded,	438
Those of headquarters commodious......	438
Established in houses, tents, or open air,	438
Near water, and removed from enemy..	438
Provided with litters, stretchers, &c.....	438
Severely wounded sent at once to them,	438
Slight wounds staunched on the spot....	438

THE END.